COOKING IN PARADISE

COOKING
IN PARADISE

CULINARY VACATIONS
AROUND THE WORLD

JOEL & LEE NAFTALI

Illustrations by Greg Koller and Erica Ritter

ST. MARTIN'S GRIFFIN   NEW YORK

www.stmartins.com

ISBN 0-312-24297-2

First Edition: April 2001

10   9   8   7   6   5   4   3   2   1

CONTENTS

INTRODUCTION • VII

1 • FRANCE • 1

2 • ITALY • 76

3 • ASIA • 178

4 • UNITED STATES AND CANADA • 218

5 • MEXICO • 250

6 • AUSTRIA, BRAZIL, ENGLAND,
GREECE, IRELAND, MOROCCO, SPAIN,
AND TURKEY • 269

INTRODUCTION

 IF THE HEART of a home is the kitchen, then the soul of a region is the cuisine. The cooking vacations in this book lead you into bustling, colorful open-air markets around the world. They teach you the history of traditional dishes, and regional variations, passed down for generations. They bring you the camaraderie of the kitchen, where strangers become friends over simmering pots and exotic spices. They serve you the joy of cooking and the bliss of eating.

You can spend a week in Provence, living in a chateau and learning how to cook authentic Provençal cuisine. You'll taste the region's best wines, go truffle hunting, and share leisurely meals on a garden terrace with local chefs and other guests. Between meals, you can go horseback riding or hot-air ballooning, lounge by the pool with a book, putter around the herb garden, or visit an Armagnac distillery, goat cheese farm, museum, or medieval hilltop town.

Or you might want to float on the canals of Gascony, explore the food shops of Paris, taste the Camembert and calvados in

Normandy, or discover the flavors of Bordeaux, Burgundy, Alsace, and other regions.

Perhaps you're more interested in Italy? You can stay in a farmhouse in Tuscany, a restored palazzo in Venice, a private estate in Sicily, or a fourteenth-century convent converted into a luxury hotel in Amalfi. You can live at the family homes of aristocrats or farmers (or, for that matter, of aristocrat-farmers), and study cooking under the direction of famous cookbook authors, celebrity chefs, or home cooks who use recipes handed down from their grandmothers' grandmothers.

Or you could visit Mexico, Thailand, Turkey, Greece, Brazil, England, China, Australia, Spain, Morocco, Bali, or India. Or stay closer to home—vacationing and cooking in the Pacific Northwest, Colorado, California, West Virginia, or New Mexico.

You will delight in the tastes of world cuisine—and in your new-found ability to prepare it. In Italy, you'll prepare Wild Mushroom Fricassee, Ravioli with Leeks and Truffles, Scallops in a Creamy Pumpkin Gratin, and Tuscan Bread Soup. In France, you'll make a Salad of Goat Cheese, Mesclun, and Balsamic Figs, Roast Pork Stuffed with Prunes and Shallots, Grilled Duck with Chestnuts and Wild Mushrooms, and crème au chocolate with wild stawberries. In Mexico, you'll cook Chile Poblanos Stuffed with Squash Flowers and Oaxacan Cheese, wrapped in puff pastry and served with cilantro sauce and pomegranate seeds. In Basque country in Spain, you'll learn a recipe for Andalusian Gazpacho with Lobster; in Vienna, Pike in Horseradish Sauce with Saffron Rice; in Morocco, Chicken Stew with Pickled Lemon and Olives; and in Thailand, Hot and Sour Barbecue Beef with Chile-Lime Dressing. You can focus on fish or pastry or appetizers or vegetarian dishes or whatever else you have a taste for—most programs are very flexible, and will teach you exactly what you want to know.

But cooking and eating are just the beginning. You can also visit the sunken gardens in Venice or a remote temple on Bali. You can have a guided tour of Pompeii or a lesson in falconry or a day of visiting artisans' studios. You can dine with friends of your hosts, and be invited into the kitchens of Michelin-starred restaurants. You can attend a silent truffle auction, visit the Picasso Museum, attend local festivals (from harvest fetes in France to Day of the Dead festivals in Mexico), explore the outdoor markets of Vietnam, enjoy a Brazilian "high coffee," or go snorkeling, windsurfing, and sea-kayaking. Golf courses, tennis courts, swimming pools, and horse-back riding facilities are common, as are opportunities for hikes and bike rides, lazy days by the beach or in the garden, and shopping for antiques, art, crafts, clothing, gourmet foods, and more.

The possibilities are almost endless: Some people even fall in love.

. . .

After she was laid off from her job in advertising, Cynthia Nawrot decided she needed two things: a vacation, and a new career based on her love of food and cooking. She heard about a cooking vacation program in Mexico, and was on her way.

"I arrived at the school—Mexican Home Cooking (page 262) in Tlaxcala," she says, "and fell in love with the food, the history, and the area. The food is *nothing* like you get in the States, or even in most restaurants here in Mexico. The recipes were passed down to Estela, one of the chefs, from her grandmother—the 'alta' cuisine of Mexico.

"And Tlaxcala is a charming colonial city—one of the first things I did was visit a baroque church nearby, the church of Our Lady of Ocotlan. While I was there, I asked the Virgin of Ocotlan to send a loving and sincere man into my life.

"After my week was up, I returned home. But there was much more to learn before I could start a catering business, so I asked Estela and her husband, Jon, if I could come back and apprentice with them for three months.

"They agreed, and it was incredible. Not only did I learn to cook, but Estela and Jon brought me into their family and their traditions. And I met one of Estela's brothers, Rene, a lawyer who lives in Mexico City.

"For him, he says it was love at first sight. For me, it took a little longer. But now, well, the wedding is this September, at Our Lady of Ocotlan Church.

"I never planned to stay and live here in Mexico—but I definitely got what I asked for."

. . .

There are more than a hundred and fifty cooking vacations in this book. They range from two-day intensives to monthlong, multiple-country tours, from formal, elegant, dress-for-dinner resorts with world-famous chefs to casual, homey, gather-around-the-kitchen-table-with-a-bottle-of-wine programs with home cooks. There are programs that focus on travel, with two or three cooking classes over the course of a two-week vacation, and there are programs that focus on cooking, with four or five hours a day spent in the kitchen. But most are vacations first and schools second: If you want to cook all day, you can. If you want to go sightseeing and return home for a meal, you can do that, too.

Some offer lectures on history, culture, and art. Some offer spa services, from massage to yoga to prana therapy. Some offer classes in art, crafts, language, and sports. Some have full days planned—you might bike thirty miles, go on a private tour of a museum, stop at the market for shopping, and cook a five-course meal before having dinner and drinks at a beautifully set table in front of the medieval fireplace. And some will just point you in the direction of interesting attractions and then encourage you to wander around. Some have set menus. Some will customize their meals to meet any dietary needs.

We spoke to students or read testimonials from every program in this book. There's no question that each program is perfect for some people. But how do you find the ones that are right for you?

The first thing, of course, is to browse this book. Then, after you've narrowed down your choices, contact all the programs in which you're even marginally interested. Our experience in writing this book has been that the people who offer these programs love travel, food, and people. They will be happy to answer your questions. Here are some concerns to keep in mind when you speak with them:

Cooking Lessons

Some programs emphasize teaching and some emphasize vacationing—be clear about which you want, and be sure the program provides it. Ask if the lessons are hands-on or demonstration, or both, how many lessons there are, and how long they last.

The Chefs

Many programs are taught (or guest-taught) by cookbook authors and celebrity chefs—Patricia Wells, Anne Willan, Marcella Hazan, Jacques Pépin, and more. And many others are taught by enthusiastic, knowledgeable, home cooks. Do you want the excitement of cooking with a world-famous chef, or the informal fun of cooking like a native?

The Food

Some of the cooking vacation programs are entirely based on your preferences—they can't even begin to teach you until they know what you want to be taught. Others have set classes, but are eager to customize them for you. And still others offer specific courses at specific times and aren't able to significantly alter classes for the needs of each student. If you have specific dietary requirements—you're vegetarian, kosher, diabetic, or on a low-fat diet (or a high-cream diet!)—or want to learn specific skills—making pastry or soup or matching food with wine—most schools will go out of their way to help you. But be sure to ask.

The Lodging

Would you rather stay in a five-star château or a stone farmhouse? Karen Herbst, of The International Kitchen (which represents more than twenty cooking vacations; see page 73), has a client who chartered a private plane to fly to France for his cooking vacation— and then stayed at a homey, casual, low-budget agriturismo. Although cost was clearly not an issue, he wanted an informal experience, and that's exactly what he got.

Sightseeing and Other Activities

How much tour guidance do you want? All programs offer recommendations and advice, virtually all offer some guided sightseeing, and many offer excursions every day. Some emphasize hiking in the nearby hills and sitting by the pool, while others offer daily trips to exotic locations, dinners at excellent local restaurants, and lectures offered by hometown experts and international authorities.

If you're traveling with someone who's less than enthusiastic about spending hours in the kitchen, make sure that there are alternative activities for noncooks. Often, in addition to sporting activities (golf and tennis are everywhere), many programs offer a variety of classes: in photography, landscape painting, writing, language, history, and much more.

Family

Some programs will arrange baby-sitters, offer children's activities, and seem to delight in the prospect of hosting families with children of any age. Others are not able to accommodate children. There are excellent programs in both categories, so whether you want to hear the pitter-patter or not, you're in luck.

The Details and the Cost

Although the details and the costs of the programs were accurate when we wrote them, everything changes. Double-check our information to be sure it's still correct. And in the area of international exchange rates, everything changes quickly and radically. When possible, we quoted prices in both the foreign currency and US dollars. If you're interested in checking the current exchange rate, there are many Web sites that can help you. We used the currency converter at www.xe.net/ucc.

International Telephone Calls

Contacting overseas schools is far easier with e-mail than by telephone. Unfortunately, a scattering of vacation programs do not, as of this writing, have e-mail. First, search on the Web to determine if the program is on-line yet. Then, if you must phone, remember that 011 is the international access code for the US, which you must dial to get overseas, and if you're having trouble, speak to your long distance operator. And, of course, there's always the forgotten art of letter writing—which may be the most efficient way of contacting several of the programs.

Vacationing with Professionals

Many of the cooking vacations in this book are affiliated with US-based travel organizations and guides—from agencies that represent dozens of programs to family members of the hosts, who were raised on the estate at which you'll be staying. There are many benefits of dealing with a vacation that has a US contact: from the ease with which you'll be able to get in touch to the ability to make recommendations from among several trips. The more formal agencies may charge a small premium, but it's often worth it. However, don't disregard programs simply because they have no US contact—some

of the best vacations have not yet affiliated with a US representative.

Another "travel professional" issue is membership in the
International Association of Culinary Professionals (IACP). Many
programs in the book are members. Many are not. Although neither
membership nor its absence guarantees that you'll have a wonderful
vacation, you may be more comfortable knowing that your cooking
vacation program is part of an international community of people
offering culinary services. For more information on the IACP,
check its Web site at www.iacp.com or 502-581-9786 or 800-928-
4227.

Assorted Details—Insurance, Health, and Passports

Travel insurance can cover medical costs (which may not be covered by your regular policy), trip delay or cancellation costs, legal
assistance, traveler assistance programs, and many other situations.
The majority of travelers don't carry travel insurance, but an
increasing number do. If you're interested, speak to your travel
agent or insurance company.

You do not currently need vaccinations to travel to any of the
countries in this book. However, the Centers for Disease Control
has an automated twenty-four-hour hotline, which provides updat-
ed information on vaccination recommendations: 404-332-4559.
This is a wonderful free service—unfortunately, it's often busy. If
you can't get through, check out the CDC's traveler's Web site at
www.cdc.gov/travel/travel.html.

You do not need a visa or passport to enter Canada or Mexico.
A passport is required for travel to all of the other countries in this
book (usually with a time limit of sixty–ninety days), with the
exception of the following, which require a passport *and* visa:
Australia (but not New Zealand), Brazil, India, and most Asian and
Pacific Island nations (but not Hong Kong, Indonesia, Japan,
Singapore, or Thailand). Again, these things change, so ask your

travel agent or the cooking vacation program for current information.

And, finally, if you have a great time, or a less-than-great time, at any of the programs listed in this book, we'd love to know about it. If you had a great or less-than-great time at a cooking vacation program *not* in this book, we'd love to know about that, too. Please feel free to contact us with suggestions, questions, rants, kudos, observations, or bons mots. You can e-mail us at CookinParadise@aol.com

Enjoy!

COOKING IN PARADISE

·1·

FRANCE

FROM PARIS to Gascony to Provence to Burgundy—all the regions of France are open to you, with their colorful and fragrant outdoor markets, favorite local wineries, and unique regional cuisines. You can watch beekeepers spin honey into glass jars, follow shepherds on their cheese-making rounds, or play croquet on an expansive château lawn, wine glass in hand. You can soar in a hot-air balloon over the vineyards of Bordeaux or hunt wild boar on a private estate in Limousin. You'll meet famous chefs and truffle hunters, professional sommeliers and master potters, traditional cobblers and the finest wine makers.

And you'll learn to cook: simple meals composed of ingredients harvested fresh from the kitchen garden, and complex sauces elegantly paired with the perfect wine. But more than cooking—more even than enjoying elaborate, multicourse meals—is learning a new pace. A pace arranged not around "to do" lists and crisis management, but around the French love of food—a regard that begins in

the fields and farms, blossoms in boisterous markets, and finally flowers in the kitchen and around the table.

· AT HOME WITH PATRICIA WELLS ·

If you've read any of Patricia Wells's many excellent cookbooks and culinary guides to France (such as *The Food Lover's Guide to France* or *Patricia Wells at Home in Provence*), the emphasis of her cooking vacation will come as no surprise. Patricia opens her home several times a year to teach guests about the food, wine, and culture of Provence—from the freshest ingredients to Patricia's own organic red wine to traditional Provençal recipes.

Patricia's home, *Chanteduc*, is a classically restored eighteenth-century Provençal farmhouse located in Vaison-la-Romaine, about thirty miles from Avignon. Vaison-la-Romaine is a lively village with extensive Roman ruins and fabulous open-air markets full of seasonal fruits and vegetables—asparagus, artichokes, peaches, pears, figs, cherries, grapes, and berries—fresh lamb, farm-raised pigeons and chickens, olives and olive oils, and goat's and sheep's milk cheeses. It's also the heart of the Côtes-du-Rhône wine region (Patricia's farm produces an organic Côtes du Rhône, *Clos Chanteduc*), and your meals will be accompanied by local vintages.

The hands-on cooking classes take place in Patricia's home kitchen (which boasts a *La Cornue* range, rotisserie, and a wood-fired bread oven, fed with vine clippings from the vineyard) and emphasize simplicity, fresh ingredients, and good kitchen habits. You'll cook with herbs freshly picked from the garden, grapes from the vineyards, and olives from the groves. The recipes are largely based on traditional Provençal specialties such as *Saumon Entier Roti en Papillotte*, *Salade Gourmandine aux olives*, *Soupe au pistou*, *Pommes de Terre au Foin*, *Gratin de Courgettes*, *Tarte aux Abricot and Amandes*, and *Tarte Tatin*.

When not enjoying the meals you've prepared or sipping homemade aperitifs with Patricia and the rest of the group, you can slip into the village to view the ruins, tour one of the many local vineyards, go hiking, biking, or swimming, or play tennis. You'll also go on several trips to local bistros for a truly Provençal dining experience.

Once a year, Patricia also offers a black truffle workshop. This four-day event includes a truffle hunt, a trip to one of the silent truffle markets, and a tour of one of the better truffle processing plants, where Patricia says, "just breathing the fragrant air is a rarefied experience." Wine tastings and truffle discussions also enhance the workshop, and of course you'll learn how to cook with truffles.

Accommodations are not included in either of Patricia's programs, but she's happy to make lodging recommendations.

THE DETAILS: The regular cooking program runs five days and is offered May through September. The truffle workshop runs four days and is offered in February. Group size is limited to eight. The cost for each program includes all meals, excursions, and cooking lessons.

Cooking Program: $3,000
Truffle Workshop: $3,000

Contact:
Deborah Orrill
7830 Ridgemar Drive
Dallas, TX 75231
Phone: NA
Fax: 214-343-1227
E-mail: deborahorrill@usa.net
E-mail: cookingclasses@patriciawells.com
Web site: www.patriciawells.com

From the kitchen of Patricia Wells

❂

SOUPE AU PISTOU:
PROVENÇAL VEGETABLE SOUP
SERVES 12

1/2 cup extra-virgin olive oil
3 plump fresh garlic cloves, peeled and halved lengthwise
Bouquet garni (several bay leaves and sprigs of thyme wrapped
    with the green part of a leek and tied securely with cotton
    twine)
Sea salt to taste
1 pound fresh small white (navy) beans in the pod, shelled, or
    8 ounces dried small white beans
1 pound fresh cranberry (pinto) beans in the pod, shelled, or
    8 ounces dried cranberry (pinto) beans

VEGETABLES 1

3 medium leeks, white and tender green parts only, scrubbed, quartered, and finely sliced

8 medium carrots, scrubbed and cut into thin triangles (*paysanne*)

2 medium onions, halved and cut into thin rings

1 pound potatoes, peeled and cubed

10 plump, fresh cloves of garlic, peeled and quartered lengthwise

VEGETABLES 2

12 ounces zucchini, cut into thin triangles (*paysanne*)

12 ounces tomatoes, cored, peeled, seeded, and chopped

2 tablespoons tomato paste

1 pound green beans, trimmed at both ends and quartered

3 quarts (12 cups) cold water

Sea salt to taste

1 cup very fine pasta, such as angel hair pasta or orzo

1 cup Parmigiano-Reggiano cheese, freshly grated

1 cup imported Gruyère cheese, freshly grated

PISTOU SAUCE

4 fresh garlic cloves, peeled and minced

Sea salt to taste

2 cups loosely packed fresh basil leaves and flowers

1/2 cup extra virgin olive oil

In a large, heavy-bottomed 10-quart stockpot, combine the oil, halved garlic, bouquet garni, and salt. Stir to coat with the oil. Sweat over moderate heat until the garlic is fragrant and soft, about 1 minute. Add the fresh or prepared dried beans (see note, below), and stir to coat with the oil. Cook for 1 minute more.

Add the leeks, carrots, onions, potatoes, and quartered garlic

(Vegetables 1) and soften over moderate heat, stirring regularly, for about 10 minutes. This will give a lovely color and rich flavor to the final soup.

Add the zucchini, tomatoes, tomato paste, green beans, and three quarts of cold water (Vegetables 2) and salt to taste. Simmer gently, uncovered, until the navy and cranberry beans are tender, about 30 minutes. (Cooking time will vary according to the fresh-ness of the beans. Add additional water if the soup becomes too thick.)

Add the pasta and stir frequently to keep the pasta from sticking to the bottom of the pot, simmering until the pasta is cooked, about 5 minutes. Taste for seasoning. Remove and discard the bouquet garni.

For the pistou sauce: If you have a mortar and pestle, mash the garlic and a little salt to form a paste. Add the basil, little by little, grinding the two together to form a paste. Slowly add the oil, con-tinuing to form a paste until all the oil has been absorbed and the mix is homogenous. Taste for seasoning. Stir before serving.

If using a food processor, place the minced garlic, salt, and basil in the bowl of a food processor and process to a paste. Add the oil and process again. Taste for seasoning. Stir before serving.

(The pistou can be stored, covered and refrigerated, for 1 day, or frozen up to 6 months.)

Serve the soup very hot, passing the pistou sauce and cheese to swirl into the soup.

Note: If using dried beans, first rinse and pick them over to remove any pebbles. Place the beans in a large bowl, add boiling water to cover, and set aside for one hour. Drain the beans, discard the water, and add to recipe when needed.

· THE CHÂTEAU COUNTRY ·
COOKING COURSE

The *Domaine de la Tortinière*, a nineteenth-century manor house converted into a château-hotel, is located in the heart of the Loire Valley. It has been the home of the Capron family for many years, and when you arrive Denise Olivereau-Capron and her son, Xavier, will join you for an aperitif in the salon.

The next day, your cooking lessons begin. During the week you spend at *la Tortinière*, your classes will progress through the order of a meal: First, you learn starters and sides, then fish dishes (using fish that arrives daily from local rivers), then meats and sauces, and finally, desserts. And after spending mornings in the kitchen, you spend afternoons sightseeing.

On Monday, you'll visit the caves of one of the finest producers of Vouvray wine in the region, for a tour and a tasting. On Tuesday, you'll visit the *Château de Chenonceau*, also known as the Château of Six Women, celebrated for its fascinating history, magnificent architecture, and lavish grounds. Before returning to *la Tortinière*, you'll stop at the *ferme Bellevue*, where you'll learn about the production of goat cheese and taste the fromage de chèvre with a glass of local wine.

You will spend Wednesday in Tours, the economic and cultural center of the region, and home of one of the largest flower markets in France. You'll have lunch at a typical Breton creperie, and can then visit the *Musée des Beaux-Arts* or go antique shopping on the *Rue de la Scellerie*.

On Thursday, you'll have a picnic in the countryside before visiting the sixteenth-century gardens of the *Château de Villandry*. Thursday is also market day in the medieval village of Chinon (the home of Rabelais)—you'll stop to explore the market and town.

And you'll devote Friday, your last full day, to an exploration—and comparative tasting—of many of the outstanding wines for which the Loire Valley is famous.

You can also wander along the wooded paths of the château park which lead down to the banks of the Indre River, dive into the heated swimming pool, play tennis, go fishing or boating on the river, and stroll throughout the thirty-acre park. Golf and horseback riding are available nearby.

DETAILS: The program runs one week and is offered March, April, October, November, and December. Group size is limited from eight to twelve. The cost includes accommodations, all meals with wine, cooking lessons, and excursions.

The Cost: 11,000 francs (approx. $1,765)
Single Supplement: 1,500 francs (approx. $240)

Contact:
Le Domaine De La Tortinière
37250 Montbazon-en-Touraine FRANCE
Phone: 247 34 35 00
Fax: 247 65 95 70

• CHEZ MADELAINE COOKING TOURS •

Madelaine Bullwinkel taught French cooking at the Chez Madelaine Cooking School for more than twenty years before, in 1994, she formed a partnership with the Count and Countess de Sainte Croix. Now the Count and Countess ("Jacque and Claude to their guests," Madelaine says), open their impeccably restored eighteenth-century château, *Château de Sannat*, to Madelaine's cooking trips three times a year.

The château, a listed historic monument with a formal park and a commanding view of the surrounding countryside, is tucked away in the Limousin region of France, about two hundred miles south of Paris. "The Count and Countess are both present to welcome us,"

Madelaine says. "To travel with us around the area and give informal tours of this great house. It's a very personal experience for the guests: living, cooking, and eating seasonal specialties in a château filled with the warmth and hospitality of a private home."

Madelaine offers several tours per year: **French Delicacies: Foie Gras and Truffles**, *Grandes Vacances*, and **Hunting and Mushroom Gathering**. All the tours highlight the medieval flavor of Limoges. You'll see the beautifully restored *Rue de la Boucherie*, the miniature chapel to St. Aurelian (the patron saint of butchers), the bustling city market housed in a building designed by Gustave Eiffel, the massive eighteenth-century two-story kiln on the outskirts of town, and the porcelain museum.

French Delicacies: Foie Gras and Truffles also includes visits to the Foie Gras Festival in Brive-la-Gaillarde and Europe's largest wholesaler of wild mushrooms and truffles, and lunch in Brive at the renowned restaurant, *La Cremaillere*, with a special menu prepared by Chef Charles-Raoul Reynal. You'll also attend two cooking classes in the château kitchen featuring foie gras of duck and goose, confit of duck, and fresh black truffles.

Highlights from past trips include: a trip to the Haviland factory; lunch in the home of J. Paul and Danielle Pouret; a stroll into the town of Bellac for a tour of the famous eleventh-century *chassé* (reliquary); shopping in Limoges; and visiting the village church that houses the enameled reliquary of St. Etienne.

The *Grandes Vacances* program begins with a day trip to the tapestry center of Aubusson, during which you'll tour both the royal factory St. Jean and the city's tapestry museum. You'll have lunch at an elegant restaurant, travel to Lac Vassiviere, stroll the forested modern Sculpture Park and Aldo Rossi's Contemporary Museum (accessible by footbridge on an island in the lake), and participate in an evening celebration of Bastille Day in the old town of Bellac. You'll also attend two cooking classes featuring summer produce from the château's eighteenth-century-style kitchen garden and Blazon Rouge (Red Label) Limousin beef.

Other highlights: a dinner in the Renaissance château of the Count and Countess du Monstiers-Merinville; attending a mass sung in Gregorian chant; and a visit to the small abbey museum in Châteauponsac.

The **Hunting and Mushroom Gathering** tour provides opportunities to hunt upland game, roe deer, and wild boar on private lands, forage for wild mushrooms with a trained specialist, and go on a guided walking tour of the Monts de Blond, an area studded with ancient dolmans and charming hamlets. Two hands-on cooking classes in the château kitchen focus on cooking with game meats, wild mushrooms, and locally grown nuts and apples.

At the end of your stay at *Château de Sannat*, you have the option of spending an additional weekend in Paris. This includes two nights in a small hotel in a charming neighborhood, customized group and self-guided touring by foot and Metro, and two dinners in restaurants offering fresh interpretations of classic French cuisine.

In addition to gourmet travel, Madelaine offers many workshops in her home in Hinsdale, Illinois.

THE DETAILS: All of the programs run eight days. French Delicacies: Foie Gras and Truffles is offered in February, *Grandes Vacances* is offered in July, and Hunting and Mushroom Gathering is offered in October. The Paris Weekend is offered at the end of each of the three trips. All group sizes are limited to twelve. The cost for each program includes accommodations, most meals (with the exception of a handful of restaurant meals), two cooking classes with Madelaine and one in a local restaurant kitchen, and excursions. The Paris Weekend includes accommodations and some sightseeing.

French Delicacies: Foie Gras and Truffles: $2,500
Grandes Vacances: $2,500
Hunting and Mushroom Gathering: $2,500
Hunting license (required for hunters): $300

Hunting fee per day: $200
Single Supplement for each program: $500
Paris Weekend: $500

Contact:
Chez Madelaine Cooking Tours
Madelaine Bullwinkel
425 Woodside Avenue
Hinsdale, IL 60524
Phone: 630-655-0355
E-mail: chezmb@aol.com
web site: www.chezm.com

From the kitchen of
Chez Madelaine Cooking Tours
◦

CHOCOLATE CHERRY BABKA

MAKES 20–24 SLICES

3/4 cup unsalted butter
  (6 ounces), plus 1 tablespoon at room temperature
1/3 cup ground almonds, plus
  2 tablespoons
1 1/2 cups confectioner's sugar
4 large eggs, separated, at
  room temperature
2 cups unbleached flour
  measured after sifting

1/2 teaspoon sea salt
1 tablespoon baking powder
1/2 tablespoon powdered
  vanilla
3/4 cup milk, warmed
1/2 cup dried sour cherries
1 tablespoon high quality
  cocoa dissolved in
  1 tablespoon hot water

Preheat the oven to 300°. Use the tablespoon of butter to gener-
ously butter a bundt pan. Sprinkle with the 2 tablespoons of ground
almonds. Set aside.

Beat the butter for 3 minutes with a paddle attachment in an electric mixer. Add the sugar and beat another 2 minutes. Beat in the egg yolks, one at a time and continue beating another 2 minutes.

Sift together the sifted flour, salt, baking powder, and powdered vanilla. Add it to the butter and eggs in three installments alternating with the warm milk.

Beat the egg whites to firm peaks. Fold the whites into the batter in three installments. Fold in the cherries.

Spoon the batter into the prepared mold. Drizzle the chocolate mixture and the almonds over the top and swirl them into the batter with a circular motion using a fork.

Bake for 50 minutes. The internal temperature of the babka should reach 200°. Cool on a rack for 10 minutes. Unmold and allow to cool to room temperature before slicing.

• COOKING IN BURGUNDY •

Encounters, Ltd.

This cooking vacation is based in a two-hundred-year-old farmhouse hidden among the hills of Burgundy, below the floodlit ramparts of the fortified village of Grancey le Château. The classes are strictly hands-on, and cover traditional French cuisine adjusted to modern cooking styles. Flavor and presentation are emphasized, and classes include such highlights as collecting wild mushrooms and asparagus with an expert guide in the local forests.

Penny Easton and Chef Michel, who run the program, describe their cooking as "traditional French with a modern touch, using fresh seasonal ingredients." Michel was trained in Paris, and ran a hotel and restaurant in a small château for twenty years. Penny, trained in England, took years off to raise her family; then, in the early nineties, she converted her French farmhouse for the purpose of offering cooking classes and, with Michel's help, has been doing so ever since.

The farmhouse has been completely modernized, but still retains its characteristic stone walls and beamed ceilings. The surrounding area offers lovely walks through the French countryside and activities such as horseback riding, golf, and swimming. Afternoon visits are made to the food market in Dijon—which is only about a half-hour's drive from the farmhouse—as well as to various vineyards in Beaune and other parts of Burgundy. Dijon, the capital of Burgundy, is home to Gothic cathedrals, ancient architecture, canals, shopping, and entertainment. In the fourteenth and fifteenth centuries it was an international arts center—it currently hosts eight museums (including, of course, a mustard museum) and its reputation as a gastronomic city is growing.

Spouses are easily accommodated. Children are welcome as well, space permitting (you may have to be housed at another establishment).

THE DETAILS: The program runs one week and is offered May through October. Group size is limited to ten. The cost includes accommodations, most meals with wine at main meals, and cooking lessons.

The Cost: £695.00 (approx. $1,150)

Contact:
Penny Easton
Encounters, Ltd.
Garden House, Orchard Court
Chillenden, Kent CT3 1YA
ENGLAND
Phone: 44-13 04 84 11 36
Fax: 44-13 04 84 11 36

• COOKING WITH FRIENDS IN FRANCE •

The Cooking with Friends program is housed in two homes nestled on a Provençal hillside among olive trees, cypress trees, and vineyards in the ancient town of Châteauneauf de Grass. But these are no ordinary houses: They're the former homes of cooking legends Julia Child and Simone Beck, who lived here while they wrote their cookbook, *Mastering the Art of French Cooking.*

The houses, *La Pitchoune* and *La Campanette*, are classic Provençal farmhouses with tiled roofs, colored shutters, and homey kitchens. The comfortable, informal kitchens are emblematic of the Cooking with Friends program: A guest writes, "We were all surprised to find only a standard stove in *La Pitchoune's* kitchen. No fancy, costly equipment. In fact, the only unique feature was a large yellow Peg-Board with outlines of each utensil drawn around its hook (Paul Child built it to help Julia stay organized). And Kathie's [Kathie Alex, the founder and chef of Cooking with Friends] approach to teaching is just as reassuring as the surroundings."

"The focus," Kathie says, "is on taking the fear out of experimentation by learning basic cooking techniques and adaptable recipes. Guests meet, work, and dine with local residents and chefs, and truly get to know their surroundings as I guide them through the markets and boutiques on a cook's tour of Provence. I want to give them a real experience of the French people, food, and local color."

Cooking classes, during which you prepare lunch, begin after breakfasts of fresh juice and homemade croissants. A sample lunch menu is onion and anchovy pizza, lamb shoulder stew thickened and flavored with garlic, potato gratin, and herbed zucchini. Or you might cook warm Camembert in a flaky crust with mixed greens and walnut vinaigrette, followed by salmon with artichokes in a pesto sauce.

The program includes three days of cooking and two days of

excursions. The first excursion is to the Forville Market in Cannes, featuring a walking tour of a cheese ripening cave and a butcher shop, and lunch at the Michelin two-star, *Le Palme d'Or* restaurant, where you'll have the opportunity to meet the chef, Christian Willer. The second excursion is to the Michelin two-star *La Terrasse* Restaurant in Juan les Pins (near Antibes) for a cooking lesson and lunch with Chef Christian Morrisset.

Afternoons are free for exploring the surrounding area. You could visit the tea room at the Villa Ephrussi de Rothschild, or have dinner at *Le Chevre d'Or* in the medieval village of Eze, enjoying a drink with a panoramic view of the coast. Nice is also close by, with its antique and flower shops, Niçoise specialties like *trucha omelette* (made from pine nuts and Swiss chard) and *socca* (a chickpea crepe cooked in an enormous round dish), and the Chagall and Matisse museums. Or you could visit the waterfall in Courmes, the medieval village of Tourettes, the Fragonard Perfume Factory, the Croisette promenade, or glassblowing or pottery workshops. And there's also horseback riding, golf, and tennis.

Kathie's love of French cooking and culture began in 1979, when she attended Simone Beck's cooking school in Provence. Since then, she's trained at Roger Vergé's restaurant, *Le Moulin de Mougins*, and has attended Lenotre's Professional Cooking School, *La Varenne*, *Le Cordon Bleu*, and *Marie-Blance de Broglie*. She has developed recipes for Michel Richard's cookbook, *Home Cooking with a French Accent*, and is at work on her own cookbook featuring traditional Provençal recipes.

THE DETAILS: The program runs six days and is offered weekly May through June, and September through November. Group size is limited to eight. The cost includes accommodations, breakfast, lunches, some dinners, cooking lessons, and excursions. Noncooking guests are welcome to attend the program; the price listed below includes accommodations, most meals, and excursions.

The Cost: $1,850
Single Supplement: $200
Noncooking guest: $1,135

Contact:
Cooking with Friends in France
Suzanne Wenz
c/o Jackson and Company
29 Commonwealth Avenue
Boston, MA 02116
Phone: 617-350-3837
Fax: 617-247-6149
E-mail: suzanne@jackson-co.com

In France:
Kathie Alex
La Pitchoune, Domaine de Bramafam
06740 Chateauneuf de Grasse FRANCE
Phone: 33-493 60 10 56
Fax: 33-493 60 05 56
E-mail: CWFinfo@aol.com
Web site: www.cookingwithfriends.com

• COOKING AND WINE TASTING TOUR •
TO AIX-EN-PROVENCE

Cultural Homestay International

Learning to cook Provençal cuisine, visiting markets and food producers, and going on excursions all offer a window into the true
Provence. But living with a local family—as guests on Cultural
Homestay's program are invited to do—does more than provide a
window: It opens a door into everyday Provençal life.

"I stayed with a lovely woman about my age, a widow, who has a gorgeous house," said a recent guest of the program. "She didn't speak a word of English, so I had to practice my high school French, which was exactly what I wanted. We laughed a lot and had a terrific time together." Many houses and hosts are available in Aix-en-Provence, or you can choose to stay in a private apartment or hotel. The city itself is the elegant former capital of Provence. It's called "the water city"—due to all the fountains—and is home to an art quarter, elegant mansions, French gardens, the St. Sauveur Cloister, and many other places of cultural interest.

Demonstration classes are taught by Chef Marc Hercle and held in *Château d' Arnajon*, a circa–seventeen hundred mansion. Some typical dishes are magrets de canard, gratin de figues, and tarte au melon.

During the first week, you'll visit a chocolatier, the aquaduc de Roquefavon, the village of Ventabren, *Château de Beaupre*, an olive oil museum, *La Rognes D'antheron*, *l'abbaye de Silvacanne*, a goat cheese factory, and will have a full-day excursion in Aix-en-Provence.

The weekend brings a two-day trip to Arles (for sightseeing, wine tasting, and theater), Nimes (where you'll visit Roman arenas and aquaducts, *Château de Montfaucon*, and the wine shops of Châteauneauf du Pape), and Avignon (for a guided tour of the Pope's Palace). You'll stay in bed-and-breakfasts, and enjoy regional cuisine for lunch and dinner.

Then you'll return to Aix-en-Provence for more classes, wine tastings, museum visiting, and a boat trip to *Château d'If* (made famous in *The Three Musketeers*). Toward the end of the second week, you'll travel to Cassis for a boat ride to view the clanques, visit the cellars and sample the wines of *Coteau du Var*, have lunch at a restaurant on the Ilse of Bander and, finally, enjoy a farewell dinner.

THE DETAILS: The program runs for fifteen days and is offered in May. Group size is limited to eight. The cost includes round-trip airfare, accommodations, some meals, cooking lessons, and all ground transportation in France.

The Cost: $2,985

Contact:
Richard Scammel
14445 Galiliee Court
Grass Valley, CA 95945
Phone: 530-272-3419
E-mail: chefs@jps.net

Cultural Homestay International
2455 Bennet Valley Drive
Suite 210B
Santa Rosa, CA 95404
Phone: 800-395-2726
Fax: 707-523-3704
Web site: www.chinet.org/group.html

From the kitchen of
Cooking and Wine Tasting Tour
to Aix-en-Provence
⊚

TARTE MENTONAISE (ORANGE PIE)

3 oranges	Pinch of fresh ground pepper
1 cup flour	Orange zest (optional)
1 teaspoon baking powder	Olive oil (enough to make
2 tablespoons brown sugar	paste, below)
1/2 cup water	Orange marmalade
1 teaspoon salt	

Use a knife to make about eight score marks on the oranges, extending from top to bottom. Then cut the oranges horizontally into slices of a quarter of an inch, at most.

In a food processor, mix the flour, baking powder, brown sugar, water, salt, and black pepper (and the orange zest, if using). While the processor is running, add the olive oil until a paste forms.

Spread the paste in a circle on a cookie sheet or pie pan, cover with the marmalade, then lay the orange slices on top to cover. Spread more marmalade over the orange slices.

Bake in a preheated oven at 350° for about half an hour. Cut into wedges and serve.

• COURS DE CUISINE PROVENÇALE •

In 1995, Madeleine Hill traveled to Arles, a two-thousand-year-old city in the south of France. Three days into her stay, she met Erick Vedel, and asked to borrow his bicycle for a quick trip to the beach—she ended up dining in his kitchen every night for a week, and then marrying him. Now she acts as his translator (she's fluent in French and Japanese, as well as her native English), hostess, assistant, and business manager, promoting his unique cooking workshops.

Erick is not only a chef, but an "archeologist of Provençal cuisine"—he has spent twelve years reconstructing more than a thousand Provençal recipes dating from antiquity to the nineteenth century. He studies ancient texts, archives, letters, and journals to rediscover lost recipes and combines historical and culinary knowledge to present a new view of Provençal cuisine.

"If you read of the Greeks or the Romans in history books," Erick says, "they remain abstract. But if you eat the same dishes they ate, you say to yourself, 'I share the same tastes as these people thousands of years ago,' and they become familiar."

Erick teaches guests to prepare a variety of historical dishes: One may have been cooked for Rabelais as he passed through Provence, another eaten by mariners as they worked their barges up the Rhône. He may teach a dish prepared by fishermen of the Camargue, enjoyed by dukes in elegant estates, or found in Carthaginian and Roman cooking pots of antiquity.

Typical dishes include *papeton d'aubergine avec un coulis froud de tomates au basilic frais*, *moules marinieres Provençale*, tapenade, *brandade de morue*, *quinquebine* (salted cod and leek stew), *les legumes fracies* (stuffed vegetables), and artichokes a la *barrigoule*.

Guests visit the largest open-air market in Provence, taste the creations of a Provençal pastry specialist, meet the Vedels' favorite boulanger who still makes his bread in a wood-fired oven, visit a sheep-cheese-maker and local wineries, and gather herbs in the hills surrounding the city.

For wine lovers, the Vedels offer personal tours and tastings at some of the best (both well- and less-known) local wineries in the region. You'll visit Côtes du Rhône, Costieres du Gard, Pic St. Loup, Languedoc, and many more. Then, every evening, you'll help prepare a meal based on the offerings of the local market and enjoy the dishes paired with the day's wines.

The Vedels also offer an historically oriented vacation featuring the cuisine of ancient Rome. Menus focus on the fish of the Mediterranean, wild game and fowl, cheese and cream produced on sheep and goat farms, herbs of the hills, fruits and nuts of local trees, spices of the Orient, and the ancient art of wine making. In addition to preparing (and enjoying) Roman menus, you'll visit the *Musée d'Arles* Antique and Roman monuments in Arles and the surrounding region.

And for nature lovers, the Vedels offer a cooking vacation featuring the Rhône river and the Camargue wildlife sanctuary, home to the eponymous bulls and white ponies, thousands of pink flamingos, sea salt gathering, and great expanses of wide, windswept beaches. The menus focus on dishes favored by mariners of the Rhône, fishermen of the Camargue, and enjoyed in local inns for centuries.

Many local activities and expeditions are also available. You can visit Roman ruins (such as the arena, the outdoor theater, the baths, and the aqueduct), medieval monuments (such as the Church of St. Trophime, known for its elegantly carved allegorical entryway), and museums, or just wander through the winding streets. Golf, horseback riding, biking, hiking, tennis, bird watching, and swimming are all available nearby.

As of this writing, the Vedels are shopping for an estate in which they can house guests. But they do not currently offer housing— they are, however, more than happy to suggest local hotels: There are excellent two- to four-star hotels in the area, as well as a number of very pleasant bed-and-breakfasts.

There is a "traveling companion" option by which noncooking travel companions can join the meals. And Madeleine would be happy to help guests with children plan activities, pick the hotel, etc., to make this vacation appropriate for families with children.

THE DETAILS: The programs range from one day to more than a week and are offered year-round. Group size is limited to eight. The cost includes lunch and dinner, cooking lessons, and day trips (which include picnics packed with local delicacies).

Single cooking class: 500 francs (approx. $80)
Four to eight day classes: 3,600 francs (approx. $575) to 6,300
   francs (approx. $1,000)

Contact:
30 rue Pierre Euzeby
13200 Arles FRANCE
Phone/Fax: 33-490 49 69 20
E-mail: actvedel@provnet.fr
Web site: www.cuisineprovencale.com

From the kitchen of
Cours de Cuisine Provençale
⊘

LA MORUE EN RAITO
(SALTED COD IN RAITO SAUCE)
SERVES 4

This is an ancient recipe, traditionally served on Christmas Eve.

FOR THE SAUCE:
1 onion
3 tablespoons olive oil
1/4 cup flour
4 small, or 2 large, tomatoes diced
4 1/2 cups dry red cooking wine
2 cloves of garlic crushed and chopped
1 liqueur glass of vinegar
3 tablespoons capers
1 bay leaf
1/4 cup black olives
1/4 cup green olives

FOR THE FISH:
2 1/4 pounds salted cod, soaked overnight (fresh cod may also be
    used if salted cod is not available)
1/3 cup flour
1/3 cup cornstarch
Vegetable oil for frying

First, desalt the cod by rinsing it thoroughly, then submerging it in
a bowl of cold water. Change the water frequently over the next
twenty-four hours, until it is entirely desalted.

For the sauce: Mince the onions and simmer lightly in olive oil
until they take on a little color. Add the flour and stir to make a

caramel colored roux, allowing the onions to become crispy brown
as well. Add the tomatoes and stir together, follow with the red
wine, the capers, the olives, the garlic, and the bay leaf. Let simmer
45 minutes.

For the fish: Cut the desalted cod into individual serving
morsels, lightly cover with the cornstarch and flour, and fry until
golden in the vegetable oil.

Dress the cod with the sauce, and serve immediately, accompanied with a strong red wine with flavor and body.

• CUISINE EN PROVENCE •

Each morning of your vacation with Cuisine en Provence starts
with pots of steaming coffee, flaky croissants, and fresh juice—in
either the courtyard of *Château de Vins sur Caramy*, a sixteenth-
century château overlooking the river Caramy, or the *Château les
Lonnes*, a bastide from the twelfth century which has been converted into a four-star hotel.

Then, after breakfast, you're off to the market—*marche de Coti-
gnac*—to inspect, discuss, select, and purchase the ingredients you'll
be cooking for the day's menus. You'll choose the fish for the *soupe
de poisson*, the vegetables for the ratatouille, and the meat for the
daube Provençale. You'll taste the seasonal creations of the local producers—of cheese, olives, saucissons, olive oil, bread, and more.

On the way back to the château, you'll stop at a local vineyard
for a lesson in enology (and, of course, a tasting), before gathering
for a barbecue on the terrace. The afternoon is free for swimming,
tennis, sightseeing, enjoying a siesta, or relaxing in the garden with
a chilled rosé.

Classes reconvene in the late afternoon. Depending on the
morning market visit, you may make a meal of tapenade (puréed
olives), *poivrons grillés* (roasted peppers), *soupe au pistou* (vegetable
pesto soup), *loup grillé* (grilled sea bass you bought that morning),

tian de courgettes (braised zucchini in tomato sauce), *salade de mesclun* (a typical Provençal mixed salad), and *tarte aux bales* (berry tart). And to round it off, a digestif and coffee around the fireplace.

Your teacher is Provence native Chef Jean-Marie Carret. Chef Jean-Marie trained in France and has worked at top restaurants in France, the United Kingdom, the United States, and Spain. He is also a private caterer who has served such notables as Prince Andrew, Margaret Thatcher, John Cleese, Sean Connery, and Michael Caine.

Cuisine en Provence also offers a long weekend dedicated to the truffle (only in season—November through March) during which guests visit a truffle plantation, go truffle hunting, learn truffle recipes, and, most important, enjoy the taste of the "black diamond." Contact them for more information on this specialized trip.

THE DETAILS: The program runs one week and is offered in June, July, and September. Group size is limited to fourteen. The cost includes accommodations, cooking lessons, wine, organized excursions, two free aperitifs, two meals at local restaurants, and visits to vineyards (with wine lessons and wine tastings.)

The Cost: $1,950
Single Supplement: $400

Contact:
Judy Ebrey
Cuisine International
PO Box 25228
Dallas, TX 75225
Phone: 214-373-1161
Fax: 214-373-1162
E-mail: Cuisineint@aol.com
Web site: www.cuisineinternational.com

In France:
38 Cours Pierre Puget
13006 Marseille FRANCE
E-mail: jean-marie@cuisine-en-provence.com
E-mail: charleric@cuisine-en-provence.com
Web site: www.cuisine-en-provence.com

• THE CULINARY TRAVEL COMPANY •

Built in the eighteenth century, *Labonne Etape* is an eighteen-room estate located in the Haute-Provence district and surrounded by wild lavender and cypress and olive trees. You'll stay at *Labonne Etape*, and study regional Provençal cuisine under the direction of your hosts Arlette, Jeannie, and Pierre Gleize.

After visiting the local markets each morning to buy the ingredients for your meals, you'll head to the kitchen for four cooking lessons, where you'll learn about thirty-five traditional dishes made from local ingredients.

In the afternoons, you are free to explore the surrounding countryside on your own, or join one of CTC's arranged excursions to local vineyards, olive oil producers, goat-cheese farmers, and beekeepers (for fresh lavender honey).

You'll also have the chance to visit the towns of Banon, Les Mees, and Forcalquier for a peek into the true Provence and to visit open-air markets to browse for antiques, textiles, and local crafts.

The Culinary Travel Company also offers a cooking vacation in Tuscany (for more information see page 110.)

THE DETAILS: The program runs one week and is offered in May, June, September, and November. Group size is limited to eight. The cost includes accommodations, breakfast and dinner with wine, cooking lessons, and excursions.

The Cost: $1,995
Single Supplement: $300

Contact:
The Culinary Travel Company
P.O. Box 14330
Chicago, IL 60614
Phone: 888-777-0760
E-mail: dan@theculinarytravelco.com
Web site: www.theculinarytravelco.com

• ECOLE DES TROIS PONTS •
COOKING INSTITUTE

Ecole des Trois Ponts offers food, wine, sightseeing, optional language classes, and, above all, relaxation. As Margaret O'Loan, who runs *Ecole des Trois Ponts* with her husband, Rene Dorel, likes to say, "the only thing you need to worry about is packing your suitcase."

From the relaxed family atmosphere to the chef's willingness to adapt menus for guests who range from rank amateurs to gourmet cooks—and to prepare meals for a vegetarian along with a card-carrying carnivore—*Trois Ponts* offers a taste of the French way of life and love of food.

In fact, Margaret seems to enjoy the challenges that can be presented to the chef. "See how well Chef Jean copes with having a low-fat food lover alongside a give-me-all-the-cream-you-can guest in the same class. It takes real flair—he will make a sauce without any butter (a real challenge in France) and then make the same sauce with a heavy dose of butter and cream. It's like having Laurel and Hardy on the same team . . . or maybe I should say Jekyll and Hyde!"

The culinary emphasis for the **French Provençal Cuisine** course is on traditional French country cooking. A typical meal might include a market garden salad, Provençal chicken, guinea hen roasted in five spices, sausage-shaped fish mousse, lemon tart, and raspberry soufflé. Other recipes are tomato, zucchini, and basil tart, roast anglerfish with young leeks wrapped in ham, Provençal-style chicken cooked in a hot pot, and apple and apricot tart. The courses are taught by Chef Jean, who has worked in two- and three-star Michelin restaurants, as well as run his own restaurant.

Classes and lodging are both at *Château de Matel*, which was completely renovated in the early seventeen hundreds. The château used to be the home of Andre Citroen of car making fame, sits on thirteen acres of park and woodland, and even has a canal. It's located near the Burgundy and Beaujolais wine regions, the extinct volcanic area of Auvergne, and is about two miles from the center of Roanne, a small city known for the three-star Michelin restaurant *Troisgros*.

An optional wine appreciation class is also offered, as are **French and Cooking** classes, where you spend mornings learning conversational French and the afternoons learning how to prepare typical Provençal country dishes, sauces, and desserts.

When you're not studying, you can swim, play Ping-Pong, golf, or tennis, visit markets and shops, go sightseeing in medieval villages, and go horseback riding.

The Culinary Institute prides itself on catering to all kinds of guests. One guest may want to try everything, another may want mostly to watch, wine-glass in hand, and a third may need a little encouragement to get involved. They've even had guests who were intent on learning to cook a special menu for a wedding anniversary. "We suggest adding a bottle of champagne in case there are any small accidents," Margaret says "A bit of bubbly will smooth over anyone's mistakes."

Ecole des Trois Ponts is happy to host noncooking partners, friends, and children. It's not unusual for a partner to wander into the kitchen with wet hair after a dip in the pool to peek at the delights being created by cooks. And if a noncooking partner has any special interests they'd like to pursue—from kayaking to rugby to choral music to yoga to handicraft—just let Margaret and Rene know, and they'll try to help.

The château also has the space and facilities (a pool, swings, toys, and plenty of space to run) to make it a great place to bring children. For younger children, the school can organize baby-sitters if desired. And they even have space for dogs and cats.

THE DETAILS: The programs run one week and are offered from June through October. Group sizes are limited to eight. The French Provençal Cuisine program includes accommodations, all meals, cooking lessons, and some excursions. The French and Cooking program includes accommodations, all meals, cooking lessons, and French language lessons. Costs for both programs vary according to the quality of the room (i.e. shared/private bath).

French Provençal Cuisine: 5,900–7,700 francs (approx. $950–$1,225)
French and Cooking Program: 7,200–9,000 francs (approx.
$1,150–$1,450)

Contact:
Ecole des Trois Ponts
Château de Matel
42300 Roanne France
Phone: 00 33-4 77 71 53 00
Fax: 00 33-4 77 70 80 01
E-mail: info@3ponts.edu
Web site: www.3ponts.edu

• FRENCH KITCHEN AT CAMONT •
AND *JULIA HOYT* CANAL CRUISES

While in Holland, Kate Hill Ratliffe bought the *Julia Hoyt,* a classic eighty-five-foot barge that for fifty years hauled firewood and cheese over the inland seas of northern Europe. She sailed south along the waterways of Europe until she arrived home: the Garonne River Valley in Gascony. Although she bought the barge as a home, she soon transformed it into a bed-and-breakfast, with a picture window saloon and dining room, a bistro-galley, a garden deck, and two queen-size staterooms with private baths.

Kate now offers culinary adventures aboard the *Julia Hoyt* and cooking vacations (that include days on the barge) at Camont, her charming eighteenth-century farmhouse set on a two-acre park on the banks of the canal. In the original brick hearth kitchen, you'll learn the secrets of seasonal Gascon cuisine: tender asparagus in the spring, succulent tomatoes in the summer, grapes, game, and mushrooms in autumn, and foie gras, confit, ham, and sausage in the winter.

While at Camont, you'll visit village markets and harvest vegetables from Kate's potager garden before settling on a menu for your cooking class du jour. One morning you'll visit a neighbor's farm to buy fresh poultry, which you then cook using the traditional farmhouse methods of braising, stewing, and grilling. Another day is spent focusing on desserts and digestifs. You'll also learn to cook complete meals, from aperitifs to *grandmère*'s favorite country desserts: A typical meal might be sautéed foi gras, pan-roasted duck breast, gratin of garden vegetables, *salade verte* and farmhouse cheeses, and *crème au chocolate* with wild strawberries, capped off with a vintage Armagnac. Other dishes you might learn to make are roasted bread with herbed sea salt, carrots glazed with rosé wine, grilled ham with figs, radish leaf soup, roast pork stuffed with prunes and shallots, and goat cheese with Armagnac and honey.

Daily excursions include visiting traditional village bistros, top restaurants (such as Marie-Claude Gracia's *A La Belle Gasconne* in Poudenas), medieval villages, Armagnac distilleries, and wineries. And, of course, you'll spend time aboard the *Julia Hoyt*. You'll cruise the canals, stopping to explore local markets, and visit with Kate's friends and neighbors along the "long village": the fifty-mile-long community of people living on barges and in canalside homes and farms, running restaurants, wineries, shops, and markets in nineteen villages and towns connected by twenty-one locks and sixty-eight bridges. You'll sip wine on deck as the tranquil French countryside slips by, drifting past fields of sunflowers and medieval villages.

Kate is the author of *A Culinary Journey in Gascony: Recipes and Stories from My French Canal Boat*. She has run a bakery, cooked on charter boats in the Caribbean, and was the chef for a travel group in East Africa. And she's taught French cooking at Camont since 1991. She has lived in the Garonne River Valley since 1988.

THE DETAILS: The program runs from three to seven days, and is offered year-round. Group size is limited from six to eight. The cost for the less-expensive program includes accommodations, all breakfasts, one restaurant lunch, cooking lessons, and a market tour. The cost for the more expensive program also includes lunches, dinners, various excursions, canal cruises, and ground transportation.

The Cost: $895 (three-day workshop) to $3,250 (seven-day gastronomic tour)

Contact:
Kate Hill Ratliffe
European Culinary Adventures
5 Ledgewood Way #6
Peabody, MA 01960
Phone: 800-852-2625; 978-535-5738
E-mail: JuliaHoyt@aol.com
E-mail: KateHill@compuserve.com

• HOLIDAYS IN THE SUN IN • THE SOUTH OF FRANCE

"The other people were the best part of the experience," says a guest
who enjoyed a "holiday in the sun" living and cooking in Sylvie
Lallemand's home. "Sylvie's program is cozy and homey—and also
quite artistic, as Sylvie is a painter in addition to being a chef—so
all of us were comfortable and relaxed."

Sylvie, who's the author of *The Tastes and Colors of Provence*
(which she also illustrated), learned to cook at her Provençal
mother's knee, and then honed her talents at the Roger Vergé cooking school. She puts guests up in her home, *les Megalithes*, in
Provence, near Gordes and about forty minutes from Avignon.

The house is secluded in the woods, and you can spend the days
hiking, by yourself or with Sylvie, or just lounging by the pool. And
the cooking classes are equally unpretentious. They focus on country cooking—lots of garlic, and fresh vegetables you pick out that
morning in the market. Some sample dishes are ratatouille Niçoise,
soupe au pistou, eggplant au gratin, lamb shoulder with rosemary,
and fish terraine with charlotte russe (with Bavarian cream and lady

fingers) or *oeufs à la neige* (literally, snow eggs—poached egg whites served in a cream sauce) for dessert.

Other activities in the area include horse or bike riding, tennis, golf, visiting museums and historic sites, and shopping.

THE DETAILS: The program runs one week and is offered March through July and September through November. Class size is limited to six. The cost includes accommodations, meals, and cooking lessons.

The Cost: 3,800 francs (about $630)

Contact:
Sylvie Lallemand
Les Megalithes
84220 Gordes FRANCE
Phone: 33-490 72 23 41

• LA VARENNE •

Anne Willan, the founder of *La Varenne*, has more than thirty years of culinary experience as a cooking teacher, food writer, and American television host. She's a leading authority on French cooking and culinary history, and has published many cookbooks including *La Varenne Pratique*, which has sold more than five hundred thousand copies worldwide and has been translated into six foreign languages.

A cooking vacation with Anne begins at *Château du Feÿ*, an historic North Burgundy estate which Anne and her husband, Mark, purchased in 1982 and lovingly restored. Anne and Mark will greet you and give you a tour of the estate, ending with the château's wine cellars—just in time for a tasting of French cheese and wine.

The next morning, you get to work. The program at *La Varenne*

combines hands-on cooking with Anne, observation of local master chefs, and meals at fabulous local restaurants. You'll spend the first morning in a three-hour master class, possibly making salmon *en meurette*, apple *tarte tatin*, goat cheese puffs, and hot chocolate mousse. Then you'll spend the afternoon at a two-hour demonstration of contemporary French recipes such as ravioli with escargot and wild mushrooms, and will have dinner at a wonderful local bistro in the evening.

Most of the days follow this pattern—master class in the morning, lunch and demonstration in the afternoon, and a special dinner. And there's still time for excursions. You'll experience the hustle and bustle of one of Burgundy's finest markets—learning how to select the finest of ingredients, the key to good French cooking. You'll spend an afternoon with a retired baker who fires up the bread oven at the château to demonstrate the creation of croissants and specialty breads—and the pizzas you'll have for dinner. You'll also spend an afternoon in Auxerre, admiring the river views of this charming town before having dinner at *La Chamaille*, one of Anne's favorite country restaurants, which has earned a one-star Michelin rating.

The morning of your final day at *La Varenne* is spent touring a well-known Chablis winery. Then you return to the château for a lunch that features novel ideas for home entertaining. In the afternoon, you travel to the cooking school of *Côte St. Jacques*, where you'll watch the master chefs prepare some of the dishes you'll enjoy that evening for your farewell dinner at the restaurant (one of only twenty in France to receive three Michelin stars).

La Varenne also offers courses at the Greenbrier resort in the United States (see page 235 for more information).

THE DETAILS: The program runs five days and is offered both summer and fall. Group size is limited to ten. The cost includes accommodations, meals with wine, excursions, and transfer to and from Paris.

The Cost: $2,950
Single Supplement: $400 (if available)

Contact:
La Varenne
PO Box 25574
Washington, DC 20007
Phone: 202-337-0073; (800) 537-6486
Fax: 703-823-5438
E-mail: lavarenne@compuserve.com

In France:
Château du Feÿ
89300 Villecien FRANCE
Phone: 33-386 63 18 34
Fax: 33-386 63 01 33
Web site: www.lavarenne.com

· LA CUISINE DE PROVENCE ·

Inland Services

L'Isle Sur la Sorgue is a charming village, located just a half-hour from Avignon—on an island in the middle of the Sorgue River. It's well known for its many Provençal antique shops, and is also the home of the recently restored *Domaine de la Fontaine*, which offers a cooking vacation in a relaxed French countryside atmosphere.

Hands-on lessons meet every day for three hours, after which you sit down with Chef Jean-Claude Aubertin to enjoy the meal you prepared. You may learn how to make *caviar d'aubergines* (eggplant purée), *soupe au pistou, escalopes de lotte cote d'azur* (monkfish with zucchini and eggplant), *legumes farcie "grandmère"* ("Grannie's" stuffed vegetables), and *fondant au poire* (pear cake) for dessert.

Noncooking activities include excursions to an open-air antique market, a chocolaterie, and several wineries for tastings. Sojourns for historical interest are made to *Palais des Papes* (Palace of the Popes) in Avignon and to *Oppede le Vieux* for its ancient castle and view of the Luberon valley, and you'll have a chance to see other Provençal villages such as Gordes, Roussillon, and Le Baux, as well. You can also stay close to home, enjoying the pool or strolling through the countryside.

Jean-Claude owns *Aubertin* Restaurant, located in a twelfth-century building in Villeneuve Les Avignon, has won numerous cooking competitions, and is a member of *Academie Culinaire de France*.

Noncooking partners or spouses are easily accommodated on this trip and are included in most activities and meals. Inland Services also arranges two culinary trips to Italy (see page 122 for more information.)

THE DETAILS: The program runs one week and is offered in April, October, and November. Group size is limited to twelve. The cost includes accommodations, meals, cooking lessons, and excursions.

The Cost: $1,995
Single Supplement: $350

Contact:
Ralph P. Slone
Inland Services, Incorporated
360 Lexington Avenue
New York, NY 10017
Phone: 212-687-9898

• LE CASTEL DE BRAY ET MONTS •

Maxime and Eliane Rochereau invite you to stay at their eighteenth-century manor in the Loire Valley to learn how to cook "á la française" and to explore the countryside from a French rather than tourist perspective.

The manor is located in the vineyard village of Bréhémont on the banks of the Loire River in the center of the French château region. Mornings are spent with the Rochereaus in the professional kitchen watching Chef Maxime, who was the head chef at the Ritz in Paris as well as the Ritz Carlton in Chicago, demonstrate traditional French recipes. With three-hour classes every morning, you'll learn such recipes as *velouté* of seafood, filet of fish *beurre blanc*, chicken *à l'Angevine*, filet of beef in a *marchand de vin* sauce, and *feuilleté de framboises* sauce chantilly.

The afternoons are reserved for excursions throughout the Loire Valley. One day is spent visiting the château of *La Belle au Bois Dormant* (Sleeping Beauty), built in the sixteeth and seventeenth century, and the medieval city of Jeanne d'Arc. Other châteaux you'll visit include *Azay-Le-Rideau*, built on an island in the Indre river in the sixteenth century, and *Langeais*, the site of Charles VIII's marriage to Duchess Anne de Bretagne, built in the fifteenth century and recently donated to the Institut de France, which has restored it to its original splendor.

You'll also see the Vallandry gardens, visit a famous equestrian school in Saumur, shop in Plumeraus, one of the oldest towns in Touraine (which hosts an excellent kitchen store and an Arbona store which sells elegant porcelain figures, crystal, and fine silver), and go wine tasting in the vineyard village of Bourgueil.

THE DETAILS: Classes run one week and are offered in March, April, May, October, and November. The cost includes accommodations, meals, cooking lessons, and excursions.

The Cost: 9,800 francs (approx. $1,575)

Contact:
Mrs. Eliane Rochereau
Le Castel de Bray et Monts
37130 Bréhémont Langeais FRANCE
Phone: 33-247 96 70 47
Fax: 33-247 97 57 36
E-mail: cooking-class-infrance@wanadoo.fr
Web site: www.cooking-class-infrance.com

From the kitchen of Le Castel de Bray et Monts

❧

VEMOUTE D'ARTICHAUTS
(ARTICHOKE SOUP)

2 tablespoons of melted butter	1 1/2 quarts of chicken stock
6 raw artichoke hearts, finely sliced	2 cups of heavy cream
2 white leeks, minced	1 bunch of chives, chopped
	Salt and pepper to taste

In a large pot, put the melted butter and artichokes, and let them sauté on a low heat for three minutes. Add the minced leeks and the chicken stock and simmer for thirty minutes.

While the soup cooks, whip the heavy cream until firm and then add the chopped chives.

When the soup is done, pour it into a blender and purée it for two to three minutes. Pour it back into the pot and add salt and pepper to taste. Serve in bowls with a large dollop of whipped cream and chives in the center. Serve very hot.

• LA COMBE EN PERIGORD •

La Combe is an eighteenth-century *maison de maitre*, a gentleman's house, on thirty acres of farmland and woods in a secluded valley near the Vezere River in southwest France's Perigord Noir. The main buildings of *La Combe* are arranged around a rustic courtyard; one side is a restored Perigordine stone barn which houses private guest suites, and the other is the main house, with a drawing room (featuring a massive stone fireplace), a comfortable dining room, a book-lined library, a wine cellar, and a newly converted country-style kitchen which opens onto a *potager* garden.

Perigord—also known as the Dordogne—is best known outside France for its prehistoric cave paintings and medieval castles and villages. But within France it is also known for its cuisine, based on local ingredients such as truffles, walnuts, wild mushrooms, and foie gras. Which is why Wendely Harvey and Robert Cave-Rogers spent two years scouring the Peregordine countryside for the perfect base for their culinary and cultural programs.

Wendely is the publisher and editorial director of many award-winning cookbooks (including the forty-three-volume Williams-Sonoma Kitchen Library), and has worked closely with many of America's leading cookbook authors and chefs. Robert worked for years in hotel management (for the Mandarin Hong Kong and Oriental Bangkok hotels), and spent two years supervising the restoration of La Combe while researching culinary and cultural programs in the region.

With Wendely's cooking connections, *La Combe* has been able to attract wonderful guest chefs, such as Georgeanne Brennan, Joyce Goldstein, Diane Holuigue, Joanne Weir, Monique Hooker, and Linda Gassenheimer. Each guest chef prepares a customized vacation week, typically including three or four afternoon classes, market visits, field trips, and meals at notable restaurants.

But there's more to a vacation at *La Combe* than cooking. On one day, you might shop at the Sunday market in nearby St. Cyprian, see fifteen thousand-year-old cave paintings in the Lascaux caves, and have dinner at *Auberge de La Vieille Cure* in historic St. Chamassy. On the next day you might travel to Sorges la Gourmande, the capital of Perigord truffles, where you'll sample a traditional menu *grandmére* at the *Auberge de la Truffle* and visit the Truffle Museum.

Other possible trips include exploring the old river port of Bergerac, winetasting, shopping for antiques, or visiting castles, cathedrals, and churches (Perigord has more listed historic monuments than any other part of France except Paris). You can also meet local artisans, tour a walnut pressing mill and a subterranean mushroom farm, and bicycle, canoe, hike, horseback ride, or just relax by the pool.

THE DETAILS: The program runs one week and is offered year-round. Group size is limited to twelve. The cost includes accommodations, all meals, cooking lessons, excursions, and transfers to and from recommended flights.

The Cost: $2,350–$2,950
Single Supplement: $400

Contact:
Le Combe en Perigord
3450 Sacramento Street #436
San Francisco, CA 94118
Phone/Fax: 888-522-6623
E-mail: info@lacombe-perigord.com
Web site: www.lacombe-perigord.com

• MAS DE CORNUD •

Mas de Cornud is an eighteenth-century Provençal farmhouse which has been renovated into a six-room country inn. It's fewer than two miles from Saint Remy, and is near Arles, Avignon, Aix-en-Provence, Nimes, the Luberon, and the Camargue. "The area is full of attractions," says David Carpita, co-owner with his wife, Nitockrees, of *Mas de Cornud.* "And St. Remy itself has Roman antiquities, the hospice where Van Gogh spent fourteen months doing some of his best work, and is also the birth-home of Nostradamus. It has tree-lined streets, pots of geraniums in windowsills, lively cafés, good shopping, and excellent dining. It is, to use that overworked phrase, the quintessential Provençal town."

David and Nitockrees offer many vacation options: from one-day cooking classes and wine tasting excursions to weeklong Provençal home cooking programs to master classes (taught by notable guest chefs) to vacations organized around the olive harvest, Christmas, and local festivals. The culinary emphasis is on Provençal cuisine using fresh ingredients, on "hands-on" cooking classes, on cooking techniques and practical hints, and on dishes you can duplicate with ingredients back home. Classes are held in a custom-built teaching kitchen with ten workstations, a full range of equipment, and granite working surfaces.

Typical menus use artichokes, garlic, tomatoes, zucchini, and red peppers, usually from the kitchen garden. Main dish ingredients are spring lamb, free-range chicken, rabbit, and fresh fish. And desserts are made from fresh fruits from the garden, such as strawberries and figs, and homemade pastry dough. All this is, of course, paired with excellent wines of the Rhône valley.

A variety of excursions are also available. During the home cooking weeks, guests visit goat cheese makers, olive oil mills, beekeepers, artisan chocolatiers, candied fruit processors, etc. They also attend wine tastings and cultural events, and go on a walk in the footsteps of Vincent Van Gogh. Other options include eating at the Carpitas' favorite bistros, watching a parade of sheep in St. Remy during the *Fête de la Transhumance*, browsing in art galleries and farmer's markets, touring medieval castles, and taking to the backroads for days of bicycling.

Nitockrees teaches the cooking classes. Born in Cairo to a prominent Egyptian family, Nitockrees learned to cook at her mother's side, using the fresh ingredients common to both sides of the Mediterranean. She has taught in the Middle East, Eastern Europe, France, and the United States, and her recipes appear in several cookbooks, such as *Pedaling through Provence*, *The Backroads Cookbook*, and *Fromages Fermiers*.

Guest chefs who have taught at *Mas de Cornud* include Philippe Théme and Jean-Pierre Novi of La Riboto de Taven, Jean-Pierre Michel of La Regalido, Robert Brunel of Brunel, François Perrot of La Maison Jaune, Alain Assaud of Le Marceau and Jacques Pépin, the noted cookbook author.

Noncooking partners and children are welcome. Baby-sitters can be arranged.

THE DETAILS: The programs run for one, three, four, or seven days. Group size is limited to ten. The cost for a weeklong program includes accommodations, all meals, cooking lessons, and excursions. The costs for other programs do not include accommodations.

Weeklong Program: $2,100–$2,800
One-day Program: $90
Three- to Four-day Programs: $540

Contact:
Judy Ebrey
Cuisine International
PO Box 25228
Dallas, TX 75225
Phone: 214-373-1161
Fax: 214-373-1162
E-mail: CuisineInt@aol.com
Web site: www.cuisineinternational.com

In France:
David and Nitockrees Carpita
Mas de Cornud
Route de Mas Blanc
13210 Saint-Remy-de-Provence FRANCE
Phone: 33-490 92 39 32
Fax: 33-490 92 55 99
Voice mail/Fax: 33-153 01 31 15
E-mail: mascornud@compuserve.com
Web site: www.mascornud.com

• MOVEABLE FEAST IN PROVENCE— •
A WALKING TRIP WITH
A CULINARY TWIST

The Moveable Feast in Provence combines walking, eating, sightseeing, and cooking lessons. It begins just a few steps from the *Cours Saleya*, the tile-paved pedestrian esplanade and produce market in Nice. You'll explore the market and then go on a walking tour of the city—you'll wander through the shaded, narrow streets of vieux Nice and discover fragrant food shops and colorful fabric stores before stopping for dinner and drinks.

The next day, you might decide to visit the Matisse Chapel and have a dip in the hotel pool before traveling to the hilltop town of Mougins, home of Roger Vergé's restaurant and cooking school. There you'll have a lesson and dinner: asparagus and artichoke *barigoule*, sautéed duck breast with Provençal honey and lemon, and crisp apricot biscuit with pistachio ice cream for dessert.

On your second day in Cote d'Azur, you'll visit *les Alpes-Maritimes*, the hills behind Nice, for a leisurely lunchon at Patricia Robinson's farmhouse and cooking school, *le Mas du Loup* (or A Taste of Provence—see page 65). You'll sample homemade vin d'orange, Provençal-roasted lamb, ratatouille, and tapenade. Weather permitting, you'll feast outside under the old olive and fruit trees. You'll then have the chance to walk off your feast by exploring the villages of les Alpes-Marities on foot.

On the third day of the Moveable Feast, you'll drive past Antibes, Cannes, and Aix-en-Provence for a walk to the Michelin-starred Bistro *d'Eygalieres*. After lunch at the bistro, you'll arrive at your home in St. Remy, *Mas de la Brune*, a family-owned château surrounded by flower gardens and lavender. The next morning, you'll shop at the market in St. Remy and return to the *Mas* to prepare a market-day feast, followed by a cooking class and dinner.

Depending on your inclination, you can spend your fifth day doing serious walking in the hilly surroundings, or (equally serious) sightseeing and shopping. Some highlights: Les Baux-de-Provence, a perched village, the Michelin-starred *Oustau de Baumaniere*, and the lunarlike landscape of the *Alpilles* (little Alps). In the evening, you'll gather for an art history walking tour followed by a special cooking class and dinner at *Mas de Cornud* (see page 40).

The final two days of the Moveable Feast you'll spend in Avignon—after a vintner's buffet lunch and wine tasting in the Rhone wine village Châteauneuf-du-Pape. You'll stay in the Hotel de la *Mirange*, a former fourteenth century palace built by the cardinal-nephew of Pope Clement V, which has a Michelin-starred restaurant.

The next morning, you'll tour the city: You can visit the *Palais des Papes* and the *Musee du Petit Palais*, and go on any of the many enchanting walks around the city and the nearby Ile de Barthelasse (an island in the middle of the Rhône). Finally, on that last night, you will have a cooking class in the hotel's kitchen, where Chef Jean-Claude Aubertin will help you prepare a farewell feast.

THE DETAILS: The program runs eight days and is offered in May and June. Group size is limited from sixteen to twenty-four. The cost includes accommodations, most meals, cooking lessons, and all excursions.

The Cost: $5,950
Single Supplement: $830

Contact:
Butterfield and Robinson
70 Bond Street
Toronto, Ontario
CANADA M5B IX3
Phone: 800-678-1147; 416-864-1354
Fax: 416-864-0541
E-mail: info@butterfield.com
Web site: www.butterfield.com

• THE MURRAY SCHOOL OF COOKERY •

The Murray School offers a cooking holiday in the Dordogne region in southwest France. Guests stay at *La Perdrix*, a center for painting holidays, where they enjoy a "house party" atmosphere, with both cooks and painters enjoying the tranquil setting and learning to create their art.

The course combines half-day hands-on cooking sessions using local produce with plenty of spare time for other activities or sightseeing. The dishes prepared during the class will form part of the evening meal, which may be served in the dining room or on the terrace under the vines. There is also an evening planned at a local restaurant.

The Murray School of Cookery was formed in 1989 when Paulette Murray purchased part of Winkfield Place, a cookery and finishing school near Windsor. Since that time, she and her husband, Keith, have developed the business to offer several activities for cooks and those wishing to learn the techniques of fine cuisine.

They also offer a variety of nonvacation cooking programs, such as one-day demonstration classes (including a three-course lunch, a glass of wine, and afternoon tea); master classes (a cookery day preparing a three-course dinner party for four to take away); and four- and twelve-week cookery certificate courses.

The Murray School of Cookery also offers a trip to Sicily (see page 131 for more information).

THE DETAILS: The program runs seven days and is offered in the summer. Group size is limited to eight. The cost includes accommodations, most meals with wine, and cooking lessons.

The Cost: £400 (approx. $655)

Contact:
The Murray School of Cookery
Glenbervie House, Holt Pound
Farnham, Surrey ENGLAND
Phone: 44-1420 23049
E-mail: KMPMMSC@aol.com
Web site: www.theonly.net/murray.cookery/

• PROMENADES GOURMANDES IN PARIS •

Join a small group for daily cooking classes and culinary expeditions around Paris: to colorful open-air markets, a prizewinning butcher, the famous *Poilane* bakery, and the kitchen of the prestigious *Hotel de Crillon*'s restaurant. You'll visit the bistros of rising young chefs, Louis XIV's vegetable garden at Versailles, and *Dehillerin*, Paris's famous kitchen equipment emporium.

Your promenade around Paris begins at the home of your guide, Paule Caillat, a Cordon Bleu–trained chef who has worked as a caterer, cooking teacher, and food consultant. Paule's home is in northern end of the Marais, in a neighborhood which has maintained its charming ambiance: typical Parisian family-run food shops, an open-air market, eighteenth- and nineteenth-century architecture, art galleries, and cafés.

Most cooking lessons begin with a morning market visit, which benefits from Paule's local knowledge of Paris: You'll hunt out the finest foie gras, the crustiest baguette, the creamiest cheese, and the most exquisite chocolate. Paule may then introduce you to fellow food enthusiasts, from chefs and wine experts to food writers and artisan producers, or, if you're interested, you may go on a short trip to the countryside to discover the roots of France's finest produce. You'll then return to Paule's kitchen to learn a repertoire of menus and techniques that are easy to recreate at home. All cooking lessons include learning to prepare a starter, main dish, and a dessert such as crème brûlée or soufflé. Lunches are served with wine and the appropriate cheese.

Accommodations are not included in this program; consider joining the program when you are already in Paris, or the International Kitchen will arrange accommodations for you.

THE DETAILS: The program runs for a half day, full day, and two days. Group size is limited to eight. The cost for each program includes a cooking lesson, lunch, and a market visit. The cost for the full-day program also includes a gourmet walking tour. And the cost for the two-day program includes two cooking lessons and two walking tours.

Half day: $200
Full day: $360
Two days: $560

Contact:
The International Kitchen
1209 N. Astor #11-N
Chicago, IL 60610
Phone: 800-945-8606
Fax: 312-654-8446
E-mail: info@intl-kitchen.com
Web site: www.intl-kitchen.com

• PROVENÇAL GETAWAYS •

"We specialize in personal and customized vacations focusing on the food and wine of Provence," says Eileen Dwillies of Provençal Getaways. "Guests live in our small restored house in the ancient village of Curnier and enjoy the life of the countryside and our tiny village."

Eileen and her husband, Paul, offer a **Cooking/Touring** program and a **Bed-and-Breakfast** program that can include cooking lessons. The Cooking/Touring program consists of morning cooking classes and afternoon excursions. In the Bed-and-Breakfast program, the guests tour by themselves during the day and return to cook in the early evening. "This is often the choice of people who are well traveled in France and want to spend more time sitting in cafés enjoying the street scene or sunbathing by our pool," Eileen says.

The recipes are typically Mediterranean, Northern Italian, and of course, Provençal. A typical dinner menu is green salad with cilantro and balsamic dressing, Moroccan chicken, polenta soufflé with "baked" green beans, and classic *clafouti*. For lunch you might have a "perfect" omelet along with raspberry sorbet and chocolate biscotti. The classes are geared toward casual cooks and, because they are very small, can be adapted to meet the needs of the guests and focus on, for example, pastry, bread, soufflés, or custards.

During the afternoon drives you'll visit antique shops, potters' workshops, wine caves, lavender presses, olive mills, and the colorful outdoor markets for which the south of France is famous.

There are many options for wine lovers, too, as Curnier is in the Côtes-du-Rhône wine region. There are also walks and hikes nearby, as well as quiet roads for cycling, and the garden has a small dipping pool and several secluded spots for reading. Eileen and Paul teach all their guests how to play *boules*—the national pastime of the locals—and, Eileen says, "we often have a racy game of croquet!"

Although there is much for adult noncooking travel partners to do, children are not encouraged.

THE DETAILS: The programs run six days. Group size is limited to five. The Cooking/Touring program is offered in May, June, September, and October. The cost includes accommodations, meals, and cooking lessons. The Bed-and-Breakfast is offered April through June and September through November. The cost includes accommodations and breakfasts.

Cooking/Touring: $1,000
Bed-and-Breakfast: $50 per day, plus $60 per cooking class.

Contact:
Paul and Eileen Dwillies
11373 Kingcome Avenue
Richmond, BC, V7A 4W1
CANADA
Phone: 604-271-8722
Fax: 604-271-1497
E-mail: eileen@bc.sympatico.ca

• PROVENCE IN THREE DIMENSIONS— •
THE ART OF THE TABLE

The Art of the Table begins with an exploration of local markets and food producers, as you follow the transformation of local produce from market stall to dinner table. You tour wineries and olive oil producers, visit bakers, pastry makers, and cheese and honey producers, attend wine tastings and discussions given by local experts, and enjoy meals in authentic local bistros.

On a typical morning, you'll visit the markets for seasonal produce: asparagus, tomatoes, strawberries, melons, grapes, and the black truffles and olives for which Carpentras is famous. You'll also tour some of the regional vineyards—Châteauneuf, Cotes du Rhône, Ventoux, Luberon, and Alpilles—which will open their cellar doors for visits and tastings.

After returning from market, you cook lunch during a demonstration and hands-on class. Then you choose a wine that complements the day's dishes, and enjoy an aperitif, wine tasting, and lunch.

The *Château de la Roseraie* in Carpentras is your home during the program. It was built in the nineteenth century and offers shaded gardens, a renovated kitchen, and a convivial dining room in an enchanting setting in the heart of the city.

Robert Reynolds (see page 57 for more information about

Robert) and Michel Depardon are the chefs at Provence in Three Dimensions. Michel is the chef/proprietor of a celebrated restaurant, *Sette e Mezzo*, in St. Remy de Provence. He comes from a long line of chefs, and, in fact, his grandfather was chef to the royal kitchens of Greece and the Vanderbilt family.

Courses are available year-round with Michel. If you're interested in learning from two chefs at once (which will, we promise, not spoil the broth), you may want to visit Michel with Robert, who regularly travels to France to teach at Provence in Three Dimensions. Contact him for specific times.

THE DETAILS: The program runs five days and is offered year-round. The cost includes accommodations, continental breakfasts, lunches at the *Château de la Roseraie*, dinners in bistro-style restaurants, cooking lessons, and excursions.

The Cost: $2,250

Contact:
Robert Reynolds
222 S.E. Eighteenth
Portland, OR 97214
Phone: 888-733-3391: 503-233-1934
E-mail: rowbear@ibm.net
Web site: www.RobertReynoldsCooks.com

In France:
Provence in Three Dimensions
Michel Depardon
Alee des Tilleuls
Carpentras 84000 FRANCE
Phone: 33-490 67 02 90
Fax: 33-490 67 02 91

• PROVENCE ON YOUR PLATE •

"Every year, we discover something new," says Connie Barney of Provence on Your Plate. "We always visit many of the places described in *Markets of Provence* [for which Connie was the recipe consultant], which offer the glorious best of Provence. But last year, for example, we also found a baker who produces bread in an eighteenth-century stone oven—he builds a wood fire in the oven during the wee hours of the night, so the loaves will be ready at dawn. We discovered beekeepers near Apt, who let us watch them spin their honey into glass jars. And, after years of polite refusal, the chocolate makers in Châteauneuf du Pape are finally willing to let me and my guests tour their facility!"

Connie offers Provence on Your Plate programs in two private villas. One is among the lavender fields near the perched village of Roussillon, convenient to the markets in Apt, l'Isle sur la Sorgue, and St. Rémy, and the second is in la Môle, in the vineyards about seven miles from the St. Tropez market. Both of the villas are grand private homes with large swimming pools, spacious bedrooms (with private bathrooms), and loads of Provençal charm.

If you decide to stay at *Roussillon* (famous for the beautiful ochre colors mined out of its hills), the first morning of your vacation begins—after a hearty breakfast—with a visit to Châteauneuf du Pape. There you'll have a private tour of an award winning chocolatier, a château tour and wine tasting at *Château de la Nerthe*, and lunch at the Michelin one-star restaurant, *Château des Fines Roches*. Then you'll return home for an evening cooking class and a light meal.

On the second day, you'll start the morning in cooking class preparing savory tarts, patés, salads, and other dishes for a picnic lunch in the vineyard overlooking the valley. Then you'll visit the village of Gordes and the eleventh-century Abbey of Senanque, before returning home for swimming, relaxing, and dinner.

Thursday is spent strolling through Rousillon, past the open-air ochre mines to see the pink, salmon, golden, rust, burnt sienna, and peach colors in the ground, and on the walls of the homes, shops, and schools. You'll visit craft and interior design shops, and a café that serves what Connie calls "the best ice cream concoctions you ever had." Afterward, you'll visit Bonnieux, lunch at a cozy village bistro, and go to the *Domaine de la Citadelle* for wine tasting and a look at the corkscrew museum. Finally, you'll wander through Mernerbes, the town made famous by Peter Mayle in *A Year in Provence*, and will return home for a cooking class and dinner by the pool.

Other excursions include shopping at the market in l'Isle sur la Sorgue, a wine tasting session at a wine bar, lunch in a lovely Michelin-starred restaurant, and a visit to Fontaine de Vaucluse, one of the deepest springs in the world, known since pre-Roman times. You'll also travel to the village of Ansouis, on the other side of the Louberon mountain range, for a visit and cooking class with Chef Aline d'Aquilante, followed by lunch and a tour of her town.

And there's still time to enjoy the garden, take long walks on the country roads, swim, or sleep in, and attend cooking classes emphasizing the produce Provence is famous for: artichokes, eggplant, tomatoes, garlic, fresh herbs, zucchini, honey, wine, olives, and olive oil.

If you decide to stay at La Môle, your vacation will be equally full. You'll visit the small but lively market in Ramatuelle, a perched village with tiny streets and byways, have lunch of bouillabaisse at the beachfront restaurant, Chez Camille, take a twenty-minute ferry ride to the Island of Porquerolles for a day of sightseeing, shopping, and picnics, and enjoy a tour and wine tasting at *Domaines Ott*.

Other highlights of the la Môle trip include: browsing the market in St. Tropez, traveling to the Maures Forest, where you'll see a tenth-century monastery and hermitage, and touring a goat farm (where the young cheese maker—"a real character, a 'salt of the earth type' "—will demonstrate how he makes his award winning cheeses). You'll also visit Collobrières, a sleepy town known for the chestnut trees that shade its streets, and the chestnut cream you can buy from the little factory; swim, sun, and sail in the bay of St. Tropez; and enjoy a farewell meal at the cozy *Auberge de la Môle*.

Connie, in addition to being the recipe consultant for *Markets of Provence*, earned the *Grand Diplôme* from La Varenne Cooking School in Paris, and directed the Roger Vergé Cooking School in Nice.

Connie is currently planning "pilot" trips to the Dordogne region in the southwest of France and to Greece and Tuscany.

THE DETAILS: The programs run eight days. Group size is limited to eight. The cost includes accommodations, most meals, cooking lessons, and all excursions.

The Cost: $2,495

Contact:
Connie Barney
Provence on Your Plate
915 East Blithedale, No. 7
Mill Valley, CA 94941
Phone: 415-281-5644; 800-449-2111
Fax: 415-389-0736
E-mail: Conbarn@aol.com
Web site: www.provenceonyourplate.com

From the kitchen of Provence on Your Plate

ə

TIAN DE COURGE (PUMPKIN GRATIN)

SERVES 8

2 pounds of French *musquee de Provence* pumpkin or red kuri or
   butternut squash
2 tablespoons flour
2 tablespoons dried thyme (less if using fresh)
1 teaspoon salt
$^1/_2$ teaspoon cayenne pepper
$^1/_4$ cup olive oil
$^1/_2$ cup grated Gruyère cheese (or Swiss)

Preheat the oven to 350°.

Cut the pumpkin into manageable pieces, and remove the seeds
and any stringy bits. Peel it and cut into 1-inch cubes.

Mix together the flour, thyme, salt, and cayenne pepper, and
sprinkle this mixture onto the pumpkin cubes. Toss the pieces to
coat them.

Lightly oil a shallow baking dish with part of the olive oil. Place
the cubes in the dish, scattering them evenly. Drizzle the olive oil
over the top and bake for 45 minutes, until the pumpkin is tender.

Remove from the oven and sprinkle the grated cheese on top.
Return to the oven for another 15 to 20 minutes, until the cheese
has melted and browned slightly. Serve hot.

• RHODE SCHOOL OF CUISINE •

"I felt more at home here than at my own home!" wrote one guest
of the Rhode School's trip to Théoule-sur-Mer. That's the effect of
living in a beautiful modern villa on the coast, with breathtaking
views of land and sea, and enjoying the Mediterranean breezes, bril-

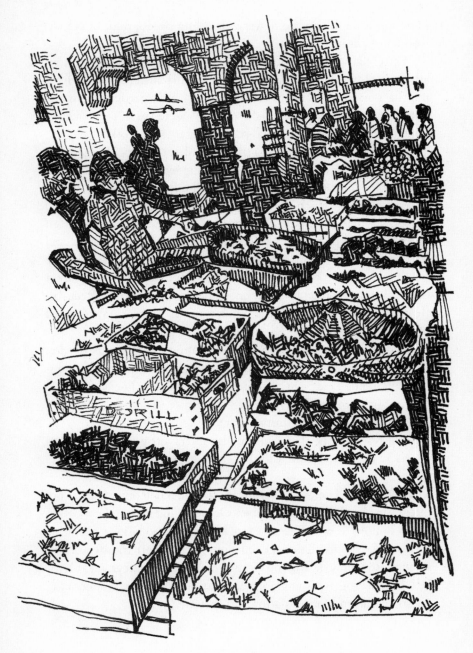

liant sunshine, blooming flowers, sparkling ocean, and, of course, wonderful cuisine.

The cooking lessons include morning and late afternoon demonstrations of fine French dishes such as bouillabaisse, salmon with a morille sauce, and lamb with saffron. You will participate in the cooking, and also observe Chef Frédéric Rivière (who has cooked at several Michelin one- and two-star restaurants) at work.

Many of the meals are enjoyed dining al fresco at poolside, under a large market umbrella. And when dining by candlelight at night, you can see the city lights of Cannes and Cap d'Antibes.

Free time, of which there is plenty, is often spent in or around the pool which overlooks the ocean. Or, if you can tear yourself away from the pool, you can enjoy picturesque guided walks and bike rides, visits to the famous glass blowing factory of Biot, the medieval hilltop town of Saint Paul de Vence, the open-air market of Forville in Cannes, a local goat cheese farm, the Château St. Roseline Vineyard, and picnic lunches on the islands off the coast of Théole-sur-Mer.

French chef Frédéric Rivière studied at *Les Sorbets in the Vendée*. Before teaching at the Rhode School he was chef for several restaurants including *Père Bise* (Michelin two-star), *Hielly Lucullus* in Avignon (Michelin one-star), *Auberge du Jarrier* (Michelin one-star), and *La Pyramide* (Michelin two-star).

The Rhode School of Cuisine also offers a trip to Tuscany (see page 132 for more information).

THE DETAILS: The program runs for six and a half days. Classes are offered in April, May, September, October, and November. Group size is limited to ten. The cost includes accommodations, all meals with wine, cooking lessons, excursions, and airport transfers. High season rates apply during the months of May, September, and October. Low season rates apply in April and November. Noncooking guests can attend for substantially discounted prices.

Standard room: $2,195–2,495
Premium room: $2,395–2,695
Single Supplement: $300

Contact:
Tim Haydon-Stone
216 Miller Avenue, Suite 8
Mill Valley, CA 94941
Phone: 800-447-1311
Fax: 415-388-4658
E-mail: tstone3954@aol.com

• ROBERT REYNOLDS •

"Golden sunlight filtered through drawn drapes and louvered doors," Robert Reynolds writes. "The windows were shuttered fast against the heat. Jacqueline went to open them, then paused as she turned the handles. Outside waited a seemingly endless panorama of grain and pasture, wood and field, still and yellow in the afternoon light.

"With a grand flourish of invitation she opened them: 'Voila, Robert—*la douce France.*'

"I don't know what the equivalent is in English for the words 'la douce France,' but in French the words sum up a totality of experience. The words roll off your lips like an excess of honey, or the jam that overflows a piece of bread. It is an automatic response full of tender emotion, and it acknowledges an appreciation, an awareness of the beauty of place. All that is France can be felt looking through the windows of this old house."

Robert offers four- and eight-week intensive apprenticeship courses for serious students of gastronomy, and shorter programs for more casual cooks. "One or two people can join us for a week at a time during the apprenticeship session," he says, "and they don't need to be professionals. For them, the program can be a vacation class. It works out for everyone, as the long-term participants take turns showing off what they know for the short-termers."

The first week of the apprenticeship course is a tour of France, starting in Paris. You then travel through Burgundy and stop near Lyon, where you stay overnight and dine in one of the restaurants for which the city is famous. You'll also attend two days of classes which Robert gives at the five-star hotel *La Mirande*, visit the region of Châteauneuf du Pape to drink the wine and eat at Michel Depardon's restaurant and travel to a small village outside of Agen, where you'll meet Kate Hill Ratliffe (see page 29) and spend the night on her barge.

The following morning you head north, past Bordeaux to Niort, just north of Cognac. You then settle in and devote the next three to seven weeks to an intensive course in food and wine: from culinary techniques to menu planning to wine tasting. While the focus is gastronomic—centered on methods and techniques—Robert also teaches an understanding of food in the context of the culture, geography, and the season which produces it.

Two typical meals you might learn to make: from Brittany—*petit choux farcis* (small stuffed cabbages), fish soup with greens, chicken with bacon and raisin dumplings, brittany cake with prunes; and from Burgundy—eggs poached in red wine, duck with chestnuts and wild mushrooms, farmstead cheeses, savarin with kirsch.

Robert was the proprietor/chef of *Le Trou* Restaurant in San Francisco for fifteen years; he is a consulting chef to the Cook Street School of Fine Cooking in Denver, he has conducted teaching programs in France for twelve years, and he travels and teaches at schools around the United States. He was trained by Josephine Araldo and, later, by Madeleine Kamman.

Robert also hosts vacation weeks at Provence in Three Dimensions, of which he is also the vice president. See page 49, for more information on Provence in Three Dimensions. And he teaches Master Classes at his Center for Advanced Culinary Study in Portland, Oregon.

THE DETAILS: The four-week program is offered in March, October, and November and includes 225 hours of class/kitchen time. The eight-week program is offered in October and November and includes 450 hours of class/kitchen time. Both include housing, food, some travel and tours, and the occasional restaurant meal. The one-week program includes accommodations, some meals, cooking lessons, and tours (all of which vary from year to year and person to person). Group sizes for all programs range from four to six.

One Week: $2,250
Four Weeks: $4,500
Eight Weeks: $7,500

Contact:
Robert Reynolds
222 S.E. Eighteenth
Portland, OR 97214
Phone: 888-733-3391; 503-233-1934
E-mail: rowbear@ibm.net
Web site: www.RobertReynoldsCooks.com

From the kitchen of Robert Reynolds

⊙

FROMAGE BLANC WITH
TOMATO AND HERBS

Fromage blanc
Crème fraîche
One tomato
A few drops of cognac
  (optional)
Herbs (parsely, chives, tar-
  ragon, and chervil, alone
  or in any combination)
Coarse sea salt
Fresh ground pepper

FOR THE VINAIGRETTE:

1 part vinegar
1 teaspoon mustard
1 to 2 tablespoons diced
  tomato
Hot pepper (optional)
Salt and pepper
3 to 4 parts olive oil

Shape a quenelle (a scoop from two soupspoons) of fromage blanc and set it on a flat soup bowl or dinner plate. Shape a quenelle of crème fraîche and set it beside the fromage blanc.

Drop the whole tomato into boiling water and count to twenty. Remove the tomato to cold water. Remove the stem and peel the tomato whole. Cut in half horizontally. Remove the seeds, and dice. Do not salt.

Chop the herbs finely and mix.

Prepare the vinaigrette by adding the vinegar, mustard, 1 to 2 tablespoons of diced tomato, salt, and pepper to a small blender, and mixing thoroughly. Then slowly add the oil, whisking. Taste and adjust seasoning.

Pour the vinaigrette over half the bottom of the plate. Sprinkle a few drops of cognac over the tomatoes and toss. Garnish the plate, scattering 1 to 2 tablespoons of the diced tomato. Scatter the herbs over the plate. Sprinkle the sea salt and fresh ground pepper, and serve.

• SAVOUR OF FRANCE •

"I'm in the business of selling happiness. That's how I respond when people ask me what I do for a living—I sell the happiness, discovery, learning, art, beauty, romance, relaxation, laughter . . . pure joie de vivre," says Darrin Anderson of Savour of France. If you're looking for a few regional cooking lessons to spice up a tour of France that focuses on sightseeing and feasting, Savour of France offers just that, in Burgundy, Provence, Alsace, Champagne, or the Riviera.

The trip to **Burgundy** starts on a Sunday at the *Château de Vault-de-Lugny* near Avallon, where you can explore the park and dungeon or brave a trip across the moat for a cocktail in the village square. You may also want to visit an antique dealer or other local shop before sitting down to a candlelit dinner in the château's banquet hall.

Monday is your first cooking lesson. You'll have a lesson in French "home cooking" at a private home, possibly making escargot or roasted squab for lunch. Then you'll visit the basilica of Vezelay, where Richard III preached the Second Crusade, before going to *L'Espérance*, a Michelin two-star restaurant, for a cooking demonstration lead by Chef Marc Meaneau, followed by dinner.

The next two days offer a trip to the medieval village of Noyers, lunch and a demonstration class at a Michelin-starred restaurant, and a late afternoon trip to the wine town of Irancy for aperitifs. You'll also float down the Burgundy Canal on a private bateau while enjoying an informal wine class taught by a professional sommelier. On the evening of the fourth day, you'll move to a new location, the *Château de Gilly*, originally built for the Priors of the Cistercian abbey.

Thursday is reserved for wine tasting. You'll discover *Côte d'Or*, Burgundy's famous wine route, and might go on an optional hot-air balloon ride with views of the region's vineyards.

Friday is your final full day, and includes a walking tour of the streets of Beaune, the food and wine capital of Burgundy, and a visit to the seventeenth-century *Hospices de Beaune*, where the world's largest wine auction is held. That night is spent at the manor house of Chef Jacques Lameloise, in Chagny. And the farewell dinner is held at the Chef Jacques' Michelin three-star restaurant, *Lameloise*.

Savour of France's trip to **Provence** begins on Sunday in Avignon, at the sixteenth-century Hotel Europe. You'll be treated to a private tour of the "Popes' Palace" before sitting down to dinner in the hotel's Michelin-starred dining room.

On Monday morning, you'll scour the market at Cavaillon with Chef Prevot, who received a three-forks mention from the Michelin guide, for the ingredients for your first cooking lesson. After your lesson, you'll spend the afternoon touring the Provençal countryside, stopping in Arles for an informal lecture from a Van Gogh expert and visiting a Roman amphitheater.

Tuesday also starts at the market, this time with Mme. Manguin, who treats you to a Mediterranean cooking lesson in her home. Ratatouille and olive tapenade are often on the day's menu: Watch out for that first glass of rosé that Mme. Manguin will offer you at ten A.M. (of course, "when in France . . ."). The afternoon is reserved for wine tasting along the Côtes-du-Rhône wine route, and dinner is at a cardinal's fourteenth-century residence in Avignon.

The next day you'll travel to the heart of "Peter Mayle country" to stay at *Maison de Garrigues*. You'll have lunch at a private home before exploring four beautiful Provençal villages. Dinner that evening is a truffle feast in the village of Vénasque.

The following day is spent on the Mediterranean coast in the fishing village of Casis, where you'll cruise in a private boat around the Mediterranean coast. You'll also visit Aix-en-Provence, a favorite town of Cezanne's, full of wonderful cafés and boutiques.

Friday, your final full day, begins at the clifftop town of Les-

Baux-de-Provence, which offers remarkable views of the country-side, a château, ramparts, and a feudal dungeon. That evening your farewell dinner is at the Michelin-starred *l'Oustaù du Baumanière*.

For more information on the trips to Alsace, Champagne, the Riviera, or to *L'Ecole du Vin* (Burgundy's foremost school of wine), contact Savour of France or check out their Web site below.

THE DETAILS: The programs run one week. Group size is limited to fourteen. The cost usually includes accommodations, most meals, all wines and wine tastings, cooking lessons, and excursions.

The Cost: $2,000–$3,500

Contact:
David Geen
2450 Iroquois Avenue
Detroit, MI 48214
Phone: 800-827-4635; 313-331-4568
Fax: 313-331-1915
Web site: www.savourfrance.com

In France:
Darrin Anderson
18 rue St. Antoine
58290 Moulins-Englibert FRANCE
Phone/Fax: 33-386 84 24 30

From the kitchen of Savour of France in Burgundy

❧

EGGS MEURETTE
SERVES 4

1 bottle of Burgundy red wine (pinot noir)
Salt and pepper
3 cloves of garlic, crushed
1 bouquet garni (fresh bay leaf, parsley sprigs, thyme, and celery stalk, tied together)

1 tablespoon butter
1 tablespoon flour
3 1/2 ounces of diced bacon
8 eggs
8 slices of bread, toasted (optional)

Place wine in a large pot and add salt, pepper, garlic, and bouquet garni. Bring to a boil, then simmer over low heat for 20 minutes or until the liquid is reduced to half. Strain. Place back on a low heat.

Mix the butter and flour by hand. Set aside.

Brown the bacon. Set aside.

Break open the eggs gently, placing unbroken egg yolk and egg white one at a time in a shallow bowl. Slip into liquid (take pot off the heat while doing this). Let each egg poach 3 minutes. When done, remove with a slotted spoon and keep warm.

Strain the sauce again; check the seasoning. Place back on low heat and add the butter and flour mixture. Give the pot a few shakes without stirring with a spoon. The sauce will remain constant if you don't stir, but the butter will dissolve slowly.

Place the eggs on the toast or just in a shallow bowl or plate. Cover with the sauce and sprinkle with the bacon pieces.

Serve immediately, if not sooner.

From the kitchen of Savour of France in Provence

❂

VERONIQUE'S RATATOUILLE

3 onions	Olive oil
2 red peppers	Sage
1 green pepper	Bay leaf
5 zucchini	Thyme
4 eggplants	4 cloves of garlic
6 tomatoes	Salt and pepper

Coarsely chop the onions. Wash the peppers, remove the seeds, and cut into 1- to 2-inch pieces. Wash the zucchini and coarsely chop. Peel the eggplant and chop. Coarsely chop the tomatoes.

Sauté each vegetable separately in olive oil until just beginning to soften.

Place all the vegetables back together into one large pot. Add the herbs, crushed garlic, salt, and pepper. Stir to blend.

Simmer for 30 to 45 minutes before serving.

• A TASTE OF PROVENCE •

"In the last thirty-five years, I've traveled to all corners of France and eaten my way through most of its provinces," says Tricia Robinson of A Taste of Provence. "But my heart and my gastronomic compass always guide me back to Provence and to my summer home at *le Mas du Loup*."

A restored Provençal farmhouse, *le Mas du Loup* sits high on the hills above Côte d'Azur, between Grasse and Vence, about forty minutes from Nice. Behind the eighteenth-century stone façade of *le Mas du Loup* is a spacious home with an open kitchen, plenty of indoor and outdoor levels with unexpected corners and terraces, and both rustic charm and modern amenities. A stroll through the grounds reveals acres of old olive, cherry, apricot, peach and fig trees, and flower and vegetable gardens top several stone terraces surrounding a large swimming pool.

But more important than the farmhouse and its surroundings is the food: "My first trip to France was to visit the family of the French students who rented a room in my parents' home in the north of England," Tricia says. "Their parents were wine makers in Provence, and the experience was like traveling to another planet. For the first time, I discovered olive oil, garlic, fresh herbs, wines, cheeses, breads, and exotic vegetables. I wanted to emulate a lifestyle in which food, wine, and family meals were the most important things and in which time and care went into preparing food and eating."

This lifestyle begins in the market, where you'll shop for local ingredients. Then, in the early evening, you'll meet on the kitchen terrace for an aperitif and dish of olives before learning to prepare the regional specialties you'll be having for dinner. Tricia emphasizes market-based cooking with a respect for traditional dishes, plus a large pinch of originality: You'll make tapenade, aioli, vegetable gratins (*tians*), roasted lamb, rustic tarts with fruit from the garden, and many other authentic dishes a la Provençal.

In the mornings, breakfast of warm croissants, brioche, or baguettes is served with homemade preserves and lavender honey, bowls of café au lait, or tea and fresh fruit, either on your terrace or in the dining room. Then you meet the other guests and mingle and cook in the kitchen.

During the day, you may go on a trip to a local marketplace (Vence, Nice, Antibes, or Grasse) where you'll buy ingredients for dinner. Then, after wine tasting and picnic at a local vineyard, you'd return to the *Mas* to cook and feast. Or you might attend a morning cooking class at the Roger Vergé *Ecole de Cuisine* in Mougins, where you'll enjoy the fruits of your labor for lunch and then spend the afternoon exploring the surrounding area on your own.

There's also plenty of time to explore the rich natural and cultural attractions of the area: "It doesn't take long," Tricia says, "before guests are returning with discoveries of every sort—flea market treasures, an unusual wine from a one-of-a-kind wine maker, or enough local fruit to last the week."

Once a year A Taste of Provence also offers a Guest Chef Week. The program is similar to the regular cooking tour, except led by a famous chef; Georgeanne Brennan, award winning cookbook writer, was the guest chef in 1999. Tricia also offers the Art of Living in Provence, a week of not only food and wine, but also painting, art, decoration, gardens, flowers, linens, and interiors. Most mornings are spent on the terrace, attending a hands-on workshop in faux and decorative painting taught by an artist who has worked on projects for the Prince of Wales and the Sultan of Brunei. Contact Tricia for more information about either of these programs.

THE DETAILS: The program runs one week and is offered in May, June, September, and October. Group size is limited to eight. The cost includes accommodations, most meals with wine, cooking lessons (including a session at the Roger Vergé cooking school), and excursions.

The Cost: $1,800
Single Supplement: $350

Contact:
A Taste of Provence
Tricia Robinson
925 Vernal Avenue
Mill Valley, CA 94941
Phone: 415-383-9439
Fax: 415-383-6186
E-mail: info@tasteofprovence.com
Web site: www.tasteofprovence.com

In France:
A Taste of Provence
Tricia Robinson
Le Mas du Loup
694 Chemin de St. Jean
06620 Le Bar sur Loup FRANCE
Phone/Fax: 33-493 42 43 05

From the kitchen of A Taste of Provence
∘
SALAD OF GOAT CHEESE, MESCLUN, AND BALSAMIC FIGS

"We're fortunate enough to have two enormous ancient fig trees on the property," says Tricia Robinson of A Taste of Provence. "So I'm always thinking up new ways to use the cornucopia of figs that descend on us twice a year."

2 very ripe figs
8 to 12 ripe figs
4 tablespoons balsamic vinegar
3 to 4 handfuls of baby salad greens
2 tablespoons olive oil
Salt and pepper
4 to 6 ounces fresh goat cheese

Peel the two very ripe figs. In a food processor, blend them with the balsamic vinegar.

Cut the remaining 8 to 12 figs in half and baste the cut sides with the fig-balsamic mixture. Grill the figs, cut-side down, over medium coals (or on a griddle), for 5 to 10 minutes, or until soft.

Toss the greens with the olive oil, season with salt and pepper, and arrange on plates. Slice or crumble the goat cheese over the greens. Arrange the warm, grilled figs around the plates, nestled in the greens, and serve immediately.

· A WEEK IN BORDEAUX · WITH DENISE AND JEAN-PIERRE MOULLÉ: TWO BORDELAIS

If you're looking for an authoritative week of food, wine, and walking in Bordeaux or the Pyrénées, look no further. Denise and Jean-Pierre are both from Gascony, Denise's family owns several well-known wine *châteaux* in Bordeaux, and Jean-Pierre is head chef at Chez Panisse in Berkeley, California.

If you visit **Bordeaux**, you'll stay in the *Château de Mouchac*, a country estate dating back to the seventeenth century and kept in perfect condition by the resident owners. You'll cook either in a professional kitchen at *Château la Louviere*, an eighteenth-century château, or the private kitchen in the Moullés' own farmhouse—an old, stone-walled, traditional kitchen. Cooking classes at the farm focus on down-to-earth food: grilling in the fireplace, spit-roasting poultry, and preparing vegetables from the garden. At the château, the cooking is more elegant, for parties and dinners.

This is also a week of walks and sightseeing. You'll walk on side roads, past old châteaux, medieval villages, and romanesque churches, stopping at vineyards (from very famous to obscure but charming), and markets. The walks are not strenuous—never more than six to eight miles a day—and there is a backup car available.

You may also visit the market in Libourne, or walk from Mouchac to Château Bonnet, the home of Denise's parents, for a tour of the cellars and a discussion and tasting of Bordeaux wines. You can visit a barrel maker or an oyster farm, or have lunch in the cellars of cheese master Jean D'Alors, who owns one of the few cheese shops in France that buys cheese directly from shepherds all over the country and ages them in the cellars beneath the shop. You'll have a private tour and cheese tasting, then back to the farmhouse or château for cooking, dinner, conversation, and relaxation.

The Moullés also offer a tour to **Cathar Country in the Pyrénées**. This trip is offered only once a year—the shepherds in the area lead very private lives, and hesitate to allow visitors to wander, however lightly, over their meadows.

Cathar Country is largely undiscovered by tourists. It's located under Carcassonne at the foothills of the Pyrénées, with stunning mountains and beautiful valleys. The area is packed with historic sights—twelfth-century abbeys, fortresses perched high on pinnacles of rock, prehistoric caves, and artisans who are preserving the ancient arts of making canes, wooden clogs, horn combs, and tools.

The program begins before you even arrive in the Pyrénées—you'll stop in the secluded village of Eugenie les Bains, home of the famous French chef Michel Guerard, to enjoy both the food and the spa. Then, once you arrive in the Pyrénées, you'll visit cheese and wine producers and enjoy a picnic in the mountains and dinner at a local inn. The next morning, wake up early and climb to meet the shepherds and watch them make cheese. Dinner by Jean-Pierre and singing with the shepherds round out the day.

A typical day exploring the region might be a morning trip to the market at Mirepoix, a medieval fortified town, for local produce and artistan's goods. Then lunch and a carriage ride at a farm that breeds *merens*, the sturdy black horses of Ariege. After lunch, you can climb the steep slopes to the fortress of *Montsegur*—3,960 feet above sea level.

You will also visit a small sheep-cheese maker in the Aude valley, taste the offerings of local wineries, go for a dip in the Mediterranean, view prehistoric art at *Grotte de Niaux*, and visit a small farm perched in the mountains where a couple of Parisian expatriates raise small goats for their mohair fur. You'll also go on trips to a bell maker (the bells that sheep, horses, and cows have around their neck each ring with a different tone, so shepherds can recognize animals by sound), a duck farm that makes foie gras and confit, and an Armagnac producer.

Although the programs are intended for people who love cooking, there are enough noncooking activities to entertain a less food-loving guest. These programs are not, however, for children.

THE DETAILS: The Bordeaux program runs one week and is offered in June and September. The Pyrénées program runs one week and is offered in September. Group size for both programs is limited to twelve. The cost for each program includes accommodations, all meals, all wines and drinks at the properties visited and during the meals, and cooking lessons.

Bordeaux: $3,200
The Pyrénées: $3,200
Single Supplement: $300

Contact:
Denise Lurton-Moullé
PO Box 8191
Berkeley, CA 94707
Phone: 510-848-8741
Fax: 510-845-3100
E-mail: jdmoulle@pacbell.net
Web site: www.twobordelais.com

From the kitchen of A Week in Bordeaux
(Jean-Pierre Moullé)

●

DUCK BREAST IN CASSIS SAUCE

2 duck breasts, from one
   whole duck
1 small carrot
1 medium onion
1 medium celery stalk
4 tablespoons butter
2 tablespoons olive oil
$^1/_2$ cup red wine

$^1/_4$ cup red vinegar
1 bouquet garni (fresh bay
   leaf, parsley sprigs, thyme,
   and celery stalk, tied
   together)
2 cloves of garlic
$^1/_2$ cup cassis liqueur
Salt and freshly ground pepper

Bone the duck breasts and legs (and save the legs for another use—Jean-Pierre recommends grilled duck legs on a salad of curly endive to serve after the duck breast course). Cut up the duck bones and coarsely slice the carrot, onion, and celery.

In a heavy saucepan, brown the duck bones in 1 tablespoon each of butter and olive oil. Add the vegetables and cook for five minutes. Deglaze the pan with the red wine and vinegar. Bring to a boil and reduce to three-quarters. Add just enough water to cover, bring to a boil again, and skim the surface. Add the bouquet garni and garlic, and simmer for one hour. Skim the stock and reduce by one third. Strain and reserve.

Season the duck breasts with salt and pepper. In a heavy skillet, heat 1 tablespoon each of butter and olive oil over medium heat. Cook the duck breasts, skin-side down (to render some of the fat from under the skin) for 3 minutes, and then roast them in a preheated 450° oven for 12 to 15 minutes. Keep warm until served.

Pour the fat from the skillet and deglaze with the duck stock. Add the cassis and reduce the sauce. Whisk in the remaining 2 tablespoons of butter. Season to taste and strain the sauce. Keep warm until served.

Slice the breasts, arrange on a plate, and spoon some sauce over. Serve immediately, with sautéed apples and a celery purée.

• THE ART OF LIVING TOURS •

The Art of Living Tours offers several excellent trips to Provence and the Loire Valley—as well as trips to Italy, Spain, and in the United States. See page 324 for more information.

Contact:
The Art of Living Tours
c/o Sara Monick
4215 Poplar Drive
Minneapolis, MN 55422
Phone: 612-374-2444
Fax: 612-374-3290
E-mail: Monick4215@aol.com

• THE INTERNATIONAL KITCHEN •

Karen Herbst of The International Kitchen had been a travel agent for six years, planning and conducting specialty travel to France and Italy. Then, in 1994, she decided to combine her travel experience with her lifelong interest in gourmet cooking. She offers about ten cooking vacation programs in France, ranging from bicycling and cooking tours to elegant five-star trips to farmhouse vacations. The following is a small sampling of her trips (others can be found scattered throughout this section).

A Fall Feast in Normandy takes place at the fifteenth-century *Château de Saint Paterne*, once the love nest of Henry IV and now surrounded by gardens full of delphiniums, larkspur, and foxgloves. Charles Henry de Valbray, whose family owns the château, will be your guide for the week as you visit farms and villages, tasting ripe cheeses and fresh cider made the traditional way. You'll learn how to prepare such delicacies as filet of sole a la normande and *poulet vallee d'Auge* in hands-on cooking classes in the château's restaurant kitchen. Other activities include a morning tour of the old village of Camembert, dinner at the home of friends of Charles Henry's, lunch in a creperie, an afternoon of antique shopping, and a morning visit to the market in Alençon. You'll also go on a calvados tasting tour, followed by a cooking class focusing on calvados, cider, and apples. French language classes can be arranged for those interested.

Another of Karen's programs is the **Food and Wine of Alsace with Michel Husser**. This trip features the tastes of Alsace: a perfectly ripe golden Muenster cheese accompanied by a glass of Gewurztraminer, a slice of poached Alsatian foie gras with a Tokay pinot gris, *tarte flambé* (a thick, creamy onion tart), and *matelot a l'alsacienne* (fish stew with a Riesling sauce).

You'll be wined, dined, and introduced to the secrets of classic and contemporary Alsatian cuisine by Chef Michel Husser, a two-star Michelin chef (and a fourth-generation chef) who leads this program's hands-on cooking classes. In addition to cooking, you'll go on a boat tour, see the Alsatian museum, have a private tour of the magnificent cheese caves of Monsieur Antony, master cheese maker in Ferrette (where you'll enjoy a special dinner featuring the perfect marriage of cheese and wine), and go mushroom hunting. And you'll visit Chef Robert Husser's (Michel's father) herb garden, have Sunday lunch with the Husser family in the garden, and tour the vineyards of Alsatian wine maker Mosbach.

The *Hostellerie de Levernois* is a Michelin-starred hotel and restaurant at which former French president Mitterrand hosted the French-German Summit in 1995. The château was built in 1750, and is located three miles from Beaune in the village of Levernois, on ten acres of fields, woods, gardens, and streams. It is owned and operated by Chef Christophe, who spent five years in the kitchens of Troisgros, Bocuse and Giardet (all Michelin three-star restaurants), and his family.

Cooking classes in the hotel's professional kitchen begin on the day of your arrival and end with breakfast on the fifth day. Chef Christophe and his wife, Gaby, will teach you to cook foie gras, poultry, meat, seafood, escargot, pastries, and desserts. Specific dishes include *rossini* of lamb with truffles, eggs *muerette* (a typical Burgundian dish), and smoked salmon with scalloped potatoes and purée of watercress.

This trip includes excursions to the caves and vineyards of nearby wineries, to a local goat cheese farm, and to Beaune, the capital of Burgundy wine, where you'll have the opportunity to shop the historic city's quaint boutiques.

THE DETAILS: A Fall Feast in Normandy and the Food and Wine of Alsace run one week. The costs include accommodations, all meals including aperitifs and wine, cooking lessons, and excursions. The trip to *Hostellerie de Levernois* runs six days and includes all meals, cooking lessons, and excursions. Group size is limited to ten. Spouses and guests are welcome on any of the trips.

A Fall Feast in Normandy: $2,490
The Food and Wine of Alsace: $2,900
Hostellerie de Levernois: $1,684
Single Supplements: $200–$300

Contact:
The International Kitchen
1209 North Astor #11-N
Chicago, IL 60610
Phone: 800-945-8606; 312-654-8441
Fax: 312-654-8446
E-mail: info@intl-kitchen.com
Web site: www.intl-kitchen.com

·2·

ITALY

 THE TASTES OF ITALY: handmade gnocchi and wood-baked pizza; fresh mozzarella and perfectly aged Parmesan; organic porcini mushrooms and Adriatic-caught fish. And that's just the beginning. There's also: homemade tiramisu and garden-fresh tomatoes; wild leeks and newly ground polenta; fine wines and Amalfi-made *limoncello*.

You can live in a renovated haybarn, a medieval fortified town, or a working estate farm still owned and operated by the aristocratic family that has lived there for generations. You can stay in an elegant hotel that was built as a convent in the ninth century or in an historic villa that hosted Napoleon and the Duchess of Windsor. From Pompeii to the Dolomites, from opera in Spoleto to ruins on Sicily, the treasures of Italy—its history, culture, countryside, fashion, and, of course, cuisine—await you.

These cooking vacations give you an opportunity to see Roman mosaics and Renaissance architecture and Etruscan pottery; to make your own pizza in a wood-fired oven and to taste fresh-pressed olive oil. You will dine in Michelin-starred restaurants and local trattoria, watch a crossbow competition, sail to Elba, and attend Italian language classes. And you will prepare lavish meals and simple country fare, and enjoy them both with spectacular bottles of wines, enthusiastic good company, and the pleasure of knowing that this is a feast of your own creation.

• BADIA A COLTIBUOUNO— • THE VILLA TABLE

Badia a Coltibuouno—the name means "Abbey of the Good Harvest"—was founded almost a thousand years ago in the heart of Tuscany as a place of worship and meditation. And of wine making: The monks of Coltibuono were the first to cultivate vines in Chianti, and to develop the wines which made the Chianti Classico one of the most famous wine producing regions in the world.

Almost two centuries ago, *Badia a Coltibuono* became the residence of the Stucchi Prinetti family, and they live there still. The estate is an hour from Florence and surrounded by rolling hills planted with vineyards and olive groves. It now houses a restaurant, guest rooms (located in the fourteenth-century corridor), extensive gardens and woods, and a swimming pool. And, of course, a cooking class.

Lorenza de' Medici Stucchi, the author of *Italy Today: The Beautiful Cookbook*, *The Renaissance of Italian Cooking*, and *The Villa Table Cookbook*, opens her home for cooking classes only ten weeks each year. She lives and works with a small group of guests, sharing with them her very personal style of cooking and entertaining—simple, elegant dishes that can easily be prepared in the home kitchen, based on seasonal ingredients whose flavors are accentuated by fresh herbs and greens.

In the afternoon, guests either relax on the estate or go on excursions, exploring the Tuscan countryside. And on several evenings, guests are invited to dinner in the private villas, castles, and beautiful homes as guests of Lorenza's gracious friends.

THE DETAILS: The program runs five days and is offered in April, May, October, and November. Group size is limited to fifteen. The cost includes accommodations, meals with wine, cooking lessons, excursions, and transfers to and from Florence.

The Cost: $3,500
Single Supplement: $600

Contact:
Judy Ebrey
Cuisine International
PO Box 25228
Dallas, TX 75225
Phone: 214-373-1161
Fax: 214-373-1162
E-mail: CuisineInt@aol.com
Web site: www.cuisineinternational.com

In Italy:
Badia a Coltibuono
Gaiole in Chianti
Siena ITALY
Phone: 39-577-749498
Fax: 0-39-577-749235

• CAPEZZANA WINE AND • CULINARY CENTER

Originally built for a member of the Medici family, the *Tenuta Di Capezzana* estate, nestled in the hills above the village of

Carmignano, twenty-five minutes west of Florence, now houses Count Ugo Contini Bonacossi and his family. The Capezzana cooking vacation offers a chance to experience Tuscan life firsthand, as various members of the Contini Bonacossi family will escort you to open-air markets, restaurant kitchens, wine classes and winery tours, art exhibits, and museums. You'll learn how to pick olives and make extra virgin olive oil, and will visit the estate winery, which produces traditional Tuscan wines such as Carmignano, Chianti, and *Vin Santo* (dessert wine)—as Beatrice Contini Bonacossi says, "You can't divide the food from the wine in Italy."

You will spend much of your time in the three dining rooms: baking bread or pizza in the wood oven in one, grilling fresh meats from a local master butcher in another, or tasting wine in the third. You'll learn to cook homemade pastas and sauces, *ignudi* (naked ravioli), Tuscan bread soup, guinea hen with grapes or *visanto*, filled rabbit *brasato al carmignano*, and desserts such as biscotti *di prato*, tiramisu, *panna cotta*, and olive oil cake. Recipes for the program change each session according to the season and the guests' desires.

Your chefs at *Tenuta Di Capezzana* are Patrizio, a native Tuscan, who is the Contini Bonacossi's chef and has been with them for more than ten years; Jean-Louis de Mori, the chef-owner of *Locando Veneta, Ca'Bea, Ca'Del Sole, Il Moro,* and *Allegria* in Los Angeles; and Faith Willinger, author of *Eating in Italy* and *Red, White and Greens: The Italian Way with Vegetables*, and a contributing editor to *Gourmet* magazine.

Spend your free time by the outdoor swimming pool, or walking or jogging on the many pathways. *Tenuta Di Capezzana* prides itself on its flexibility: They will help you find separate housing or baby-sitters for spouses and children, or will include them in the excursions.

THE DETAILS: The program runs five days. Group size is limited from twelve to fourteen. Capezzana offers roughly ten sessions per year in the spring and fall. The cost includes accommodations, meals with wine, cooking lessons, and excursions.

Shared room/shared bath: $2,350
Shared room/private bath: $2,600
Single Supplement: $400

Contact:
Lili Rollins
1607 Pearl St.
Alameda, CA 94501
Phone/Fax: 510-865-8191
E-mail: lrrol@pacbell.net

In Italy:
Beatrice Contini Bonacossi
Tenuta di Capezzana
Via Capezzana 100
59011 Loc. Seano
Carmignano (PO) ITALY
Phone: 39-55-8706005
Fax: 39-55-8706673
E-mail: Capezzana@dada.it
Web site: www.capezzana.it

From the kitchen of Tenuta di Capezzana

•

BISCOTTI DI PRATO

MAKES 4 DOZEN COOKIES

4¹/₂ cups (2¹/₄ pounds) cake
    flour
2 ²/₃ cups sugar
3 egg yolks
5 whole eggs
1¹/₂ teaspoons baking powder

1 teaspoon salt
1 cup melted butter
1 cup whole toasted almonds
1 tablespoon grated orange zest
2 egg yolks, to brush over the
    biscotti

Preheat oven to 350°.

Pour the flour in a mound on a work surface. Make a well in the center and place the sugar, whole eggs, egg yolks, baking powder, and salt in the well. Add the melted butter and gradually mix with your hands until smooth. Knead the almonds and orange zest into the dough thoroughly and keep kneading, sprinkling with additional flour if needed. It should take you 4 to 5 minutes in all. Be careful not to overwork the dough.

Butter and flour two baking sheets that are at least 15 inches long. Divide the dough into quarters. Roll each piece of the dough on a floured surface into a 2 to $2^{1}/_{2}$-inch-wide flat log and place the logs at least 2 inches apart on the baking sheets. Beat the 2 egg yolks and brush over the dough logs.

Bake for 35 minutes. Remove from the oven and reduce the temperature to 325°. Cut the logs diagonally into $^{3}/_{4}$ to 1-inch slices and lay them back on the cookie sheets. Return to the oven for another 5 minutes and then cool on racks.

• CASA CAPONETTI— • AGRITURISMO IN TUSCANIA

"Our favorite saying is, 'A guest can become a friend.' And we know it's true because it's been happening for fifteen years—and now we have friends all over the world," says Laura Caponetti, who runs *Casa Caponetti* with her husband, Giorgio, and their children.

Laura's cooking lessons are based on the seasonal availability of produce, often incorporating wild herbs and fruits, vegetables from her own *orto* (the vegetable garden is one of the passions of her life), and homemade *marmellata* and other preserves. Some class themes are: the Warm Italian Winter; Spring in Full Bloom; Tomato Feast; Grapes, Wines, and Preserves; the Time of Golden Oil; and Last Taste of Autumn.

Depending on the season, you will prepare wild fig preserves, cannelloni filled with nettles and ricotta cheese, mint omelets, or hazelnut biscuits. Or you might make *tagliatelle al* pesto, *zuppa* with pecorino cheese, or *timballo del Gattopardo* (a huge tart made with sweet pastry and filled with pasta and every sort of delicious filling: small chicken meatballs, green peas, meat gravy, pine nuts, boiled eggs, diced ham, and mushrooms).

A typical vacation begins with dinner at the casa and a night tour of Tuscania, with a café stop for *aperitivi*. The next morning, you shop at the local market, have a cooking lesson, and then explore the estate (stopping to gather herbs for use in your next cooking lesson). From the garden, you can enjoy a view of the medieval towers of Tuscania, on the grounds you can visit an Etruscan necropolis, and nearby is the sea and the Marta river valley. "We are surrounded," Laura says, "by a land kissed by the Goddess of Fortune."

The following day, you'll visit the Isola Bisentina (a private island with architecture from the sixteenth century), where you'll have lunch by the lakeside in a typical trattoria. You'll spend the afternoon in a three-hour cooking lesson followed by dinner and a talk about local dishes and traditions. Over the next few days, you'll visit Romanesque basilicas, an archaeological museum, the thermal spa *Terme dei Papi* (where the Romans and the Popes used to bathe), and will travel along an ancient Etruscan road to the medieval town of Viterbo. You'll taste local cheeses, wines, hams, sausages, and ricotta, will have many more cooking lessons, and will travel to Tarquinia where you'll enjoy dinner at a seaside fish restaurant.

Laura's background is as a hotel and restaurant consultant, and she has a degree in Italian gastronomic history, as well as years of experience in Italian "eating culture."

Noncooking guests are welcome at *Casa Caponetti* and may consider taking language or horseback riding lessons from Laura's husband, Giorgio, or lessons in falconry, calligraphy, photography, or ballooning offered by various family friends.

THE DETAILS: The program runs one week. Group size is limited from two to six. The cost includes accommodations, meals, cooking lessons, and excursions.

The Cost: $1,460
Single Supplement: $487
Non-cooking Guests: $1,150

Contact:
Casa Caponetti
Tenuta del Guado Antico
01017 Tuscania VT ITALY
Phone: 39-761-435792
Fax: 39-761 444247
E-mail: caponetti@iol.it
Web site: www.touring.it/caponetti/uk.html

• CENTRO KOINÈ— •
PANE, VINO, E LINGUA

Centro Koinè offers a course in Italian language and cooking, which they call "Bread, Wine, and Language." This is not the most elegant course—there's no ancient villa, no aristocratic family, and no breathtaking views from the rooms. But the optional language lessons—which focus on conversation skills for tourists who want to learn about Italian art, history, politics, food, and wine—are guaranteed to deepen your appreciation of the culture, and the food is authentic, delicious, and enthusiastically paired with the wine.

The program is a collaboration between the *Centro Koinè* language school and *Enoteca de' Giraldi*, a local wine bistro. The school and the bistro are both located in the *Palazzo Borghese*, an ancient building in the center of Florence that was once the palace of Prince Borghese, Napoleon's son. Classes take place in a professional kitchen with a Renaissance ceiling, stone columns, and cross vaults. You'll learn to make simple Tuscan meals with an emphasis on pure ingredients: *pappa al pomodoro, zuppa di farro, ribollita, crostini toscani, trippa alla forentina* (tripe), *inzimino,* and *tiramisu e torta della nonna.* The classes combine demonstration and hands-on cooking, and include a pasta making session and several wine tastings.

But the course isn't just chatting and eating and cooking. You also go on sightseeing trips to local farms and vineyards and wineries. Andrea Moradei, the head of the program, says, "It's the cultural approach to wine and food, the little wine producers we found and the artisans who produce salami and cheese we use, that makes the program so special."

If you choose to take the language course, your mornings are spent in language lessons and your afternoons in cooking class. If you're interested only in the cooking, your mornings are free to explore Florence. *Centro Koinè* will arrange accommodations: You can stay at an elegant hotel, with an Italian family (enhancing your cultural immersion and your language skills), or at a student apartment, church, or youth hostel. *Centro Koinè* also arranges accommodations for spouses and baby-sitting for children.

THE DETAILS: The programs run one or two weeks and are offered in spring, summer, and fall. Group sizes are limited to ten. Costs include cooking lessons, wine tastings, and cultural excursions. Accommodations are not included.

1 week with language: 990,000 lire (approx. $540)
1 week without language: 750,000 lire (approx. $410)
2 weeks with language: 1,850,000 lire (approx. $1,005)
2 weeks without language: 1,350,000 lire (approx. $735)

Contact:
Andrea Moradei
Enoteca de' Giraldi
Via de' Giraldi 4
50122 Firenze ITALY
Phone: 39-55 213 881
Fax: 39-55 216 949
E-mail: koine@firenze.net
Web site: www.vinaio.com

In the United States
The International Kitchen
1209 North Astor #11-N
Chicago, IL 60610
Phone: 800-945-8606; 312-654-8441
Fax: 312-654-8446
E-mail: info@intl-kitchen.com
Web site: www.intl-kitchen.com

From the kitchen of Centro Koinè

RENAISSANCE ONION SOUP

SERVES 4

Traditionally known as a French dish, this is a Tuscan Renaissance version of onion soup.

2 pounds onions, finely sliced
1/2 cup almonds, skinned and
    pounded to a paste in a
    mortar and pestle
1 tablespoon sugar
4 tablespoons olive oil
White wine vinegar

Cinnamon stick
4 1/2 cups stock
Pinch white pepper
Pinch salt
Powdered cinnamon
    (optional)
4 slices bread

Put the crushed almonds and the cinnamon stick in enough vinegar to cover, and leave about 1 hour.

Heat the oil in a medium-sized pan, sauté the onions in it until soft, using more oil if necessary.

Rinse the almond paste in a sieve and add to the onions a tablespoon at a time until they are well blended. When the mixture is smooth, add the sugar, powdered cinnamon if liked, white pepper, salt, and stock.

Cook for another 30 minutes. Put a slice of grilled bread—crisp and brown—into each bowl, pour soup over it, and serve.

From the kitchen of Centro Koinè

⚬

CENCI (FRIED PASTRY TWISTS)

This popular dessert is named *cenci*, "scraps," because it looks like the fabric used for dusting and cleaning. It comes in many varieties, from long strips tied in bows and lover's knots, to the heart-shaped *dolci d'amore*.

> 1 cup, 2 tablespoons (9 ounces) white flour
> 1 egg
> Pinch salt
> 2 tablespoons (1 ounce) granulated sugar
> 1 teaspoon vanilla
> 2 tablespoons (1 ounce) butter, just melted
> 3 tablespoons *Vin Santo* (sherry or rum may be substituted)
> Oil for deep frying

Make a little volcano of sifted flour with a crater in the middle. Put the egg, salt, sugar, vanilla, and butter in the crater. Gently knead with your hands. When the dough begins to get stiff, moisten with a little *Vin Santo*, as the dough should always be quite pliable. Knead well, cover with a cloth, and leave in a cool place.

After about an hour, roll the dough out very thinly and cut into whatever shapes you like. The most traditional is a strip about 8 inches long and 1/2 inch wide tied in a bow or knot.

Deep fry these pieces 2 or 3 at a time in hot oil until they puff up and turn golden brown. Drain on paper towels and sift confectioner's sugar over the top. They can be eaten hot or cold and keep well in an airtight container.

• CHIANTI IN TUSCANY •

Podere Le Rose, which hosts the Chianti in Tuscany program, is a thirteenth-century farmhouse, a typical *casa colonica* located in the heart of the Chianti Classico area. Classes meet in *Podere Le Rose's* homey, country-style kitchen, which is large enough to hold the two spacious tables that allow all the guests to work at once—a vital consideration, as this program is very hands-on.

You'll work with a variety of kitchen equipment from the traditional *mezzaluna* knife (crescent-shaped blade) to the modern food processor, learning how to make traditional Italian recipes that have been passed down for generations in different regions of Italy. The recipes focus on the simple, familiar, and delicious, such as bruschetta, fresh pasta, gnocchi, risotto, and tiramisu. Your hosts, Chefs Simonetta and Paola de'Mari, teach the cooking skills and techniques they learned from their mother, Countess Bevilacqua.

You can sightsee on your own or through excursions arranged by *Podere Le Rose*. The farmhouse is an excellent base for many lovely walks through the countryside, and is close to the local swimming pool and a playground for small children. You can also easily drive to medieval villages, Etruscan tombs, and the *Museo Contadino*. If you're interested in slightly less common sights, you can visit the place where Machiavelli played cards, the town where Mona Lisa was born, the area that inspired E.M. Forster's novel *Where Angels Fear to Tread*, and the villa where the movie *Much Ado About Noth-*

ing was filmed. Or, if you want to stick with the culinary theme, you can visit local producers of wine and olive oil, and many other regional specialties.

In addition to offering bed-and-breakfast cooking vacations, Simonetta and Paola have a language school in Florence, and will arrange Italian language lessons, taught by the school's faculty, at *Podere Le Rose* for those interested. They are also very flexible: If you already have accommodations arranged elsewhere, you can take the cooking classes only, and if you plan to arrive with family, they will arrange for a local apartment.

THE DETAILS: The programs run five days and are offered from April to October. Group size is limited to ten. The Italian Cookery and Wine course includes one dinner at a Tuscan restaurant, a daily meal at *Podere Le Rose*, and all cooking lessons. The special weekly packages, in addition to the above, includes accommodations at *Podere Le Rose*, breakfast, two excursions, and some transport.

Italian Cookery and Wine Program: 1,100,000 lire (approx. $600)
Special weekly packages: 2,200,000–2,700,000 lire (approx. $1,195–$1,470)
Single Supplement for special weekly packages: 150,000 lire (approx. $85)

Contact:
Shona Fowler
CPV–Chianti in Tuscany
Piazza del Mercato Nuovo, 1
50123 Florence ITALY
Phone: 39-55 294511
Fax: 39-55 2396887
E-mail: info@cpv.it
Web site: www.cpv.it/chianti

• COOKING, CULTURE, AND •
COUNTRY LIFE IN A SICILIAN
VINEYARD: THE WORLD OF REGALEALI

Regaleali is the Sicilian country estate of Count and Countess Tasca d'Almerita. Located in the heart of Sicily, about an hour and a half from Palermo, *Regaleali* is one of the most important wine-producing estates in the area, as well as a working farm. The Tasca family invites guests to enjoy an authentic Sicilian experience on the estate, sharing their passion for the land, and their time-honored recipes.

Your Sicilian holiday begins on Monday, with your arrival at *Regaleali*. After settling in your room, you'll have drinks and appetizers, followed by a *spaghettata* (spaghetti dinner). Next morning, the cooking demonstrations begin. They're seasonally based, as most of the food that ends on the table begins on the farm: poultry, lamb, sheep's milk cheese, wheat, olive oil, vegetables, and fruit. And, of course, every meal is accompanied by a fine *Regaleali* wine.

Other activities also vary according to season. Some highlights are: watching the shepherds make pecorino and ricotta cheese; a risotto dinner at Anna's (the Countess's) sister's house; a tour of the winery; an excursion to the nearby Madonie Mountains (a spot still untouched by tourism) and the Greek temples of Agrigento; a bread-baking demonstration in a wood-burning oven; lunch at a local trattoria (for their special dishes made with wild mushrooms and asparagus); a visit to the market at Vallelunga; and, finally, a farewell gala dinner.

Comptessa Anna Tasca Lanza, the author of *The Heart of Sicily*, *The Flavors of Sicily*, and *La Sicilia in Cucina*, conducts and directs the cooking courses. In addition to traditional Sicilian recipes, she also teaches a more international cuisine based on the cooking of her husband's family.

THE DETAILS: The program runs three days or five days. The three-day program is offered in April and October; the five-day program is offered in May and October. Group sizes are limited to twelve. Costs include accommodations, meals, cooking lessons, and excursions.

Three Days: $1,000
Five Days: $2,200

Contact:
Judy Ebrey
Cuisine International
PO Box 25228
Dallas, TX 75225
Phone: 214-373-1161
Fax: 214-373-1162
E-mail: CuisineInt@aol.com
Web site: www.cuisineinternational.com

In Italy:
Anna Tasca Lanza
Viale Principessa Giovanna, 9
Palermo 90149 ITALY
Phone: 39-91 450 727
Fax 39-921 542 783
Office at Regaleali: 39-934 814 654
Home at Regaleali: 39-921 544 011

• COOKING WITH MARIA •
AND MEDITERRANEAN COOKING IN AMALFI

Gabriele's Travels to Italy

A cooking class that starts with dessert cannot be bad. "If my dessert is made, I'm confident," says Chef Maria Maurillo, owner of Malvarina Country Inn in Assisi. The Inn, which dates from the Middle Ages and is furnished with local antiques, is run by Maria and her son's family, giving it a distinctly homey appeal. "I cook each meal for my guests," Maria says, "as though I were cooking for my family."

Maria teaches a highly personal cuisine based on Umbrian specialties and local ingredients. You can join her in a sort of vacation-apprenticeship program, **Cooking with Maria in Umbria,** in which you don your apron each afternoon to help Maria create dinner to be served to the other guests. "This is not just practice," Maria will remind you.

You'll learn to prepare sautéed dried ham with vinegar and sage served on homemade bread, infused olive oil with hot peppers poured over spaghetti with tomato sauce, and traditional Umbrian dishes such as lentil and sausages and zucchini flowers sautéed in olive oil and cooked with eggs. And desserts such as apple *torta*, a light cake filled with cream, and a variety of biscotti.

Cooking classes meet in the late afternoon—in the morning and early afternoon, you'll have plenty of time to see Umbria. You can visit Spello to see Pinturicchio's masterful Renaissance paintings; Bevagna for its elegant piazza and Roman mosaics; Montefalco for its celebrated Sagrantino wine; Gubbio for its perfectly preserved Renaissance buildings and Etruscan pottery; Spoleto for olive oil and wine tasting; and Perugia for its underground fortress and excellent shopping. Then, after returning from a sightseeing journey, you'll spend the evenings in the converted wine cellar dining room at the Inn, relaxing while enjoying the delicious meals you've helped Maria prepare.

Gabriele's Travels, which organizes Cooking with Maria, also arranges a cooking tour of the Amalfi Coast, **Mediterranean Cooking in Amalfi**. You stay at the Hotel *Giordano* Villa Maria, which was built by a Roman nobleman and still has the flavor of an ancient patrician palace, with its beautiful furnishings and excellent restaurant.

Your teachers for the week are Ezio Falcone and Enrico Cosentino, both of whom specialize in medieval cuisine. As a food historian and writer, Ezio has spent more than thirty years researching recipes from Roman times, and Enrico is a founding member of the Italian Academy of Medieval Cuisine. You'll spend most mornings and early afternoons touring the Amalfi Coast, arriving back at the hotel for cooking lessons in the late afternoon. Each evening is spent dining on the delicacies you've prepared, emphasizing Mediterranean, medieval, and ancient Roman recipes.

As with the Umbrian tour, there's plenty to do while you're not cooking. You'll take a walking tour of Ravello and go on a boat excursion to Positano, a seaside village just a few miles down the coast. You'll visit a mozzarella factory, a *limoncello* producer (*limoncello* is an intensely sweet liquor made from locally grown lemons— typically made in Amalfi), and other local food artisans. You'll have an unstructured day, during which guests usually visit Capri, Pompeii, Naples, or Salerno—all easily accessible by public transport. Tours of villas in Ravello are also available, as are trips to Ravello's music festival; from early spring to late fall a variety of concerts are performed in villas, churches, and outdoor venues throughout town.

THE DETAILS: Both programs run one week and are offered May through November, excluding August. Group sizes range from eight to sixteen. The costs include accommodations, all meals, cooking classes, and excursions.

Cooking with Maria in Umbria: $1,899
Mediterranean Cooking in Amalfi: $2,350

Contact:
Gabriele's Travels to Italy, Inc.
3037 Fourteenth Avenue NW
Rochester, MN 55901
Phone: 888-287-8733
Fax: 507-287-9890
E-mail: gabriele@hps.com
Web site: www.travelingtoitaly.com

From the kitchen of Cooking with Maria
○

CHICKPEA SOUP

SERVES 6

3 1/3 cups dried garbanzo beans
   (about 1 pound)
1 1/2 cups chopped onion
1 cup chopped peeled carrots
1 cup coarsely chopped celery
1 cup chopped seeded tomatoes

2 bacon slices
1/2 cup olive oil
12 1/4-inch-thick baguette
   slices, halved crosswise
1 large garlic clove, halved

Place garbanzo beans in a large heavy pot. Add enough water to cover them by 3 inches. Bring to a boil, then drain the beans. Return beans to pot, again adding enough water to cover them by 3 inches.

Add onion, carrots, celery, tomatoes, and bacon. Bring soup to a boil. Reduce heat and simmer until the beans are tender, stirring occasionally and adding more water as necessary to cover beans (about 2 hours, 45 minutes.)

Meanwhile, heat 1/2 cup of olive oil in heavy skillet over medium-high heat. Working in batches, add baguette slices and cook until golden brown, about 1 minute per side. Using tongs, transfer the slices to a paper towel-lined plate to drain. Rub garlic over both sides of the baguette slices.

Purée soup in blender until smooth, thinning with more water, if desired. Return to same pot. Season with salt and pepper.

Ladle soup into bowls. Drizzle a teaspoon of olive oil over each serving. Top with the baguette-slice croutons, and serve.

• CUCINA DIVINA •

"My recipes are not upscale or trendy," says Judy Witts Francini of *Cucina Divina*. "They are simply the best that generations of Florentine families and chefs have used daily and perfected into *cucina Toscana*. People who enjoy crowding around a pot to see and smell and participate in what's cooking will love my classes!"

Judy offers hands-on cooking lessons in her home, a typical Florentine apartment on Via Taddea overlooking the bustling central market of Florence, *Mercato Centrale*. You start the day shopping for the regional and seasonal best, and finish it with a leisurely meal that you've helped plan and prepare. The accompanying wines, local selections, will be recommended by a Florentine sommelier. And the classes are informative, informal, and, above all, fun.

"We're flexible at *Cucina Divina*. I want to accommodate guests' culinary interests and travel schedule. If they only want to learn how to make *panzanella*, a Tuscan bread, and vegetable salad—we'll make it. If they want to make *ribollita*, a bean soup baked with bread—we'll make it. If they want to watch a chef prepare for the lunch crowd and then sit down to eat in the restaurant, we'll do that! Classes may focus on vegetarian dishes, appetizers, breads, fresh pasta, or desserts—you name it. And if they prefer to eat and not to cook, tasting classes are also available. But why miss all the fun?"

Judy will help you customize your vacation with an itinerary combining Florentine food, art, and culture. Some highlights of past trips are: a food lover's walking tour of Florence; lunch at a local trattoria to refuel between trips to the central market, kitchen stores, and the historic town center; a wine tasting with an expert sommelier at a local wine bar; and exploring the Chianti wine region, visiting local food purveyors and artisan workshops.

Judy has made her home in Florence since 1984. She started *Cucina Devina* (originally called *Mangia Firenze*) in 1988 with a simple goal—to share her knowledge of Italian cuisine and culinary history with fellow food lovers in and around Florence. "I've lived in Florence among food enthusiasts," she says. "Exchanging ideas and recipes, lunching with chefs, and developing my own style that is relaxed and entertaining. I get my inspiration from the Tuscan combination of strong regional traditions with an instinctive approach in the kitchen. It's the perfect combination for getting things moving—and for creating unforgettable meals."

Judy, the author of *From the Market to the Table*, has been a student of cooking for twenty years. She's worked in the United States and Florence as a pastry chef. She speaks Italian perfectly, and at one time used her language and culinary facility as a waitress in a Florence trattoria—and she's married to a native Florentine, Andrea Francini.

Accommodations are not included in the program, but Judy can book any type of housing for you: from pensiones to apartments, convents to five-star hotels. The cost for housing ranges from 60,000 to 160,000 lire ($30–$90) per night. And, although non-cooking partners are welcome, Judy can't make provisions for children under twelve.

THE DETAILS: Program lengths vary from one to six days and are offered year-round. Group sizes are limited to eight. Costs include lunches and some dinners, cooking lessons, market trips, and some wine tastings and transportation. Accommodations are not included.

The Cost: $250–$1,250

Contact:
Cucina Divina (Mangia Firenze)
Judy Witts Francini
2130 Comistas Drive
Walnut Creek, CA 94598
Phone/Fax: 925-939-6346
Web site: www.mangiafirenze.com

In ITALY:
Cucina Divina
Judy Witts Francini
Via Taddea, 31
50123 Firenze ITALY
Phone/Fax: 011-39 055-29-25-78
Web site: www.mangiafirenze.com

From the kitchen of Cucina Divina

◦

RAVIOLI GNUDI DI SALSA DI NOCI (SPINACH AND RICOTTA GNOCCHI IN WALNUT SAUCE)

Judy Witts Francini writes: "In most cookbooks, recipes with 'Florentine' in the name include spinach as a main ingredient. Not so in Florence, where it means that peas are included! For example, Veal Florentine style (*Vitello alla Fiorentina*) has no spinach, although many of us would expect that instead of peas. Blame Catherine de'Medici. When she married into the sixteenth-century French royal house at age fourteen, she brought along Tuscan cooks who introduced their cuisine to the royal court. The French incorporated and codified these recipes, giving them new names that have endured for centuries. *Còlla* became *béchamel*, *crespelle* became crepes, gelato became glacé, *pàpero al melarancio* became *canard à l'orange*, and *alla fiorentina* . . . you get the idea."

THE SAUCE:

2 slices white bread

Milk

6 ounces walnut meat

2 cloves of garlic

Salt

3 tablespoons olive oil

THE GNOCCHI:

1 pound loose spinach

12 ounces ricotta

3 eggs

3 tablespoons Parmesan

1 1/4 cup flour

Salt

Nutmeg

THE SAUCE:

Remove crusts from bread and soak the bread in a little milk, just enough to wet the bread. Place in a food processor with walnuts and garlic. Purée. Add salt to taste. Add olive oil and blend again. If too thick, thin with a little milk.

THE GNOCCHI:

Cook spinach in very little water. Drain and squeeze out all excess water. Chop finely. Place in a large mixing bowl and add ricotta, eggs, Parmesan, and flour. Blend well. Season with salt and a generous grating of fresh nutmeg.

Bring a large pot of salted water to boil, then lower it to a simmer.

Form gnocchi by using a spoon or floured hands. Drop a few at a time into water (test first with a single gnocchi to make sure it doesn't fall apart in the boiling water). They will drop to the bottom and then float to the top when done. Let simmer 20 to 30 seconds. Remove with slotted spoon or ladle and place in an ovenproof dish until all the gnocchi are cooked. (Only cook a few gnocchi at a time or they will fall apart in the water.)

Pour walnut sauce on top of gnocchi. Serve with Parmesan cheese and garnish with toasted nuts.

Another simple sauce: Sauté fresh sage leaves in butter until crisp. Pour butter and sage on top of gnocchi, toss gently, and serve with Parmesan cheese or tomato sauce.

• CUISINE ECLAIRÉE •

Cusine Eclairée offers a cooking vacation in a house party atmosphere at a restored eleventh-century estate, *Villa Catureglio*, in northern Tuscany, and in Hotel *Giordano* Villa Maria in Ravello, on the Amalfi Coast. In both programs, the cooking classes are taught by Elaine Lemm, a freelance food and recipe writer, who has appeared on television in England, the United States, and Sweden (her first cookbook will be published shortly).

"The four most important ingredients in cooking are love, care, attention, and fun," Elaine says about her relaxed and informal classes. "Great food requires having a great time, not just fancy techniques. The love put into the food is what makes it shine."

While staying in **Tuscany**, either in the villa or one of the fourteenth-century cottages located on the estate, you'll learn to make focaccia, fresh pasta, *pappa al pomodor*, *panzanella*, and baked tarts. You'll incorporate as many local ingredients as possible into your cooking, including mushrooms, beans, meats, cheeses, and locally produced olive oil. Meals are topped off with desserts such as *zuccotto*, polenta *dolce*, and petite *cantuccini* cookies dipped in *Vin Santo*. You'll also have a pizza night, where guests gather around the wood-fired oven built in 1813, tossing their own pizza dough, and smother it with toppings, and a final feast outside under the Tuscan skies, barbecuing chicken for *pollo alla diavola* while sampling local wines.

When you're not busy creating fabulous meals, you can relax by the pool, walk through the woods to a natural swimming pond, explore the old mule trail that still links the neighboring villages, slip into town to shop, spend the afternoon with the locals at a neighborhood bar, or play tennis.

The **Amalfi Coast** trip meets in Ravello, one of the small hill villages on the coast in southern Italy. You'll stay at the Hotel *Giordano* Villa Maria and will cook either in the professional kitchen at the neighboring Villa Eva, or outside, on the clifftop terrace, where you'll prepare regional meals while enjoying the private gardens and views of the Amalfi coastline.

You'll learn to cook using the abundance of fresh fruit, vegetables, fish and seafood, mozzarella, hams and salamis that the area has to offer—many of the ingredients will come straight from Villa Eva's vegetable and herb garden. Pizza and barbecue nights are also planned, as well as field trips to a local mozzarella manufacturer, and a *limoncello* (lemon liquor) producer. Also included in the course are a guided day trip to Pompeii and a half day in Positano and Amalfi.

Cuisine Eclairée welcomes spouses and partners and has accommodated children in the past. They are flexible and will try to arrange whatever you need. They can also accommodate travel partners who prefer to take classes in other subjects—*Cuisine Eclairée* offers occasional courses in wine tasting, table decorating, landscape painting, and photography.

THE DETAILS: The programs run one week. Group size is limited to twelve. Programs in Tuscany are offered in the spring and fall. Classes on the Amalfi Coast are offered in the fall. The costs include accommodations, meals, cooking lessons, and excursions.

TUSCANY
Villa: £965 (approx. $1,600)
Cottages: £865 (approx. $1,425)
Single room supplement: £300 (approx. $500)

AMALFI COAST
Double room: £1,195 (approx. $1,970)
Single room supplement: £300 (approx. $500)
Non-participating partner (including all trips): £995 (approx. $1,640)

Contact:
Elaine Lemm
Cuisine Eclairée
5 The Poplars
Newton-on-Ouse
York YO30 2BL ENGLAND
Phone/Fax: 44-1347 848557
US Phone: 888-904-6866
E-mail: CUISINE_ECLAIREE@compuserve.com
Web site: www.diningpages.com

From the kitchen of Cuisine Eclairée

●

ZUPPA DI PISELLI (PEA SOUP)

SERVES 6

2 tablespoons butter
1 tablespoon olive oil
1 medium onion, peeled and
   finely chopped
1 garlic clove, peeled and
   very finely chopped
1 1/2 pounds frozen peas
Handful of fresh mint leaves,
   chopped

5 cups vegetable stock
Sea salt and freshly ground
   black pepper
5 tablespoons Parmesan,
   freshly grated
Extra virgin olive oil

Heat a large saucepan, melt the butter and oil together. Gently sauté the onion for about 10 minutes. Add the garlic and cook for another 5 minutes. Add about 3/4 each of the peas, mint, and stock and cook gently for about 5 minutes.

Put the mixture through a food mill to make a thick purée. Return to the pan and season. Add the remaining peas and stock and cook for another 5 minutes. Check the seasoning and add the remaining mint, finely chopped.

Serve with Parmesan in the center of a soup plate, surrounded by the soup. Drizzle with extra virgin olive oil. This soup is also delicious served cold, but not chilled.

• A CULINARY ADVENTURE •
IN AMALFI AT THE
HOTEL LUNA CONVENTO

The first three things you notice about the cooking vacation at the *Luna Convento* in Amalfi are location, location, and location. First, classes are held in an ancient Saracen Tower on the Amalfian coast. Directly on the coast—the tower, which used to be a lookout for enemy ships, is perched on a cliff above the sea.

Second, guests stay in the Hotel *Luna Convento*, which was built as a convent in the ninth century, and where St. Francis founded a cloister in the thirteenth century (now a lovely garden—and a perfect setting for breakfast, afternoon tea, and evening cocktails). Not to mention that the *Luna* provided inspiration to both Henrik Ibsen (while writing *A Doll's House*) and Richard Wagner (while working on *Parsifal*).

And third, Amalfi itself—nestled on a mountainside of the Neapolitan Riviera with whitewashed buildings and brilliant flowers and the sea just below.

The cooking classes are taught by Chef Enrico Franzese, a native Amalfian who returned to his hometown after studying and cooking throughout Europe. Rosemary Anastasio is Enrico's interpreter—as well as the school director, tour guide, and all-around "mother hen" for the guests. British-born and married to an Amalfian, Rosemary (who as a young woman was the nanny for the sons of one of the Queen of England's ladies-in-waiting) accompanies the group on all excursions.

The cookbook used in class includes forty-four recipes, all designed to be easily replicated at home: *linguine alla Bella Donna*, *maccheroncelli al limone*, *nidi di rondini de convento* (swallows' nests from the convent), cannelloni *all'Amalfitana*, *melanzane a scarpone*, and many recipes for risotto, gnocchi, veal, pizza, and much more. And, of course, desserts—from tiramisu to custard cream pie to biscotti.

Rosemary will take you on walking tours of Amalfi: You'll visit an ancient handmade paper mill (still operating, although it will go out of business upon the death of the present owner—his son says he'd rather eat three meals a day than slave over a dying art), historical sites, favorite restaurants and shops, and the church of the *Luna Convento*.

You'll also explore Ravello, the most elegant of the small cities on the Amalfi coast. You'll shop for the pottery of Vietri, tour the gardens of the thirteenth-century Villa Rufelo and Villa Cimbrone (constructed in the medieval Ravello style which incorporates towers and loggia with a splendid natural setting), and enjoy afternoon teas in the gardens of Hotel *Palumbo*.

And you'll stroll through Pompeii, enjoying the ancient the-aters, temples, shops, and frescoes; shop in Sorrento for the famous local lemon liquor, gold jewelry, wooden inlaid boxes, and other local specialties; and enjoy dinner at *Don Alfonso*, a two-star Miche-lin restaurant which will provide a seven-course Neapolitan feast, tour of the historic wine cellar, and a tasting of their homemade olive oil and *limoncello*.

And there's still time for relaxing on the local beach or at the hotel swimming pool, taking casual trips, perhaps by boat, to shop or eat, and sightseeing on your own.

Spouses or partners who want to enjoy all the activities except the cooking (and the lunch following the class) receive a ten percent discount. Children who are old enough to entertain themselves are welcome—bringing younger children is not recommended.

THE DETAILS: The program runs one week and is offered in May and October. Group size is from twelve to eighteen. The cost includes accommodations, all meals, cooking lessons, and excur-sions.

The Cost: $2,400
Single Supplement: $300

Contact:
Judy Ebrey
Cuisine International
PO Box 25228
Dallas, TX 75225
Phone: 214-373-1161
Fax: 214-373-1162
E-mail: Cuisineint@aol.com
Web site: www.cuisineinternational.com

In Italy:
Hotel Luna Convento
84011 Amalfi ITALY
Phone: 39-89 871 002/050
Fax: 39-89 871 333

*From the kitchen of a Culinary Adventure in
Amalfi at the Hotel Luna Convento*
◦

RIGATONI ALLA MATRICIANA
(RIGATONI WITH BACON AND TOMATOES)
SERVES 4

3 tablespoons olive oil
1 medium white onion
  (preferably young),
  chopped
Salt
5 ounces bacon or pancetta,
  cut into strips
Red chili pepper

12 ounces fresh or canned
  plum tomatoes, crushed
Bay leaf (optional)
Chopped parsley
$1/2$ cup white wine
1 pound rigatoni
2 tablespoons Parmesan or
  pecorino cheese

Sauté onion slowly in olive oil and a little salt (which helps soften the onion) for about 10 minutes, until tender. Add the bacon or pancetta and sauté for another 10 minutes.

Add the white wine and simmer until evaporated. Add the chili pepper, tomatoes, bay leaf, and parsley. Taste for salt. Simmer from 30 minutes to 1 hour, depending on how thick you want the sauce.

In a large saucepan, boil 6 quarts of salted water and cook the pasta until al dente. Drain and place on a warm serving dish. Pour the hot sauce over the pasta. Season with grated Parmesan or pecorino and serve immediately.

(This is a perfect sauce to make in large batches and freeze for later use.)

*From the kitchen of a Culinary Adventure
in Amalfi at the Hotel Luna Convento*

PIZZE RITTE
(FRIED PIZZA)

1 package dry yeast (or 1
ounce fresh yeast)
Warm water
2¼ cups flour
2 teaspoons salt
Vegetable oil for frying
Pizza toppings (as below)

Dissolve the dry yeast in a little warm water. Place the flour and the salt on the counter and make a well in the center. Pour in the yeast and water mixture (or, if you're using fresh yeast, crumble it directly into the flour), working it into the flour gradually, adding enough extra water to make a manageable dough.

Knead for 10 to 15 minutes until the dough becomes elastic and smooth. Cover and leave in a warm place until it has doubled in size, about 1 hour. Punch the dough down and allow it to rise a second time.

After the dough has risen, divide it into small pieces and shape into rounds either by rolling it out or with your floured hands. Fry the rounds in very hot oil for a few minutes, until golden brown. Drain well on paper towels. Add toppings, and serve immediately— "while you are frying it, you should also be eating it!"

Recommended toppings: for *pizze* margherita, top with tomatoes, mozzarella, and fresh basil; for *pizze* marinara, top with tomatoes, anchovies, garlic, and oregano; and for *pizze quattro stagione*, top with tomatoes, mozzarella, ham, mushrooms, and artichokes.

• CULINARY ARTS, INTERNATIONAL •

Do you prefer Parmesan and prosciutto or truffles and risotto? Culinary Arts offers cooking vacations that cater to both preferences: a trip to Emilia Romagna that includes visits to Parmesan and prosciutto makers (and balsamic vinegar distilleries), and a vacation in Torino and Alba of the Piemonte region during which you'll hunt, cook, and feast on truffles.

Your home base in **Emilia Romagna** is the three-star Hotel Castello, located just outside of Modena. After breakfast and steaming cappuccino in the mornings, you'll go on a culinary tour of the region. You'll meet Nello Faroni, who has been a cheese maker for forty-four years. Nello makes Parmigiano-Reggiano the traditional way—the way it's been done for seven hundred years—from Vacche Rosse cows, which are no longer used commercially due to low milk production, but produce a milk that gives the cheese a distinctively rich flavor. You'll visit balsamic vinegar producers, where you'll learn the difference between the commercial variety made from wine vinegar and caramel flavoring and the way balsamic vinegar is meant to be made: from cooked grapes aged in wood for at least twelve years.

You'll also explore other parts of the Emilia Romagna region, with excursions to Modena, Parma, and Bologna, where you'll visit markets, the Tamburini food emporium, and the famous Majani chocolate shop, and will stop for wine tasting at *Bottega del Vino Olindo Faccioli*.

And, of course, you'll cook. During hands-on cooking classes, you'll learn how to make handmade pastas and classic sauces, delicious fast breads such as *gnocco fritto* and *piadina*, as well as slow rising traditional breads. You'll also attend cooking demonstrations using balsamic vinegar and Parmigiano-Reggiano, as well as an aromatic herb class taught by an organic gardener and chef.

The tour of **Piemonte** begins with three nights in Torino, at the three-star Hotel Victoria. Your first cooking lesson will be at the

Principate di Lucedio, the famous rice-growing estate of *Contessa* Rosetta Clara Cavalli d'Olivola, where the *Contessa* will teach you the secrets of cooking perfect risotto. Your second lesson in Torino will be a traditional Piemontese cooking class with Romana Bosco of *Il Melograno*. When not cooking, you'll go gourmet food shopping, attend farmers' markets, and tour the Krumiri candy factory in Casale Monferrato and a Cistercian abbey and farm.

After Torino, you'll travel to the one-hundred-year-old Hotel Savona, located in the heart of Alba, where you'll stay for four nights: studying, cooking, inspecting, eating, smelling, and living truffles. Alba is famous for its truffles—while you are there, citywide festivities take place to celebrate the truffle season. You'll even have the chance to truffle hunt with a master *trifolau* and his dogs. You'll also take a wine tasting class with Burton Anderson, wine expert and author of *Treasures of the Italian Table*.

Your guide is Pamela Sheldon Johns, author of five cookbooks, including *Parmigiano!*, *Williams Sonoma Lifestyles: Vegetarian for All Seasons*, *Balsamico!*, and *Italian Food Artisans*. In Piemonte, she is joined by *Contessa* Rosetta Clara Cavalli d'Olivola, and Cesare, a chef in Alba.

Culinary Arts also offers a larger number of cooking tours in Tuscany during the spring and fall.

THE DETAILS: The programs run one week. Trips are offered to Emilia Romagna in the spring and Piemonte in the fall. Groups of six or more can book an exclusive week. The costs include accommodations, all meals, cooking lessons, and excursions.

Emilia Romagna: $2,650
Single Supplement: $500

Piemonte: $2,750
Single Supplement: $500

Contact:
Culinary Arts, International
Pamela Sheldon Johns
1324 State St., Suite J-157
Santa Barbara, CA 93101
Phone: 805-963-7289
Phone in Italy: 39-347 471 6006
Fax: 805-963-0230
E-mail: CulinarArt@aol.com
Web site: http://hometown.aol.com/culinarart/myhomepage/
index.html

*From the kitchen of Culinary Arts, International
(from Pamela Sheldon Johns' book,
Italian Food Artisans)*

⚬

PANE SANTO (HOLY BREAD)

SERVES 6

"Holy bread" takes its name from the blessing of olive oil drizzled over the top. Massimiliano Mariotti, executive chef at *Fattoria Le Capezzine*, makes this traditional Tuscan antipasto with *cavolo nero*, ("black cabbage")—if you're unable to find it in your market, substitute kale, Swiss chard, or spinach, and steam instead of boil.

12 cups julienned *cavolo nero* (or substitute kale, chard, or spinach, as above)
3 tablespoons extra virgin olive oil, plus extra oil for garnish
3 ounces pancetta, finely chopped
1 onion, finely chopped
1 clove of garlic, minced, plus 1 whole clove
1 dried *peperoncino* (red chile), finely chopped
2 tablespoons wine vinegar
Salt and freshly ground pepper to taste
6 slices country-style bread, cut in half

Bring a saucepan of water to a boil. Add the *cavolo nero* and cook over medium-low heat until tender, about 1 hour. Drain, reserving the water.

Prepare a fire in a grill, or preheat a broiler.

In a sauté pan over medium heat, warm the 3 tablespoons olive oil. Add the pancetta, onion, minced garlic, and *peperoncino* and sauté for 4 to 5 minutes, or until golden brown. Raise the heat to medium-high, add the *cavolo nero*, and stir until well blended. Add the vinegar and continue to cook until some of the vinegar evaporates, 1 or 2 minutes more. Season with salt and pepper and keep warm.

Toast the bread on the grill or in the broiler, turning once, until golden on both sides. Remove and rub both sides of each slice with whole garlic clove. One slice at a time, dip one side of the bread in the reserved cooking water, just enough to moisten the surface.

Arrange the toast on a tray and top with the *cavolo nero* mixture, dividing evenly. Garnish with a drizzle of olive oil and a sprinkle of freshly ground pepper.

• THE CULINARY TRAVEL COMPANY •

Stay at the *Antico Casale di Scansano*, a two-hundred-year-old restored farmhouse located in the remote (and relatively undiscovered) Etruscan region, near the spa towns of Saturnia and Argentario. The Pellegrini family, who own the farmhouse, join The Culinary Travel Company as your hosts, and will teach you their family recipes which have been passed down for generations. You'll learn approximately thirty recipes for soups, pastas, sauces, poultry, lamb, pork, jams, desserts, olive oils, mushrooms, and truffles, as well as balsamic, raspberry, and blueberry vinegars.

Each morning, you wake up to fresh juice, coffee, homemade biscuits, and jams. Then, after a cooking class, you can spend the afternoon on your own, exploring the extensive estate vineyards and orchards or the nearby villages. Other afternoons you'll spend with the group, visiting cheese farms, vineyards, food markets, and olive oil producers. You'll also take trips to the towns of Siena and San Gimignano, to Orbetello which lies along the coast, and to Pitigliano which sits on a plateau above sheer cliffs and ravines carved out by the River Lente. The group always returns from field trips by early evening, and there's time to rest and relax before dinner. The meal—which you prepared in morning class—will be enhanced by local wine and lively conversation of cooking notes from class and the sightseeing experiences of the afternoon.

The Culinary Travel Company also offers a cooking vacation in Provence, France (see page 25 for more information).

THE DETAILS: The program runs one week and is offered in April, May, September, October, and December. Group size is limited to eight. The cost includes accommodations, breakfast and dinner (including wine), cooking lessons, and excursions.

The Cost: $1,995
Single Supplement: $300

Contact:
The Culinary Travel Company
PO Box 14330
Chicago, IL 60614
Phone: 888-777-0760
E-mail: dan@theculinarytrav-
    elco.com
Web site: www.theculinary-
    travelco.com

· GRITTI PALACE SCHOOL ·
OF FINE COOKING

Hotel *Gritti* Palace, a fifteenth-century palazzo that was at one time home to Venetian doges, offers luxurious accommodations complete with antique furnishings and tapestries—and combines your discovery of the splendor of Venice with the opportunity to cook and taste the distinctive Venetian cuisine. The hotel offers cooking courses such as Cooking with Fresh Herbs, Mediterranean Cuisine, the Warm Flavors of Autumn, the Doges' Cuisines, and Cooking for Important Occasions.

The Cooking with Fresh Herbs course teaches the use of both popular and obscure aromatic herbs in cooking (and includes one day devoted exclusively to vegetarian cooking). The Doges' Cuisine course teaches guests to prepare dishes based on the seas, gardens, and woods of the Venice region. The Warm Flavors of Autumn focuses on cheese, truffles, and the most flavorful of root vegetables. And Cooking for Important Occasions teaches guests holiday and special occasion recipes dedicated to festivity and celebration.

Whichever course you attend, you'll spend most mornings in a well-equipped kitchen classroom with Chef Celestino Giacomello. Menus for each day are planned with the guests, and the resulting meals are enjoyed together at lunchtime in the elegant hotel restaurant. Afternoons are reserved for food tasting trips to hidden regions of Venice, and excursions to local markets and villas. The evenings are at your leisure, perhaps for moonlit canal rides in a gondola or explorations of the ancient palaces of Venice.

Chef Giacomello has been at the *Gritti* Palace since 1990. His expertise is in fine cuisine influenced by his travels within Italy and to the United States, Germany, Jamaica, and Hong Kong.

THE DETAILS: Programs run for four days. Group size is limited from fifteen to twenty-five. Classes are held in Italian with simultaneous translation into English. Cooking with Fresh Herbs and Mediterranean Cuisine are offered in the spring, The Doges' Cuisine is offered in summer, and Warm Flavors of Autumn and Cooking for Important Occasions are offered in the fall. The costs include accommodations, buffet breakfast, and cooking course. During your stay a 30 percent discount is applied at the hotel restaurant and 25 percent at the bar.

Double occupancy: 3,310,000 lire (approx. $1,800)
Additional night: 670,000 lire (approx. $365)
Single occupancy: 2,000,000 lire (approx. $1,100)
Additional night: 450,000 lire (approx. $245)

Contact:
Massimo Feriani, General Manager
Hotel *Gritti* Palace
Campo Santa Maria del Giglio
Venice 2467 ITALY
U.S. Phone: 800-325-3589
U.S. Fax: 512-834-7598

• IL CHIOSTRO •

Il Chiostro offers customized cooking classes at the *Scuola del Colle*. The classes are held in the recently renovated original elementary school (donated by Baron Bettino Ricasoli, the second prime minister of Italy) located in *Il Colle San Marcellino*, a thirteenth-century hamlet of twenty-five people in the Chianti region. True to its name—*Schuola del Colle* means "School of the Hill"—the school is set above vineyards and olive groves, and provides expansive views of the countryside. Classes are held in the school's kitchen, and meals are served in the dining room or garden. The school is only twenty minutes from Siena, and is close to Florence, Arezzo, and Perugia.

The courses are completely customized: They last as long as you want and take place whenever fits your schedule. Excursions are designed the same way: to satisfy your personal interests. You can choose to focus on art, history, nature, crafts, shopping, enology, or whatever other element of Italian history and culture attracts you. In the past, guests have explored private, medieval castles, visited Etruscan burial grounds, watched olives being pressed at a neighborhood mill, and had shoes tailor-made for them by a local artisan cobbler.

A sample seven-day itinerary is as follows: Guests stay at a small Hotel *de Charme*, enjoying full breakfasts every day, attending five days of cooking school, and shopping for ingredients at local outdoor fresh produce markets, butchers, and specialty food stores.

They also have a private lunch and visit at *Villa di Geggiano*—featured in Bernardo Bertolucci's movie *Stealing Beauty* and owned by the Bianchi Bandinelli family for centuries (Rolando Bandinelli became Pope Alessandro III, who defeated Fredrick Redbeard, emperor of Germany, in 1150). After lunch Andrea Bosco Bandinelli gives guests a tour of the original furnishings, the lovely frescoed rooms, the Italian garden with the open-air theater, the small chapel built in the eighteenth century for a family wedding, and the wine cellar—the family produces Chianti Classico and Riserva.

The program also includes private tours of wineries and olive mills in the Chianti Classico and Brunello di Montalcino area, trips to Siena, Pienza (home of Pope Pius II), Volterra, and San Gimini-ano, and visits to beekeepers, ceramists, stained-glass makers, and hand-weavers.

Il Chiostro also offers, once a year, an Autumn Arts Festival at the Dievole winery in Tuscany and a Tuscan Country Cooking program with Maryann Terrilloin at a farmhouse villa outside of Siena, on a private Chianti vineyard.

THE DETAILS: This program is entirely customized. A representative will speak with you about your schedule, your budget, the interests of the members of your group, your previous experience in Italy and Tuscany, and help you develop a personal program. The cost varies according to the length of stay, number of guests, and custom requests, but generally includes accommodations, all meals, cooking lessons, and excursions.

The Cost: $2,500 (for the program described above)

Contact:
Michael Mele, Director
Il Chiostro
241 West 97th St, Suite 13N
New York, NY 10025
Phone/Fax 212-666-3506; 800-990-3506
E-mail: mmele@msn.com
Web site: www.ilchiostro.com

• INTERNATIONAL COOKING SCHOOL • OF ITALIAN FOOD AND WINE

"Guests are amazed by how quickly they feel at home in Bologna," says Mary Beth Clark of the International Cooking School of Italian Food and Wine. "It's a very comfortable small city, with a strong sense of family and hospitality. And it's known as 'the Gastronomic Capital of Italy'—famous for handmade pasta and *la cucina buona*, and home of Emilia-Romagna, Parmigiano-Reggiano, balsamic vinegar, prosciutto di Parma, and even Pavarotti and Ferrari sports cars!"

Mary Beth, who owns and manages the school, is the author of *Trattoria* and a contributor to *Italy: A Culinary Journey*. She's also the European editor of the *Journal of Italian Food, Wine, and Travel* and has appeared frequently on radio and television. She offers two weeklong cooking vacations: the Basics of Great Italian Cooking and the October Truffle Festival.

For both programs, you'll be cooking in the kitchens of a sixteenth-century private Renaissance palazzo in the heart of Bologna's historic center. The kitchen is modern and professional, with individual work areas and cooking equipment—but the palazzo itself is filled with antiques, marble fireplaces, oil paintings, brocades, and frescoes.

The **Basics of Great Italian Cooking** course is rooted in the lively outdoor market of Bologna, with mounds of seasonal fruits and vegetables, seafood, and specialty meats and cheeses. Cooking classes are taught by four chefs: Mary Beth, a guest executive chef, a *sfoglina* (professional pasta-maker who makes and rolls out pasta by hand) and a Neopolitan *pizzaiolo* (master pizza-maker). There's also an assistant who washes dishes and cutting boards as you cook—as Mary Beth says, "Everything is provided for the guests. All they need is enthusiasm and appetite."

You'll learn to make *antipasti*, assorted *primi piatti* of pasta, risotto, *crespelle*, polenta, and pizza (in the *forno a legno*, wood-burning brick oven); *secondi piatti* of veal, lamb, duck, fish, or game; *contorti* of seasonal vegetables; *dolci* of fruit *crostata*, *semifreddo*, biscotti, and more. And you'll taste regional extra virgin olive oils, balsamic vinegars aged in heirloom wooden barrels, prosciutto, Parmigiano-Reggiano from a gold medal–winning cheese master, and a wide array of local wines chosen to complement your meals.

Your vacation begins with an afternoon walking tour of Bologna—visiting the beautiful basilicas, cloisters, Romanesque and Gothic art—and then dinner at one of Mary Beth's favorite local trattorias. Other highlights include: learning the secrets of *La Cucina Nuova*; visiting artisan galleries; shopping at designer outlets; enjoying a festive lunch at Michelin-starred *Gaidellos*, a converted stone farmhouse restaurant serving local organic ingredients; and a demonstration class at Michelin two-starred *Ristorante La Fasca* (rated among the top five restaurants in Italy), where the chef opens his kitchen exclusively for Mary Beth's students.

The **October Truffle Festival** trip also begins in Bologna with a walking tour, a visit to the market, and lessons with the *pizzaiolo* and *sfoglina*. But this time, truffles are everywhere: You'll taste fresh white and black truffles in the market, and make a "truffle-laden feast" with *antipasti*, game, sauces, seasonal vegetables, and dessert.

Then you travel to Alba—the truffle center of Italy and home of the White Truffle Festival and Market (so popular that Mary Beth has to make hotel reservations a year in advance)—to stroll along its narrow cobbled streets, surrounded with the aroma of truffles and porcini.

And over the next few days, you attend a chocolate truffle demonstration at *Pasticceria Sacco*, enjoy an exclusive truffle demonstration class and dinner at Alba's best restaurant, stalk the elusive truffle with an expert *trifolau* and his dog on a woodland hunt on private grounds ("You always remember finding your first truffle!" Mary Beth says), and drive to *Costilgliole d'Asti* for a sensational dinner with truffles, created just for you at the two Michelin-star *Ristorante De Guido*.

And between all the truffle tastings, there's still time for drives among the hillside castles of the wine country, for outlet shopping for bargains from Italy's top designers, and (truffles, again) for watching the secretive negotiations among truffle hunters at the famous White Truffle Market.

Noncooking spouses and partners are welcome to join the meals and excursions for the full fee. Children are welcome, but the school does not provide specific activities for them. However, Mary Beth will provide a list of day trips in the area: a drive to a twelfth-century fortress in Dozza, Etruscan ruins at Marzabotto, chapels, frescos and botanical gardens at Padua, and much more.

THE DETAILS: The Basics of Great Italian Cooking runs one week and is offered from May to October. The October Truffle Festival runs one week and is offered in October. Group size is limited to twelve. The costs include accommodations, all Italian buffet break-fasts, most lunches and dinners, cooking lessons, and excursions.

Basics of Great Italian Cooking: $3,200 (first-class hotel)–
    $3,600 (deluxe hotel)
Single Supplement: $280 (first-class hotel)–$380 (deluxe hotel)
October Truffle Festival: $3,600 (first-class hotel)–$3,800 (deluxe
    hotel)
Single Supplement: $320 (first-class hotel)–$360 (deluxe hotel)

Contact:
Mary Beth Clark
International Cooking School of Italian Food and Wine
201 East 28th Street, Suite 15B
New York, NY 10016-8538
Phone: 212-779-1921
Fax: 212-779-3248
E-mail: MaryBethClark@worldnet.att.net

*From the kitchen of the
International Cooking School of
Italian Food and Wine*

❂

**TORTA DI POLENTA CON
MIELE E D'ARANCIO
(ORANGE-HONEY POLENTA
CAKE)**

SERVES 8 TO 10

"During the Feast of San Giorgio," Mary Beth Clark of the International Cooking School says, "farmers traditionally celebrate by scooping the cream off the top of the milk and pouring it over a polenta cake like this one. Now that's close to the land!"

7 tablespoons unsalted butter,
   melted and cooled
1/2 cup finely ground corn
   meal or polenta
1 1/4 cups all-purpose flour
1 tablespoon baking powder
2 generous pinches fine sea
   salt
1 large egg, lightly beaten
2 teaspoons minced orange zest
7 ounces milk

1/2 cup honey
1 1/2 teaspoons almond extract

SYRUP:
1/4 cup fresh, tart orange juice
2 tablespoons honey

GARNISH (OPTIONAL):
Powdered sugar
Fresh fruit (orange sections,
   strawberries, nectarines)

If you use polenta instead of corn meal, the cake will have a denser, moister texture, similar to pound cake.

Preheat oven to 375°.

Melt the butter, allowing it to cool without forming a crust on top.

Sift the corn meal or polenta, flour, baking powder, and salt together in a mixing bowl. Mix the ingredients, then quickly add the cooled melted butter in a steady stream, and mix for several seconds. Add the egg and orange zest, mix for a few seconds more, and scrape the bowl so all ingredients are blended.

Pour in the milk and beat until barely incorporated. Pour in the honey and the almond extract, blending the batter briefly and then scraping the bowl again. **Do not overmix** or the batter will become thick and the cake will be too dense.

Coat a 9-inch round baking pan with a little butter or nonstick spray (even if you're using a nonstick pan). Pour the batter into the pan and level it. Then place the pan on the center rack of the oven and reduce the heat to 325°. Bake for 45 to 50 minutes (or until a baking needle inserted in the center comes out clean), and transfer to a cooling rack.

Prepare the syrup by heating the juice and honey for a few minutes until it begins to boil. Remove from the heat, and brush the syrup over the surface and side of the cake, repeating until the cake absorbs all the syrup.

Serve the cake warm or cool. If desired, sprinkle it with powdered sugar, garnish with fresh fruits, or zabaglione sauce.

The cake can be covered and served for up to two days.

• ITALIAN COOKING CLASSES •
WITH MAMMA AGATA

Mamma Agata has cooked for Jacqueline Kennedy, Humphrey Bogart, Audrey Hepburn, Gore Vidal, and many other celebrities, politicians, and writers. Her cooking classes meet in her home: a gracious clifftop house a thousand feet above sea level, overlooking the Amalfi coastline, with terraces and gardens full of lemon trees, flowers, vegetables, and poultry (she produces almost all of the ingredients for the recipes she cooks).

Mamma Agata teaches traditional Italian cuisine—you'll learn how to create many wonderful pastas, including her own special recipes, and will cook with veal, fish, chicken, and seasonal vegetables. You'll make starters, pizzas, many typical Mediterranean dishes, cakes, and traditional marmalade and preserves. And every class ends with a meal you enjoy with local wines as you sit on the terrace and look out over the Mediterranean Sea.

Ravello and the surrounding area offer many opportunities for sightseeing, shopping, and exploring. In Ravello itself, you can explore the Cathedral and the two most famous villas: *Villa Rufolo*, the home of the garden that inspired Richard Wagner while he was writing *Parsifal*, and *Villa Cimbrone*, famous for its breathtaking belvedere, from which you can see, as Gore Vidal said, "the most beautiful view in the world."

Or you can visit Scala, Amalfi, Capri, or Ischia. It's a lovely one-mile walk to Scala, the smallest and oldest of the four towns. Along the way you pass an ancient bridge and a small waterfall, and once you arrive in Scala you can visit the churches of San Giovanni and San Pietro. Amalfi is an excellent destination for eating, exploring, shopping, or sightseeing—or you can visit a cathedral built in the sixth century, take an Amalfi by Night tour, or enjoy a boat trip to the *Grotta dello Smeraldo* in the bay of Conca die Marini. And while Capri can feel a bit touristy, the island of Ischia—with its hot springs, beaches, vineyards, and thermal cures—is an excellent destination.

THE DETAILS: The program runs one week and is offered, upon request, year-round. Group size is limited to four. The cost includes meals, cooking lessons, and an interpreter. Accommodations are not included, although the Amalfi Coast Service Center, which works with Mamma Agata, is happy to recommend lodging options for all budgets. It's also possible to take cooking lessons with Mamma Agata on a daily basis.

The Cost: $900
Daily cooking lessons: $150 per day

Contact:
Mrs. Chiara Lima
Amalfi Coast Service Center
Via Trinita, 31-83010
Ravello—Salerno ITALY
Phone/Fax: 39-89-858386
E-mail: chiaralm@amalficoast.it
Web site: www.webworld.co.uk/mall/Coastline

• LA CUCINA KASHER IN TOSCANA •
(KOSHER COOKING IN TUSCANY)
AND L'AMORE DI CUCINA ITALIANA
(LOVE OF ITALIAN COOKING)

Inland Services

Inland Services offers two Italian cooking vacations: One emphasizes kosher food and Italian-Jewish culture, and the other focuses
on the more general tastes and sights and culture of Italy.

Italy has one of the longest continuous Jewish histories of any
European country, and an important part of that history is, of
course, the food. **La Cucina Kasher in Toscana** offers a unique
opportunity to learn kosher Italian-Jewish cuisine.

You'll spend three hours per day in a farmhouse-like kitchen,
attending hands-on classes that emphasize preparation, presentation,
and the historical aspects of cooking. You learn to cook *panzanella*
(bread salad), *taglierini alla carrettiera* (pasta carter's style), *vitello
arrosto* (veal with sauce from stock), *peperonata* (stewed peppers),
and *castagnaccio* (chestnut cake). Following each lesson, you'll
enjoy the meal you created, accompanied by appropriate wines.
You'll prepare both lunches and dinners, with a special class pre-
ceding Sabbath dinner on Friday.

The program includes a trip to Florence, where you'll dine at a
Jewish restaurant, Ristorante Ruth, and then tour a nineteenth-
century synagogue and museum. You'll also visit with *Contessa
Corsini* at the *Villa di Maiano*, Fiesole, where the movie *Room with a
View* was filmed, and watch restorers of tapestry at the *chiostro*. Day
trips are also made to a well-known porcelain manufacturer, the
Salvatore Ferragamo shoe museum, a local olive oil producer, to
Siena for lunch and a tour of its synagogue, and to San Gimignano.

Your home during the trip is restored fifteenth-century farmhouse, *Locanda di Praticino*, in Pomino, about a half hour outside of
Florence. The farmhouse offers a relaxed country atmosphere, with

modern amenities, including private baths in each room, a tennis court, and pool.

The chefs are Cristina Blasi and Gabriella Mari, owners of *Scuola di Arte Culinaria 'Cordon Bleu'* in Florence. They are renowned olive oil experts as well as cookbook authors. Kosher certification is provided by Rabbi Josef Levi, chief rabbi of Florence, full-time *mashgiach*, and authority on Italian-Jewish culture. ***l'Amore di Cucina Italiana*** is similar in scope to the kosher program: You stay at *Locanda di Praticino*, Cristina Blasi and Gabriella Mari are your chefs (though the meals are traditional Italian rather than kosher), and the field trips, excluding the synagogue tours and Jewish restaurant, are the same. In addition, you'll visit local producers of cheese, and prestigious wineries for tastings and lunches.

Spouses are welcome on either trip and included in activities. Inland Services also arranges a trip to Provence (see page 35).

THE DETAILS: Both programs run one week. Group sizes are limited to twelve. *La Cucina Kasher in Toscana* is offered in April, May, and October. *l'Amore di Cucina Italiana* is offered in May, September, and October. The costs include accommodations, meals, cooking lessons, and excursions.

La Cucina Kasher in Toscana: $2,600
Single Supplement: $300
L'Amore di Cucina Italiana: $2,195
Single Supplement: $350

Contact:
Ralph P. Slone
Inland Services, Inc.
360 Lexington Avenue
New York, NY 10017
Phone: 212-687-9898
E-mail: incook@earthlink.net

From the kitchen of
La Cucina Kosher in Toscana

◦

BACCALÀ ALLA LIVORNESE
(COD LIVORNO STYLE)

SERVES 4

2 tablespoons of extra virgin
   olive oil for the sauce
2 cloves of garlic, crushed
Chili pepper to taste
   (optional)
2 cups tomato sauce, or 4 ripe
   tomatoes for sauce, peeled
   and diced
1 teaspoon of very finely
   chopped parsley

A pinch of salt to taste
4 slices of cod, de-boned and
   cut into 2-inch by 2-inch
   pieces
2 whole eggs, beaten
1 cup all-purpose flour
2 cups oil for frying
1 sprig of rosemary
Freshly ground black pepper

Heat the olive oil in a pan with the garlic and the chili and add the tomato sauce. Cook for about 5 minutes or until it has thickened. Sprinkle with the parsley and the salt.

Dry the fish with paper towels. Dip it first in the eggs and then the flour. Heat the oil for frying, add the rosemary and the fish, and cook both sides for a few minutes. Drain it and add it to the sauce. Let it absorb the flavor, and serve.

You may prepare the sauce in advance and cook the fish just before serving.

• LA VILLA CUCINA •

Travel an hour south of Pisa, into the Val di Cornia hills of western Tuscany, to *Tenuta La Bandita*, a seventeenth-century villa set on

more than two hundred acres. Within the estate are olive groves
and vineyards, two small lakes, and views of the Tyrrhenian sea and
the Tuscan isles. And classes in *cucina tipica Toscana*—traditional
Tuscan cuisine, based on local ingredients and seasonal availability.

If you visit *La Villa Cucina* in the spring, when the hills are covered with the yellow blossoms of the *saggina*, the breeze carries the
scent of the *acacia*, and the markets offer fresh herbs, artichokes,
wild fennel, and asparagus, your cooking will emphasize the freshest
vegetables and spices. Your excursions will include visits to Florence
to enjoy concerts and dance recitals performed in local palazzi and
churches, to Pisa for the regatta of the Great Maritime Republics,
and to the historic hill town of Massa Marittima to watch a competition of crossbow sharpshooters dressed in thirteenth-century
costumes.

In summer, when the Tyrrhenian sea delivers an abundance of fresh seafood, your recipes will reflect this harvest. You'll also visit—and eat—in the port cities of Cecina, Livorno, and Piombino. You'll go sightseeing on Elba, and will visit the medieval town of San Gimignano, known for its historic towers and Vernaccia wine, and Lucca, where you can walk the ancient walls surrounding the city and sample the local olive oil, sweet breads, and pastries.

And if you choose to travel in the fall, you'll cook hearty fare: Truffles are in season, as is game such as wild boar, rabbit, tiny birds called *tordo* (served grilled with porcini mushrooms), and chestnuts, which inspire many desserts. Fall is also the end of the agricultural year and when Tuscany celebrates *La Vendemmia* (the grape harvest). You'll go on day trips to watch the fine art of Tuscan cheese making, and to local wineries where you'll taste wines such as *Vermentino* and *Sassicaia di Bolgheri*.

The classes are held in the professional kitchen of the estate (which includes a wood-burning oven), and are taught by Chef Daniel Rosati. During each of the five four-hour classes, Chef Daniel introduces the day's recipes and ingredients, and then divides the guests into small groups, each of which is responsible for preparing one portion of the meal. At the end of class, either in the morning or afternoon, you and Chef Daniel sit down in *Tenuta La Bandita's* elegant dining room to dine on the meal you've created.

Chef Daniel has been a teacher at the New School in New York since 1989. He has been awarded numerous awards, such as the Antonin Carême bronze medal for the *Société Des Cuisiniers De Paris*. Gina Russomanno, the director of *La Villa Cucina*, has assisted Daniel for the last ten years and is a member of the Italian Culinary Institute.

THE DETAILS: The programs run one week and are offered in May, July, and October. Group size is limited to twelve. Costs include accommodations, meals, cooking lessons, and excursions.

The cost: $2,750
Noncooking guest: $2,500
Single Supplement: $300

Contact:
Gina Russomanno
La Villa Cucina
326 Broad Street
Bloomfield, NJ 07003
Phone: 973-566-9727
Fax: 973-743-6096
Web site: www.lavillacucina.com

• MOVEABLE FEASTS IN ITALY— •
BIKING AND WALKING TRIPS
WITH A CULINARY TWIST

Butterfield and Robinson

Butterfield and Robinson offers two Moveable Feasts tours in Italy:
a biking trip in Tuscany and a walking trip in the Dolomites.

The **Tuscan Moveable Feast** biking tour begins in Chianti. You
bike approximately twenty-two miles on rolling terrain, past vineyards of Malvasia, Sangiovese, and Canaiolo grapes. Then you
pass through the Colli Sensei and into San Gimignano (nicknamed
"the medieval Manhattan" for its beautiful towers that look, from
a distance, like skyscrapers). You'll stop for espresso and gelato
before arriving at your home for the next two days: *La Collegiata,* a
sixteenth-century Franciscan convent that was recently converted
into a fine hotel.

The following day, you explore Volterra, an ancient city built on
a high plateau surrounded by volcanic hills—you can either bike, if
you enjoy decidedly uphill travel, or drive there. After lunch in a
local restaurant (be sure to sample the *cinghiale*—wild boar, salted

and cured in Volterra style), you bike back from Volterra, a reward-
ing (downhill) ride.

On your third day, you begin in northern Tuscany (after a short
transfer, if you want to do less biking), cycling down quiet country
roads toward Ripoli—and a feast of your own making under the
supervision of Chef Umberto Menghi at *Villa Delia* (see page 161).
The rest of the day you spend enjoying the Villa: strolling on the
grounds, lounging at the pool, playing tennis or bocce.

After breakfast at the Villa, you set off for a loop ride through
the tiny Tuscan villages that dot the surrounding countryside—
about thirty-five miles of challenging, but not strenuous, terrain.
Then, in the late afternoon, you'll return to the villa for a cooking
extravaganza: making dinner from fresh produce and matching it
with locally produced wines.

The next morning you drive to Pisa for a walking tour of the city,
guided by a local resident. Then it's back to the villa's kitchen to
prepare dinner—or, if you'd prefer, a gentle, scenic bike ride to
nearby Santo Pietro.

Note: This trip includes twenty-two to thirty-five miles of bike
riding each day (with longer options available), although some of
the bigger hills are "flattened" by timely bus tranfers.

The **Dolomites Moveable Feast** walking trip starts with a stroll
through the vineyards at award winning Lageder vineyards before
you travel to the picturesque town of San Cassiano. There you'll
settle into your home during the trip, the Hotel *Rosa Alpina*—a
small, family-run luxury hotel and spa, originally built in 1850 as a
Tyrolean guest house.

Like many of the villages in the area, San Cassiano is a place
where three cultures and languages meet: Italian, German, and
Ladino. You'll study the cuisine, which is equally unique, under the
direction of Chef Norbert Neiderkofler, who trained with David
Bouley at *Le Bouley* in New York.

"Chef Norbert's range is tremendous," says Liz Willette, the director of the trip to the Dolomites. "From light spa cuisine to a richer style of cooking that is typical of the region. But shed any notions you have about heavy German food—you'll find a mix of the very best of Italian and Austrian cuisines, as Norbert fuses his Italian sensitivity with a more minimal and inventive American way of cooking. Every plate is not only healthy and delicious, but aesthetically pleasing, as well."

When you arrive at the hotel, you'll be greeted with cocktails preparatory to enjoying your first dinner by Chef Norbert. The next morning, breakfast is Austrian-syle: fresh fruit juice, muesli, ham and bacon, cakes, eggs, yogurt, and fresh fruit. Then you hike along La Gran Ega river to the village of La Villa, where you'll take a cable car to the peak of Piz La Ila (unless you prefer to walk—a narrow, steep footpath also climbs the mountain).

Back at the hotel you have your first cooking class with Chef Norbert and then dinner. If you prefer not to cook—or have some free time to fill—you can enjoy the spa services of the hotel. After a day of walking and cooking, an evening of eating and pampering is a fitting reward.

The next day you'll hike the pass between the Cortin and Alta Badia valleys, followed by a walk to Rifugio Scotoni in the valley of Lagazuoi—a stunning setting in which to enjoy delicious food. After a beer and some grilled polenta topped with wild mushrooms, you can visit the local museum and church before returning to the hotel for another lesson with Chef Norbert. And to cap off your day: a dinner of high Tyrolean cuisine at a nearby one-star Michelin restaurant.

On the final two days, you'll hike to a *baita*—a cabin in the woods used by local families for entertaining—where you'll have a lunch of risotto, grilled meats and vegetables with polenta, and homemade apple fritters washed down (in the local tradition) with espresso strengthened by a shot of pear liqueur. You'll have a wine lesson and tasting. You'll visit the church of Santa Croce along a pilgrimage route (complete with hand-painted stations of the cross) that has been used since the 1800s. And you'll explore local villages, enjoy simple *rifugio* food, attend two more of Norbert's classes before enjoying a farewell feast.

Note: Although the hiking isn't excessively difficult in this program, some routes do require a fair amount of physical exertion.

THE DETAILS: The Moveable Feast in Tuscany biking trip runs five days and is offered August through October. Group size is usually between sixteen and twenty-four people. The cost includes accommodations, all breakfasts and dinners, three lunches, all special events, lessons, and entrance fees, a customized Cannondale bicycle to use during the trip, all transportation during the trip, and all gratuities.

The Moveable Feast in the Dolomites walking trip runs five days and is offered in July and August. Group size is usually between sixteen and twenty-four people. The cost includes accommodations, all breakfasts and dinners, two lunches, all lessons and special events, all transportation within the trip, and all gratuities.

Moveable Feast in Tuscany: $4,475
Single Supplement: $1,500
Moveable Feast in the Dolomites: $3,450
Single Supplement: $250

Contact:
Butterfield and Robinson
70 Bond Street
Toronto, Ontario
CANADA M5B IX3
Phone: 800-678-1147; 416-864-1354
Fax: 416-864-0541
E-mail: info@butterfield.com
Web site: www.butterfield.com

• THE MURRAY SCHOOL •
OF COOKERY

"Sicily is one of the most underrated treasures of Europe. To many, it's little more than the football on the toe of Italy, home of the Mafia and Mount Etna," says Paulette Murray of the Murray School of Cookery. "But Sicily's history and culture was forged by most of the great empires of Europe and Africa. The Greeks, Romans, Normans, Spanish and French all left behind a legacy of magnificent antiquities, and enriched Sicilian cuisine with influences not always found on mainland Italy."

Guests live and learn the skills of Sicilian cookery at *Azienda Mose*, a beautiful Sicilian country house beside the Valley of the Temples at Agrigento. For centuries, Azienda Mose was the country home of the Agnello family—it is now a one-hundred-acre organic farm run by Chiara Agnello and her mother, Elena. Many of the ingredients you'll be using in the kitchen come from the farm: olives (the oil is sold exclusively to Fortnum and Mason), almonds, pistachios, eggplants, peppers, onions, tomatoes, oranges, pears, and more.

You'll spend half of each day cooking, usually in the afternoon—preparing a three-course dinner using fresh organically grown produce from the estate. And in the mornings, you can visit the Valley of the Temples, the Archaeological Museum (in which some of the exhibits were provided from the Mose estate), Piazza Armerina and its Roman Villa, market day at Agrigento, and any of the many sandy beaches within easy reach.

The evening meal is prepared by the guests and may be enjoyed either in the period dining room or on the terrace under the trees, with plenty of local wine.

THE DETAILS: The program runs one week and is offered in September. Group size is limited to eight. The cost includes accommo-

dations, some meals, cooking lessons, and transportation from England. Contact them for information about rates from the United States.

The Cost: £950 (approx. $1,570)

Contact:
The Murray School of Cookery
Glenbervie House, Holt Pound
Farnham, Surrey GU10 4LE
ENGLAND
Phone: 44-1420 23049
E-mail: KMPMMSC@aol.com
Web site: www.theonly.net/murray.cookery/

• RHODE SCHOOL OF CUISINE •

The nineteenth-century *Villa Michaela*—the site of the cooking vacation offered by the Rhode School—was rated by *Tattler* maga-

zine one of the fifty best houses in the world to rent. It has ornamental Italian gardens and exquisitely decorated drawing rooms,
dining rooms, and bedrooms, as well as swimming pools, grass tennis courts, and olive groves.

The cooking lessons at *Villa Michaela* are mostly hands-on, with
guests preparing both lunches and dinners. Some of the dishes you'll
learn to make are *Fagottini di Verdure* (vegetable puff pastry parcels);
Coniglio al Cacciatora Con Polenta ("hunter's" rabbit with polenta);
Pere Affogate (drowned pear); Gnocchi *al Quatro Formaggi* (gnocchi
with four cheese sauce); *Anatra alle Mele e Vino Rosso* (duck with
apple and red wine); *Crespelle al* Grand Marnier (Grand Marnier
crepes); *Fagioli con Gamberi* (warm cannellini and prawn salad);
and, *Saltimbocca alla Romana* (veal and prosciutto with sage.)

And you'll still have plenty of time for afternoon field trips, wine
tours, and enjoying *Villa Michaela*. The optional sightseeing trips
include visits to the Leaning Tower of Pisa, Lerici (a small fishing
village on the Gulf of La Spezi), Florence, and Villa Torrigiani
(famous for its glorious garden), located on the outskirts of Lucca.
Food-related trips include visits to a local olive press and market
and many wine tastings. A favorite of past guests has been a
leisurely stroll around the ancient walls of Lucca—just ten minutes
from *Villa Michaela*.

Valter Roman is the chef at Rhode School in Tuscany. He was
the pastry chef at the Slaley Hall Hotel near Newcastle, England,
and chef at both *Patisserie Amota* and *Patisserie Valerie* in London. He
has worked in Italy since 1983 at a variety of restaurants, including
several with Michelin stars.

Rhode School of Cuisine also offers a cooking vacation in the
South of France (see page 54 for more information).

THE DETAILS: The program runs for one week. Classes are offered
in April, May, September, October, and November. Group size is
limited to ten. The cost includes accommodations, meals with
wine, cooking lessons, excursions, and airport transfers from Nice,

Pisa, or Florence. High season rates apply during the months of May, September, and October. Low season rates apply during the months of April and November. Noncooking guests can attend for a reduced price.

The Cost: $2,195–$2,695
Single Supplement: $300

Contact:
Tim Haydon-Stone
216 Miller Avenue, Suite 8
Mill Valley, CA 94941
Phone: 800-447-1311
Fax: 415-388-4658
E-mail: tstone3954@aol.com

From the kitchen of the Rhode School of Cuisine
●

MELANZANE ALLA PARMIGIANA
(EGGPLANT PARMESAN)

2 eggplants
Olive oil
Salsa Di Pomodoro (see measurements below)
Mozzarella
Parmesan
Fresh basil
Salt

Slice the eggplants into $1/4$-inch slices and fry them in a $1/2$-inch of olive oil until a golden color. Remove the oil and put the slices of eggplant to one side.

Put a layer of tomato sauce (recipe below) on the bottom of an ovenproof dish, followed by a layer of eggplant. Then another layer of tomato sauce, then sliced mozzarella, grated Parmesan, and fresh basil leaves. Repeat the layers of eggplant, tomato sauce, and cheese 5 times, topping with a layer of Parmesan. Bake in the oven for 20 minutes at 350°.

When the dish is taken from the oven, the top should be golden. Decorate with fresh basil leaves and serve with *Ciabatta* (Italian bread) and Chianti.

SALSA DI POMODORO
$1^3/4$ pounds of cherry tomatoes
Olive oil
1 garlic clove
Salt
Fresh basil

Cut the cherry tomatoes into quarters. Heat a tablespoon or more olive oil in a frying pan and lightly fry the garlic. Add the tomatoes, salt, and basil to taste, and cook for 10 minutes.

• SICILIAN ODYSSEY •

The impact of the many great Mediterranean civilizations—Greek, Roman, Arabic, Norman, French, and Spanish—can still be found in Sicily's architecture, customs, and culinary traditions. Your discovery of this unique heritage begins in Palermo, Sicily's capital, where you'll see the Palazzo dei *Normanni*, the pink domes of *San Giovanni degli Eremiti*, the *Quattro Canti*, and other sites. You'll then spend the night near the town of Monreale and will attend two cooking lessons by Chef Jack Bruno, one of Sicily's top chefs.

After an excursion to Cefal, a town built on a narrow peninsula and dominated by a huge twelfth-century Romanesque duomo, you'll travel along Sicily's west coast. You'll stop first at Segesta to see the Greek temple and will then visit the medieval hilltop town of Erice, enjoy a wine tasting at Marsala, and travel down the coast to Agrigento, home of the Valley of the Temples. That night you'll stay at *Baglio Della Luna*, a former sixteenth-century tower and villa which is now a four-star hotel.

The next day, after a stop in Piazza Armerina, a tiny baroque town known for the Roman emperor's villa that sits nearby, you arrive in Siracusa, once the world's largest and wealthiest city-state. You'll explore the island of Ortygia with its beautiful Piazza del Duomo and many restaurants, cafés, markets, and vibrant night life. You'll see Mount Etna, the largest active volcano in Europe, and will travel to Taormina, the medieval mountaintop town where you'll stay in *Villa Diodoro*, a four-star hotel with view of Mount Etna and the Ionian Sea.

Finally, you'll join *Signora* Giuliana Condorelli for a cooking lesson in her villa near Catania. *Signora* Condorelli is an expert in traditional Sicilian cuisine; she will share recipes of the nobility which have been passed down through her husband's family for centuries.

THE DETAILS: The program runs eight days. The cost includes accommodations, all meals, cooking lessons, wine tastings, excursions, and airport transfers.

The Cost: $2,350

Contact:
The International Kitchen
1209 North Astor 11-N
Chicago, IL 60610
Phone: 800-945-8606; 312-654-8441
Fax: 312-654-8446

E-mail: info@intl-kitchen.com
Web site: www.intl-kitchen.com

• THE SPOLETO COOKING SCHOOL •

Spoleto, a small city in the Umbrian hills about seventy-five miles north of Rome, dates from prehistoric times and is richly endowed with cultural heritage and history. It offers splendid architecture (Roman, medieval, Renaissance, and later), charming piazzas, sidewalk cafés, elegant restaurants, interesting shops, spectacular views, and many treasures of art history such as the frescoes of the Renaissance master Filippo Lippi adorning the apse of the duomo.

Guests of the Spoleto Cooking School use fresh, seasonal ingredients from the region of Umbria to prepare a wide variety of dishes. Recipes range from simple casalinga (home-style) to professional, restaurant-quality meals. They include vegetable *antipasti*; *primi piatti* of pasta, risotti, *crespelle*, and polenta; *secondi piatti* of veal, lamb, duckling, fish, and *cinghiale* (wild boar); *contorni* of seasonal vegetables; and *dolci*, including biscotti, zabaglione, and *crescionda* (a Spoleto specialty tart). You'll also be taught the art of handmaking pasta (including *strangozzi*, Umbria's distinctive string pasta) under the tutelage of a master *sfoglinia* (pasta chef).

Each morning class concludes with a lunch that you prepare in the private kitchen and enjoy—along with regional Umbrian wines and mineral waters—in the school's restaurant. Among other treats, you'll taste fresh porcini mushrooms, Umbrian black truffles, and locally produced cheeses and extra virgin olive oil. The final class is devoted to making a dinner of Umbrian *salumi*, Norcia prosciutto *con melone*, *formaggi*, polenta *al sugo*, *carne alla spoletina*, and fresh-baked pastry. Dinner is topped off with homemade *grappa*.

On a typical day, you may learn to roll pasta with a wooden *matterello*, stroll through the town's *centro storico* (old town), shop on the Piazza *del Mercato di Spoleto*, visit a water-driven flour mill for a bread and pastry baking demonstration, and enjoy dinner at a local restaurant with a guest speaker on Italian food and Spoleto's history.

You'll also visit *Tartufi Urbani* (the famous Umbrian truffle company), the Monini olive oil company, and the Orvieto winery, and, if you choose, can attend Italian language classes, which concentrate on conversation and vocabulary related to *la cucina*. Many day trips can be arranged, either within or outside of Umbria.

Most guests stay at the Hotel Aurora, a two-star hotel just off the Piazza *della Liberta*. Other accommodations are available at Spoleto's Convent, *L'Instituto Bambin' Gesu*, and in private apartments. The school is happy to work with guests who have special lodging requests, whether they want a luxury hotel, spacious apartment, or need to accommodate a spouse or children. The cooking classes are conducted at *La Scuola Alberghiero di Spoleto*, a modern and fully equipped professional cooking institute.

Claudio Cesarò, the head chef at *La Scuola Alberghiero dello Stato di Spoleto*, obtained his degree in culinary arts at *L'Istituto Alberghiero di Alessio* and has worked in many fine hotels and restaurants throughout Italy. He has conducted Italian cooking courses in Charleston, South Carolina, as well as workshops in Italian culinary traditions from the thirteenth, fourteenth and nineteenth centuries.

The Spoleto Arts Symposia, of which the Cooking School is part, also offers a writer's workshop, a children's writing workshop, and a vocal arts symposium. Cooking students are encouraged to take advantage of free attendance at symposium concerts and readings.

Accommodations for family members can be arranged.

THE DETAILS: The program runs one week and is offered in July and August. Group size is limited to ten. The cost includes accommodations, all meals, cooking and Italian language lessons, excursions, and invitations to special concerts or readings given by other Spoleto Arts Symposia participants.

The Cost: $2,100

Contact:
The Spoleto Arts Symposia
760 West End Avenue, Suite 3-A
New York, NY 10025
Phone: 212-663-4440
Fax: 212-663-4440
E-mail: clintoneve@aol.com
Web site: www.spoletoarts.com

From the kitchen of the Spoleto Cooking School

*

RISOTTO CON ZUCCINE E FIORI DI ZUCCA
(RISOTTO WITH ZUCCHINI AND
ZUCCHINI BLOSSOMS)

SERVES 4

5 to 6 cups vegetable broth
2 tablespoons olive oil
1 medium onion, diced
1 celery stalk, chopped
2 medium zucchini,
   chopped
$1/2$ cup dry white wine

1 dozen zucchini blossoms,
   approximately
$1^1/2$ cups arborio rice
3 tablespoons butter
$1/4$ cup Parmesan cheese,
   grated
Salt

Bring the broth to a steady simmer on the stovetop. In a large saucepan, heat the olive oil over a medium heat and add the onion and celery. Sauté for 2 or 3 minutes, until the onion and celery are soft but have not begun to brown. Add the chopped zucchini and about a cup of the simmering vegetable broth. Cover and cook for 5 minutes.

Add another cup of the broth, all but 2 of the zucchini blossoms, and the white wine. Let this mixture cook for another 5 minutes, then add the rice and stir thoroughly, until almost all of the broth has been absorbed by the rice. Add another half cup of broth and cook for about 15 minutes, vigorously stirring in an additional half cup of broth whenever the liquid is almost entirely absorbed.

When the rice is done, turn off the heat and immediately add the butter and Parmesan and salt to taste. Coarsely chop the 2 zucchini blossoms you reserved and add them as garnish. Let sit for several minutes and serve.

• TASTING PLACES •

Tasting Places offers three culinary vacations to Italy: a rustic holiday in the Italian countryside at *La Cacciata,* an estate in Orvieto; a vacation in a private eighteenth-century villa in Sicily; and a stay in elegant accommodations near the medieval city of Verona, the home of Shakespeare's Romeo and Juliet.

La Cacciata in **Orvieto** has been a working estate farm for generations, and is known for its extra virgin olive oil and Orvieto Classico wine. Classes and lodging are in renovated stone farmhouses nestled within the vineyards—the kitchen is light and airy, and the guest rooms feature tiled ceilings and stone floors.

The region is known for the quality if its porcini mushrooms and black truffles, as well as for the open-air market in Orvieto where you'll have a chance to shop for fresh produce. You'll also attend wine and olive oil tastings and a demonstration by a local pizza maker (followed by an al fresco pizza dinner), and have dinner with the owners of *La Cacciata*. In your free time, you can swim, hike, ride horseback, and discover the many delights of favorite local restaurants.

The dishes you'll learn to prepare include Bruschetta *con Melanzane Sott' Olio* (bruschetta with eggplant preserved in oil); *zuppa di rucola tartufata* (arugula soup with truffle oil); *ravioli con porri e tartufo* (ravioli with leeks and truffles); *coda di rospo con pomodori arrosto e olive nere* (baked monkfish with roasted tomatoes and black olives); *crostata di pesche bianche e mandorle* (white peach and almond tart); and *torta di pinoli e vin santo* (pinenut and *Vin Santo* cake).

If you decide to have your cooking vacation in **Sicily**, you'll find yourself in a culinary melting pot of Mediterranean cuisine: Italian, Greek, Moorish, and French. You'll stay at the Ravida family's private villa in Menfi, cooking in the estate's huge marble and wood furnished kitchen with Ravida extra virgin olive oil from the nearby groves. You'll visit Palermo and Marsala, the island of Mozia for a picnic, the Greek monumental sites of Selinunte and Agrigento, and any of the many near-deserted, sandy beaches within walking distance of the villa. You'll also explore the markets, as the history of Sicilian cuisine is nowhere more alive than in the outdoor stalls with their bounty of seafood, meats, specialty food products, vegetables, and fruits.

While staying at *Villa Ravida*, you'll prepare focaccia stuffed with figs, gorgonzola, and prosciutto; *caponata* (eggplant, tomato, pine nut, caper, and raisin compote); stuffed swordfish with pine nuts, lemon, raisins, and herbs; almond and pistachio ice cream; and, oven-baked figs with honey and oranges.

If you holiday in **Verona**, you'll stay at *La Foresteria*, the elegant estate of Count Serego Alighieri—a direct descendant of Dante. The property has been owned by the family since 1353, and was expertly remodeled into eight elegant apartments with open fireplaces, beamed ceilings, and cypress-lined views of the hillside vineyards. Classes meet in a professional quality kitchen and make use of the estate's own produce and wines, including olive oil, preserves, balsamic vinegar, and *grappa*.

You'll be welcomed at *La Foresteria* with tea and *prosecco*, an introduction to Venetian ingredients, drinks, and dinner. Over the following days, you'll visit the market town of Soave and the famous fish market of Rialto, shop for art, antiques, and clothing, visit a rice farm and a sixteenth-century mill, and enjoy a seven-course dinner at one of Verona's most renowned restaurants. Hiking, dining, and wine tasting opportunities abound, and a golf course, *Ca'degli Ulivi*, is only twenty minutes away.

A sample of dishes taught at *La Foresteria* includes pumpkin ravioli with sage and butter, crostini with fresh *borlotti* bean purée, risotto *nero* (black squid ink risotto), Venetian mussels stuffed with sausages, *panettone* bread, and butter pudding, and Venetian rice pudding with pine nuts and *grappa*-soaked raisins.

Tasting Places works with a variety of chefs. Most cook at well-known restaurants in London, and all are highly committed to Italian cuisine. Past chefs have included: Claudio Pecorari, owner of *Al San Matino*, Tiberio's, and *Cibo*; Maxine Clark, food writer for *Food and Travel*, *County Living*, and *Good Houskeeping*; and Sophie Baimbridge, who has worked with Alice Walter at *Chez Panisse*.

THE DETAILS: The Orvieto and Sicily trips each run one week and are offered in May, June, and September. Verona runs six days and is offered in June and October. Group sizes are limited to twelve. Costs include accommodations, food, wine, cooking lessons, schedule trips, and transfers to and from recommended flights.

La Cacciata, Orvieto, Umbria: £980 (approx. $1,615)
Villa Ravida, Menfi, South West Sicily: £995 (approx. $1,640)
La Foresteria, Verona, Veneto: £1,375 (approx. $2,265)
Single Supplement: £200 (approx. $330)

Contact:
Tasting Places Limited
Unit 40, Buspace Studios
Conlan Street
London W10 5AP, UK
Phone: 44-171 460 0077
Fax: 44-171 460 0029
E-mail: ss@tastingplaces.com
Web site: www.tastingplaces.com

From the kitchen of Tasting Places

POTATO GNOCCHI WITH RED PESTO

SERVES 4

Classic potato gnocchi originated in northern Italy, where it is a staple food. It takes practice to make gnocchi really light—overworking them tends to make them a little tough.

PESTO:
1 large red pepper
$1/4$ cup fresh basil leaves
1 clove of garlic
2 tablespoons pine nuts, toasted
6 sun-dried tomatoes in oil, drained
2 ripe tomatoes, skinned
$1/2$ tablespoon tomato paste
$1/2$ teaspoon chili powder

$1/4$ cup freshly grated Parmesan cheese
$1/2$ cup olive oil

GNOCCHI:
2 pounds potatoes
Salt
4 tablespoons butter
1 egg, beaten
1 to $1 1/4$ cups flour

GARNISH:
Basil leaves

On a high heat over a gas flame burner, or in a broiler, grill the red pepper, turning occasionally, until blackened all over. Place in a covered bowl until cool enough to handle, then peel off the skin. Halve the pepper and remove the core and seeds.

Place in a blender or food processor with the remaining pesto ingredients except the oil. Blend until smooth. Then, with the machine still running, slowly add the oil.

To make the gnocchi, cook the unpeeled potatoes in boiling water for 20 to 30 minutes until very tender; drain well. Halve and press through a potato ricer, or peel and press through a sieve into a bowl.

While still warm, add 1 teaspoon salt, the butter, beaten egg, and half the flour. Lightly mix together, then turn out onto a floured board. Gradually knead in enough of the remaining flour to yield a smooth, soft, slightly sticky dough.

Roll the dough into thick sausages, 1 inch in diameter. Cut into ³/₄-inch pieces and shape into mini torpedoes. Lay on a floured tea-towel.

Bring a large pan of salted water to boil. Cook the gnocchi in batches. Drop them into the boiling water and cook for 2 to 3 minutes, until they float to the surface. Remove with a slotted spoon and keep hot while cooking the remainder. Toss with the red pesto and serve immediately garnished with basil.

Note: The pesto can be stored in a jar, covered with a layer of olive oil, for up to 2 weeks in the refrigerator.

• TASTY TUSCANY •

"Our goal is to let guests experience real Italian hospitality," says Patrizia Vecchia, who runs Tasty Tuscany with her husband, Paolo. "Guests cook typical family dishes made with seasonal produce and herbs freshly picked from the garden. Or they just relax and enjoy, sharing our meals and a bottle of good wine, and discover the hidden face of our country: little medieval villages, historic towns and art enclaves, natural oases and places known only by local people."

Tasty Tuscany custom-designs schedules and itineraries to suit their guests' preferences. For example, a tour designed for vegetarians might start with an exploration of the family garden, followed by a cooking class using herbs you just picked. Then a lunch of bean salad with herbs and fresh vegetables, and baked eggplant rolls with mozzarella, basil, garlic, and olives. Or you might have handmade *tagliatelle* in zucchini cream with basil and pine nuts, *orecchiete* in tomato sauce, and Sicilian salad with fennel and orange.

For dinner, you might enjoy a pizza party dinner at a friend's farmhouse, with a wood oven, wine, and songs. Or you might stay in the villa and have dinner of small onions with honey and cloves, polenta, pumpkin pudding with truffles, *incavolata* (traditional soup with black cabbage), and *crostata* (cake) with almonds and figs. Another dinner might be potato and leek ravioli with sage, butter, and Parmesan cheese, *sfoglie* with zucchini and tomino (a seasoned northern cheese), fresh spinach salad, and chocolate pudding with apricot cream.

You'll also visit the ancient towns of Volterra and San Gimignano, browse and shop in alabaster artisan shops, have a picnic lunch in the Tuscan countryside, visit a pottery factory that's been operating since the 1500s, and taste wines at local vineyards.

Other activities and classes include horseback riding, mountain biking, ceramic creation and decoration, wood basket weaving, shiatsu massage, and prana therapy. Tasty Tuscany is happy to accommodate children.

The villa itself, *Villa Sorgente*, was for centuries the summer residence of an aristocratic family. The property, which was recently transformed into a holiday residence, has always been affiliated with local agricultural activities—near the villa you'll find a granary, cellars, and other typical farm buildings. The villa also has a swimming pool, garden, eight double rooms, and an olive oil pressing room with a large fireplace that has been converted into a kitchen, where guests cook—and also eat, unless they're enjoying dining alfresco on the terrace.

THE DETAILS: Programs run from one to two weeks and are offered year-round. Group sizes are limited to eight. Costs include accommodations, all meals, cooking lessons, and excursions.

One Week: $945
Two Weeks: $1,890
Single Supplement: $20 per day

Contact:
Tasty Tuscany
Patrizia and Paolo Vecchia
Via Mazzana, 1
56020 Marti–Montopoli Vildarno (Pisa) ITALY
Phone/Fax: +39-0571-461-700
E-mail: tastytuscany@tin.it
Web site: web.tin.it/tastytuscany

From the kitchen of Tasty Tuscany
ӭ
EGGPLANT ROLLS
SERVES 4

This dish is perfect for hot summer lunches. It can be eaten either cold or warm, with a cool white wine.

3 medium or 2 large eggplants	$^{1}/_{2}$ cup of black olives and
$^{3}/_{4}$ pound mozzarella (enough	capers, finely chopped
for 16 slices)	1 clove of garlic
4 ripe tomatoes	$^{1}/_{4}$ cup Parmesan cheese
Fresh basil	Salt
	Olive oil

Peel the eggplant and slice lengthwise thinly (about $1/8$ inch). Grill it until brown and tender, but be careful not to burn.

Cut the mozzarella and the tomatoes into thin slices. Chop the basil, olives, capers, and garlic together, and add half the Parmesan. Put a slice of mozzarella and a slice of tomato on each of the grilled eggplant slices, and then top with a teaspoon of the basil/olive mixture. Sprinkle with a pinch of salt and drizzle with olive oil.

Roll the eggplant slices into cylinders, with the mixture inside, and close with a toothpick. (If one eggplant slice is not long enough, add another slice—without mixture—to complete the round.)

Lay the rolls in an oiled baking pan, and cover them with the remaining Parmesan. Bake in an oven preheated to 350° for 10 to 20 minutes.

Serve with grilled zucchini and tomatoes (dressed with salt, balsamic vinegar, and olive oil) and a little toasted rustic bread (any hearty, crusty bread will do) sprinkled with olive oil and oregano, and enjoy.

• TOSCANA SAPORITA •

"People dream about actually living like a Tuscan instead of peeking in from the periphery of a tour group," says Anne Bianchi, the co-owner of *Toscano Saporita*. "But to truly live like a Tuscan, you must first master a few essentials—such as learning to cook and eat as Tuscans do." *Toscano Saporita* offers entrée into the real Tuscany: quaint villages with cobbled streets, undiscovered trattorias, endless carafes of red wine, newly pressed olive oil, and unhurried lunches on shaded verandas.

Guests stay at *Camporomano*, a five-hundred-year-old country estate on seventy acres which is owned and occupied by Baron Gianfranco Pecchioli and *Contessa* Oretta Martellini, whose family has been in continuous residence since 1630. Two beautiful villas front a lawn dotted with chestnut trees and flanked by formal herb and vegetable gardens set alongside the estate's pool. The older of the two structures, built in the late 1400s, served as the original home of the estate's noble residents, and now houses *Toscana Saporita*. In addition to serving as the proprietors' home, *Camporomano* is a working agricultural estate, housing one of Tuscany's few remaining privately owned olive presses. In mid- to late-November, Baron Gianfranco personally oversees the pressing of the olives from the family's ten thousand ancient trees. (Anne says, "Our favorite saying is, 'If you want your food to taste better, simply use more oil.' We tell our guests this constantly and, by the end of the week, they absolutely believe it.") The estate also produces a limited quantity of fine wine, which is reserved for the use of the family, their friends, and *Toscana Saporita*.

Anne, who was raised in the United States (although she spent every summer of her life in Tuscany), runs the program with her Tuscan cousin, Sandra Lotti. Together, they focus on providing a truly insider experience. "Most of our food and wine suppliers have known us all our lives," Anne says. "The *Contessa* is a childhood friend, and she and her father, the Baron, are very involved with our cooking guests on a day-by-day basis. And during the week, cousins, aunts, uncles, and mothers are bound to show up at various times. By the end of the week, guests feel like part of the family."

Cooking lessons are held for three hours each morning. Classes are small, completely hands-on, and make use of all-natural, seasonal ingredients. You'll learn to make homemade pasta, ravioli, gnocchi, pizza, focaccia, risotto, bruschette, crostini, vegetable and grain soups, grilled, roasted, fried and stuffed vegetables, sweet and savory tarts, pastries, ice creams, and sorbets. Two specific recipes you'll make are homemade four-color pasta tossed with roasted red peppers and basil-infused olive oil, and radicchio-stuffed ravioli with brown butter and sage sauce.

The modern, professional kitchen occupies the ground floor of a villa built in the late 1400s. For hundreds of years, this room was used to house the estate's fine wines, stored in huge wooden barrels. The barrels are gone, but the terra cotta floors and original wood-beamed ceilings remain. Classes involving instruction in bread, pizza and focaccia making are held next door, using a wood-fired oven that baked the estate's bread for hundreds of years. In addition to learning to cook like a Tuscan, you'll also learn to eat like one— leisurely lunches on a sun-drenched lawn facing the ancient villa, and four-course dinners served in the dining hall, which has twenty-foot-high, wood-beamed ceilings and is decorated with the *Contessa's* ancestral portraits.

Daily afternoon tours are led by a professional, English-speaking guide who will introduce you to Lucca (an eleventh-century walled city surrounded by three miles of perfectly preserved walls), the hill-towns of Coreglia and Bagni di Lucca, the seaside resorts of Viareggio and Lerici, Torre del Lago Puccini, and various local wineries for tastings.

During your stay, you will live in one of suites located above the school, each of which has its own living room, bathroom, and kitchen fully supplied with breakfast provisions. Suites contain from one to four bedrooms and are decorated with Italian country antiques.

Toscana Saporita offers four classes: the Spring Festival class focuses on the foods that emerge in April and May: wild leeks, new potatoes, spring onions, wild asparagus, shellfish, and fresh new cheeses. The Summer Abundance class is organized around ripe tomatoes, fragrant basil, eggplants, peppers, apricots, peaches, and melons. Autumn Harvest emphasizes mushrooms, chestnuts, truffles, newly ground polenta, and freshly pressed olive oil. And, once in spring and once in fall, you can participate in a Celebrity Chef-in-Residence program, during which guests have an opportunity to cook alongside some of America's most famous chefs.

Anne is the author of numerous Tuscan cookbooks including *From the Tables of Tuscan Women: Traditions and Recipes, Zuppa! Soups from the Italian Countryside,* and *Solo Verdura: The Complete Book of Tuscan Vegetable Cooking.*

Sandra Lotti is *Toscana Saporita's* co-owner and managing director. Known throughout Italy for her cookbooks on Tuscan regional cuisine (*Sapore di Maremma, L'Anno Toscano,* and *Zuppe Toscane*), she also co-authored *Dolci Toscani: The Book of Tuscan Desserts.* She conducts private lessons at *Toscana Saporita* when classes are not in session.

Children and noncooking partners are welcome (and there's a Ping-Pong/swing area for children).

THE DETAILS: The program runs one week and is offered in the spring, summer, and fall. Group size is limited to twelve. The cost includes accommodations, all meals with wine, cooking lessons, excursions, taxes, and transfers.

Cost: $1,970
Private Bathroom Supplement: $150

Contact:
Anne Bianchi
265 Lafayette Street A22
New York, NY 10012
Phone: 212-219-8791
E-mail: toscana@compuserve.com
Web site: www.cyberstudio.it/saporita

The International Kitchen
1209 N. Astor, #11-N
Chicago, IL 60610
Phone: 800-945-8606
Fax: 312-654-8446
E-mail: info@intl-kitchen.com
Web site: www.intl-kitchen.com

In Italy:
Sandra Lotti
Via Emilia Sud 59
Stiava (LU) Italy 55049
Phone: 39-584 92110
E-mail: letscook@ats.it

From the kitchen of Toscana Saporita

●

PURE DI PASTINACA CON SALVIA FRITTA
(PARSNIP PURÉE WITH FRIED SAGE)
SERVES 4

2 pounds parsnips, peeled and cut into thirds
1 cup tightly packed fresh parsley leaves
Salt and freshly ground black pepper
4 tablespoons unsalted butter
Olive oil for frying
Two dozen large fresh sage leaves

Place the parsnips in a large saucepan, cover with salted water and bring to a boil. Lower the heat to medium and cook for 10 to 15 minutes or until tender. Drain.

Place the parsnips and parsley in a food processor and purée. Season with salt and pepper and whip in the butter. Keep warm.

Pour $1/2$ inch of olive oil into a skillet and place over medium heat. When the oil is hot enough, add as many sage leaves as will comfortably fit and fry for 10 to 15 seconds or until just crisp. Remove with tongs and drain on paper towels. Serve over parsnips

For a spicier flavor, purée the parsnips with 2 cloves garlic and $1/2$ of a red chili pepper.

From the kitchen of Toscana Saporita

ə

FRITTELLE DI RICOTTA
ALLA PIETRASANTINA
(LEMON-RICOTTA FRITTERS)

MAKES ABOUT 30 FRITTERS

1 whole egg, plus 1 egg yolk,
at room temperature
1/4 cup sugar
1 tablespoon freshly grated
lemon zest
1 tablespoon milk
1/2 teaspoon vanilla extract

1 tablespoon cake flour, sifted
1 1/2 cups fresh sheep's milk
ricotta or other fresh
ricotta
Vegetable oil, for frying
Confectioners' sugar, for
dusting

In a medium-size bowl, beat the egg, egg yolk, and sugar until fluffy
and smooth. Stir in the grated lemon zest, milk, vanilla, and flour,
and mix to blend all ingredients.

Press the ricotta through a fine sieve directly into the egg mixture and stir until creamy. Cover the bowl and refrigerate for 1 hour.

Heat 1 inch of oil in a large nonstick skillet over high heat until
a bread cube immersed in the center sizzles around the edges.

Drop the chilled ricotta mixture by the tablespoonful into the
hot oil. Fry until golden brown on both sides, turning once. Drain
on paper towels, dust with the confectioners' sugar and serve.

As a variation, try adding 2 tablespoons of cognac or brandy to
the eggs, sugar, lemon zest, milk, and flour mixture.

• TUSCANY ADVENTURES •

Tuscany Adventures offers two cooking vacation programs: *La
Cucina del Castello* (the Kitchen of the Castle) and a Food and
Wine Intensive.

La Cucina del Castello is located at the Castello di Tocchi, an eleventh-century fortified village twenty-five minutes from Siena. The cooking course, and many of the dinners, is held in the castle in a large, comfortable room with ancient chestnut beams, a fireplace, and murals. You'll use the ancient wood burning oven at the *Castello* for many of your meals.

Chef Giancarlo Giannelli, who has been cooking Tuscan cuisine for more than thirty years, will teach recipes and demonstrate traditions that have been passed down for generations. Some of the guests' favorite dishes in the past have been *maialino con patate alla ghiotta* (piglet and potatoes cooked in the wood-burning oven), *sorbetto all salvia* (sage sherbet), *pappa al pomodoro*, and ravioli *al tartufo*.

You'll also go on excursions. On Monday, after preparing a four-course Tuscan lunch, you'll visit San Gimignano, where you'll sample the local wine, see the restored frescoes in the Collegiate Cathedral, and shop at the artisan stores that line the medieval streets. On Tuesday, you'll visit the San Lorenzo market in Florence. On Wednesday, you'll drive to Siena to explore the stone lanes and the Piazza del Campo, where the famous Palio horse race is run, and will attend a wine tasting class at Enoteca Italia. Thurday's class focuses on pastry. After class you'll drive to Montalcino, where you'll sample Brunello wines, and the fortified village of Murlo, where you'll enjoy pizza cooked in a wood-burning oven. And on Friday you'll visit a salami factory or a cheese farm before an elaborate farewell *festa*, with many toasts and traditional Sienese songs.

Each room in the castle has a view of the forest, private garden, and pool. The rooms are all individually furnished, and each has its own unique charm: One is located at the top of an ancient watchtower.

The **Food and Wine Intensive** focus on private visits to exclusive wine estates and food and wine matching meals with the winemakers. You'll visit prestigious estates producing *Brundello di Montalcino*, *Vine Nobile di Montepulciano*, Chianti *Classico*, and Ver-

naccia di San Gimignanon. You'll have wine tastings and classes every day, as well as lessons in matching food and wine.

THE DETAILS: The programs run one week and are offered March through November. Group size is limited from six to twelve. The cost includes accommodations, most meals, cooking lessons, and excursions.

La Cucina del Castello: $2,400
Food and Wine Intensive: $2,929

Contact:
Anne Dunne
Adventures in Tuscany
Phone 800-834-2943
Phone/Fax: 206-374-6123
E-mail: ann_dunne@ibm.net
Web site: www.tuscany-adventures.com

• TUTTI A TAVOLA •

Tutti a Tavola may not be the fanciest cooking vacation in this book, but it's one of the friendliest. It's run by four women—Lele, Marisa, Mimma, and Simonetta—who open their kitchens and homes to you, not just for cooking classes, but to share a truly Tuscan community experience.

Tutti a Tavola started in one kitchen, but soon outgrew it. Classes now take place in each of the four hostesses' homes, allowing guests to cook in different kitchens and dine at different tables—with Lele at *Canvalle*, Marisa at *La Casa*, Mimma at *Muricciaglia*, and Simonetta at *Adine*. And to enjoy different specialties (for example,

Simonetta's specialties are homemade ice creams, desserts, gnocchi, and handmade pasta).

A morning at *Tutti a Tavola* might begin with an expedition to a market in Montevarchi, Figline Valdarno, or Greve. You'll wander through the colorful market stalls: violet eggplants, red and yellow peppers, dark green parsley, shiny zucchini, and peaches and plums and pears and apples and grapes . . . You'll pass *pecorino* and Parmesan stalls, herb sellers, mushroom and fresh egg stalls, all amid the narrow streets and ancient buildings of a Tuscan town.

After the shopping is done, you'll return to the kitchen for the preparation. A typical meal may start with a rich antipasto of *crostini* (slices of local bread toasted and served with liver pâté), *fettunta* (unsalted Tuscan bread, toasted, rubbed with garlic, doused with virgin olive oil and seasoned with salt and pepper), or bruschetta with fresh tomatoes.

A vegetable dish will follow: baked tomatoes, stuffed zucchini, spinach pie, sweet and sour eggplant, or Tuscan salad. Then the main course: possibly chicken *cacciatora* or veal in tuna sauce, or risotto, lasagne, *tagliatelle*, or fusilli. Dessert may be baked peaches with *amaretti*, stewed pears, *panna cotta* (cream pudding), or tiramisu. And, of course, *cantuccini* (almond biscuits) to dip in the *Vin Santo* (Tuscan white dessert wine).

Radda and the surrounding area offer a wide range of accommodations: from rooms in village houses to luxurious châteaux, and everything in between. But Lele, Marisa, Mimma, and Simonetta recommend that you stay with them. Lele houses guests in a restored tower or an independent bed-and-breakfast off the main house. Mimma offers a lovingly renovated ancient haybarn and three stone farmhouses built in the fifteenth century. Marisa has a large house on three acres, with a garden and olive trees. And Simonetta presides over a cozy house that is part of a beautiful medieval village, Adine, which consists of only five houses and a church.

Noncooking activities include wine and olive oil tastings, trekking, horseback riding, tennis, watercoloring, and Italian language classes. There are also concerts, museums, abbeys, and castles to enjoy and explore. Finally, short trips to hill towns such as Volterra, Cortona, and San Giminiano can be easily arranged, as can walking tours focusing on plants, wildlife, history, and anthropology. Noncooking partners are welcome to attend dinner for an additional fee.

THE DETAILS: The program runs three days and is offered January through November. Group size is limited to eight. The cost includes meals, cooking lessons, and excursions. Accommodations are optional (price listed below).

The Cost: $500
Accommodations: $130 per night
Dinner only for noncooking companions: $50

Contact:
The International Kitchen
1209 North Astor 11-N
Chicago, IL 60610
Phone: 800-945-8606; 312-654-8441
Fax: 312-654-8446
E-mail: info@intl-kitchen.com
Web site: www.intl-kitchen.com

In Italy:
Mimma Ferrando
Phone: 39-0577 742 919
Fax: 39-0577 742 807
E-mail: ferrando@chiantinet.it

From the kitchen of Tutti a Tavola

⚬

GELATO AGLI AMARETTI
WITH CHOCOLATE SAUCE
(HOMEMADE ICE CREAM—
ICE CREAM MAKER NOT REQUIRED)

ICE CREAM:
5 eggs, separated
1 cup sugar
2¼ cups whipped cream
¾ cup crushed *amaretti* cookies
A small glass of rum

CHOCOLATE SAUCE:
1 cup sugar
½ glass of water
5 tablespoons bitter chocolate
1 glass of heavy cream

Firmly beat the egg yolks with the sugar. In two separate bowls, whip the cream and the egg whites to firm peaks. Add the crushed cookies to the egg yolks and sugar, then add the whipped cream, the rum, and finally the egg whites.

Put the mixture into a mold lined with aluminum foil and then in the freezer for at least 6 hours.

Unmold it by rapidly putting the mold in a basin of hot water. Serve with chocolate sauce.

For the chocolate sauce, first add the sugar to the half glass of water and bring to a boil. Add the chocolate, and bring it back to a boil. Add the glass of cream. When it again comes to a boil, the sauce is ready. The sauce lasts for several days in the refrigerator.

• VEGETARIAN COOKING •
IN TUSCANY

Tenuta San Vito is a working estate in the Chianti hills that produces wine and olive oil using both traditional techniques and the modern methods of organic cultivation—and that offers vegetarian cooking vacations.

Your vacation begins in San Vito Fior di Selva, the town where the farm is located—you can relax by the pool or tour the farm before a welcome dinner featuring vegetarian dishes of Tuscany. The next day you'll visit the Medici Villa in Poggio a Caiano, have lunch at a nearby farmhouse, where the owner will prepare a typical Tuscan meal, and go on a two-hour walking tour of Florence before returning to San Vito for dinner.

Day three begins with your first cooking lesson. Your instructors will be Jacopo Efrussi and Enrica Gamba. Jacopo has worked in some of Italy's top hotels and specializes in Tuscan vegetarian and macrobiotic cooking, and Enrica studied at Angelo Parcucchi's school and worked for seven years in one of Prato's top restaurants. After a vegetarian feast and a relaxing afternoon on the farm, you'll be treated to a wine tasting and lesson with an expert enologist.

The rest of your days include: a trip to Pisa; outlet shopping; a tour of a family-run pasta factory in the village of Lari; lunch at a seaside restaurant; shopping at the open-air market at Pistoia; and tours of Chianti and Siena. You'll also travel to the Medicean villa of Artimino where Carlo Cioni of Da Delfina will give a demonstration lesson in vegetarian dishes, followed by lunch.

Your home during your holiday will be one of three old farmhouses that have been restored and converted into apartments on the farm's 130 hectares of vineyards, forests, and open land. You can also relax by the pool or in the restaurant that overlooks the gardens.

THE DETAILS: The program runs one week. The cost includes accommodations, most meals, cooking lessons, excursions, and transfer to and from Florence airport.

The Cost: $2,300

Contact:
The International Kitchen
1209 North Astor 11-N
Chicago, IL 60610
Phone: 800-945-8606; 312-654-8441
Fax: 312-654-8446
E-mail: info@intl-kitchen.com
Web site: www.intl-kitchen.com

• VENETIAN COOKING •
IN A VENETIAN PALACE

The *Palazzo Morosini della Trezza* once belonged to a branch of the Morosini family, four of whose members were doges of Venice. It now houses an elegant Venetian cookery school run by Fulvia Sesani de Sabato, the seventh generation of her family to live in the palazzo. The palazzo was renovated in the nineteenth century, but evidence of an earlier time remains: in door jambs made of rare *macchiavecchia* marble extracted from a long-depleted quarry, in collections of antique silver, and in exquisite rugs, fine painting, glasses and jugs from Murano.

Fulvia's classes cover Italian—and specifically Venetian—recipes. She teaches traditional recipes, using her imagination to inject them with a dash of originality, explaining how they changed over the years, and discussing what causes forgotten dishes to enjoy a revival.

Some dishes you might learn to create are *pasta e fagioli* (pasta and bean soup), *fegato alla veneziana* (liver cooked in Venetian style), and marinated sole (one of Venice's oldest recipes, and a particular favorite today during the *Redentore* celebrations).

When you're not cooking or eating, you'll explore the city. You can tour the magnificent Doge's Palace, view the mosaics at the Basilica of St. Mark, and see the spectacular architecture and religious art at San Giovanni e Paolo, San Zaccaria, and the *Scuola di San Giorgio degli Schiavoni*. You'll also enjoy trips to the Accademia Art Gallery, the Nason and Moretti glass factory at Murano, the secret gardens of Venice (where you'll see a collection of antique fans in a private palace), and the Peggy Guggenheim Collection on a private guided tour.

Fulvia also takes guests on a walk through the picuresque arcades of the Rialto market to visit her favorite vendors, where fruits and vegetables, grown on the islands of the lagoon, are sold together with Adriatic-caught fish. Additionally, Fulvia's friends welcome guests into their homes, giving them the opportunity to admire the interiors of palaces on the Grand Canal and elegant houses tucked away in picturesque neighborhoods.

Also included are dinner at Harry's Bar and Arcimboldo's, and lunches at *La Busa* and the new *Cip's* restaurant of the *Cipriani* Hotel on Guidecca Island. Guests stay at the residence of the Hotel *Cipriani* and Palazzo Vendrami, located on Giudecca Island and set among lush gardens.

THE DETAILS: The program runs one week and is offered in January, March, June, September, October, and November. Group size is limited to ten. The cost includes accommodations, most meals, cooking lessons, and excursions.

The Cost: $4,400
Single Supplement: $300

Contact:
Judy Ebrey
Cuisine International
PO Box 25228
Dallas, TX 75225
Phone: 214-373-1161
Fax: 214-373-1162
E-mail: CuisineInt@aol.com
Web site: www.cuisineinternational.com

In Italy:
Palazzo Morosini della Trezza
Santa Maria Formosa, 6140
30122 Venice ITALY
Phone: 39-41 522 8923

• VILLA DELIA TUSCANY •
COOKING SCHOOL

Pisa, Tuscany

"When you think of an Italian meal," says Chef Umberto Menghi of *Villa Delia*, "you think of platters of hot steaming pasta, mounds of bread, and brightly painted plates heaped with colorful vegetables, with everyone eating, drinking and (most important) talking

all at the same time. For Italians, this scene requires a talent for ambidexterity, since as most people know, Italians need their hands in order to talk!"

Located in the heart of rural Tuscany, *Villa Delia*, built in the six-teenth century, sits on a ridge above the village of Ripoli di Lari. It is set in a serene countryside of ancient cypress and rolling hills, with stone farm houses, solitary monasteries, gently preserved medieval towns, and picturesque walled villages, yet within easy driving distance of Florence, Siena, Pisa, and the Italian Riviera.

The cooking classes are taught by Umberto (who is also the author of *Umberto's Kitchen: The Flavors of Tuscany*), his sister Mari-etta (the resident chef), and regional guest chefs—native Tuscans whose culinary skills are honed by a tradition of creating clean, fresh-tasting food.

The course specializes in pasta, Tuscan bread making, *cucina povera*, and general Tuscan cuisine. Some recipes include sea bass with olive oil and tomatoes, toasted canapés, lamb with thyme, mushroom and leek risotto, lemon chicken, veal carpaccio with arugula, stuffed zucchini, and many, many desserts.

On the day of your arrival, you'll be welcomed with a buffet lunch, followed by aperitifs and dinner and an introduction to the school. Day two includes the first cooking class (which run for two hours every morning during your stay), and then a visit to a pasta factory and an olive oil tasting. Then lunch at *Gattaiola* and dinner back at the villa.

The next day you might visit Lucca or Monastero (Castelfalfi), go shopping in Siena, or visit the tiny coastal villages of Cinque Terre for a walk, a picnic, and a tasting of local white wines.

In the middle of your vacation at the villa, you'll have two treats. The Great *Bocce* Tournament in the afternoon, in which the winners receive a bottle of wine (finagle your way onto Umberto's team: *Bocce* is his childhood game, and he always wins), and for din-ner, a make-your-own-pizza feast in the outdoor brick oven in the courtyard.

The villa, while maintaining friendly old-world charm, is well equipped with modern facilities, and has a heated swimming pool, a hard-surfaced tennis court, and fifty-four acres of rolling hills to walk, jog, bike, and enjoy. Children are very welcome, and traveling partners not attending the cooking classes can stay for sixty-five dollars a day including breakfast (plus fifty dollars for lunch and fifty-five dollars for dinner, if they choose).

THE DETAILS: The program runs ten days and is offered March through November. Group size is limited to twenty. The cost includes accommodations, all meals, cooking lessons, excursions, and transfers to and from the Pisa International Airport.

The Cost: $3,700–$4,100 (depending on season/guest chef)
Single Supplement: $400–$500

Contact:
Lisa Adams
Villa Delia Tuscany Cooking School
Umberto Management
1376 Hornby Street, Vancouver
B.C., CANADA V6Z IW5
Phone: 604-669-3732
Fax: 604-699-9723
E-mail: inquire@umberto.com
Web site: www.umberto.com

In Italy:
Villa Delia Tuscany Cooking School
Via Del Bosco 9
Ripoli di Lari
Pisa, ITALY
Phone: 39-587 684-322
Fax: 39-587 684-331

From the kitchen of Villa Delia
Tuscany Cooking School

۰

CALAMARI RIPIENI (STUFFED CALAMARI)
FROM UMBERTO'S KITCHEN:
THE FLAVORS OF TUSCANY

2 pounds of squid

STUFFING:
1 tablespoon olive oil
3 ounces prosciutto
1 small onion, finely
chopped
2 cloves of garlic, finely
chopped
1 tablespoon fresh parsley,
finely chopped
2 teaspoons fresh lemon
thyme, finely chopped

1 teaspoon fresh oregano,
finely chopped
Salt and freshly ground black
pepper to taste
1 egg
¼ cup fine bread crumbs, dry
or fresh
Zest of 1 lemon
2 tablespoons olive oil
2 tablespoons butter
½ cup dry white wine
Fresh parsley, finely
chopped

Preheat the oven to 350°.

Clean the squid by removing the head and entrails. Cut off the tentacles, making sure to discard the beaklike mouth. Chop the tentacles and reserve for the stuffing.

To prepare the stuffing, heat the oil in a medium-sized sauté pan, and cook the tentacles, prosciutto, onion, garlic, and herbs over medium heat for 2 to 3 minutes. Season with salt and pepper to taste.

Remove from the heat and transfer the mixture to a bowl. Add the egg, bread crumbs, and lemon zest and mix until smooth.

Using a piping bag, fill the squid tubes (bodies) with the stuffing and seal each end with a toothpick. Season the squid with salt and pepper. Put the oil and butter in a medium-sized ovenproof skillet and brown the squid over medium heat for 3 to 4 minutes on each side.

Place the skillet in the preheated oven for 8 minutes. Remove, pour off the grease, and add the wine. Serve the squid whole or sliced in 4 even pieces. Pour the pan sauce over and around the squid.

Garnish with parsley. This recipe is best served on a bed of steamed rice.

• WALKING AND COOKING • IN TUSCANY

On the first full day of this walking and cooking vacation, you walk from San Gimignano toward San Donato, an ancient hilltop village. You follow a path through fields and woods and vineyards, cross a river, and arrive first at *Montauto*, an old castle on the Francigena road, and then at a traditional Tuscan farmhouse. There you'll enjoy an informal lunch of regional specialties such as bruschetta, *salame*, prosciutto, *pecorino* cheese, sweets, and, of course, a good bottle of Chianti. You then return to your hotel in San Gimignano to rest before enjoying a special dinner in a local trattoria, featuring five courses with five selected wines.

The next day begins in San Donato. You walk along a woodland path to the ruins of *Castelvecchio*, where you'll enjoy a view over the valley of Riguardi, and then follow a steep track to an old stone quarry and an abandoned farm with a wonderful garden. After returning to your hotel for lunch and relaxation, you transfer to *Panzano* in Chianti for your first cooking lesson taught by Franco Filieri, a private chef at villas in Chianti.

The following day, your hike begins in San Gimignano and follows the old Francigena road. You pass the parish church of Cellolle and continue to the ancient Collemuccioli village, where a path along the crest of the hill takes you to the church of Pancole, to La Piazzetta, and finally to the castle of *Villa del Monte*, where you stop for a wine tasting and light lunch. After lunch, you continue along the Francigena road through Canonica and Badia a Elmi, and, after crossing the river Elsa, arrive at Certaldo for sightseeing.

You'll also have cooking lessons with Giulietta Giovannoni, a former chef at two Chianti restaurants, in her farmhouse kitchen, and at *Villa di Riboia*, the home of Milvia Renzoni.

You'll stay at the *Villa San Paolo*, a four-star hotel just outside San Gimignano. This former country villa offers modern amenities in an authentic Tuscan atmosphere, and includes a swimming pool surrounded by mature gardens that overlook the hills and medieval towers of San Gimignano.

THE DETAILS: The program runs one week. The cost includes accommodations, most meals, cooking lessons, excursions, and transfers to and from Florence rail station.

The Cost: $1,900

Contact:
The International Kitchen
1209 N. Astor #11-N
Chicago, IL 60610
Phone: 800-945-8606
Fax: 312-654-8446
E-mail: info@intl-kitchen.com
Web site: www.intl-kitchen.com

• THE ART OF LIVING TOURS •

France, Italy, Spain, Morocco, Ireland

Sara Monick of the Art of Living Tours offers several excellent trips to Italy, as well as to France, Spain, and the United States. See page 270 for more information.

Contact:
The Art of Living Tours
Sara Monick
4215 Poplar Drive
Minneapolis, MN 55422
Phone: 612-374-2444
Fax: 612-374-3290
E-mail: Monick4215@aol.com

• CUISINE INTERNATIONAL •

Judy Ebrey founded Cuisine International in 1987 to represent cooking schools and culinary experiences around the world. Judy studied at Cordon Bleu in London—as well as with many well-known chefs in the United States, France, and Italy—and founded the company to combine her love of food with her love of travel. She now spends part of each year scouting out locations and instructors and opening new cooking vacation programs. It's a tough job, but someone's got to do it.

As of this writing, Judy represents sixteen schools, in Italy, France, England, and Brazil. Many of her programs are spread throughout this book—below are a handful of her Italian programs not mentioned elsewhere.

Villa Crocialoni, the home of Buncky and Marcantonio Pezzini, sits on thirty-five acres of land in the Tuscan countryside, surounded by fields and woods. In the park behind the villa is the private chapel where Buncky and Marcantonio's children were married and grandchildren were baptized, and the trails in the woods beyond lead down to a lake stocked with fish. The Pezzini family dates back to 1345 and the villa is filled with family antiques and paintings: You'll be using the family silver, hand-embroidered linen towels, and antique furniture.

Buncky and Marcantonio offer a friendly, family-style cooking experience using natural, organically grown and raised ingredients. Marcantonio bakes the bread in an 1886 wood-burning oven and handles the olive oil, the homegrown organic garden produce, the rabbits, the corn-fed free-range chickens and their eggs and also makes fig jam.

Buncky, who has lived in Italy for more than forty years, teaches the hands-on lessons. You'll learn to make *pappa al pomodor* (tomato-herb bread soup); fried zucchini flowers; *peperonata*, meat, tomato, herb, and veggie pasta sauces; grilled radicchio and eggplant pizzas; fish, herb, mushroom, and veggie risotto; pâté with herbs; and chickens' livers with Jack Daniels.

Meals, which include wine, are served under the chestnut tree at poolside, at the marble-topped kitchen table, or in the dining room. Some sample excursions include the Florence markets (the villa is forty-five minutes from Florence, thirty minutes from Pisa, and twenty minutes from Lucca), and Viareggio on the sea to the fish market.

Diane Seed, author of the best-selling *Top One Hundred Pasta Sauces* and other books such as *Eating Out in Italy* and *Diane Seed's Mediterranean Dishes*, is an Englishwoman who has spent more than thirty years studying, cooking, and writing about Italian cuisine. She offers two cooking vacations through Cuisine International: the Colors and Flavors of the Mediterranean with Diane Seed, and Diane Seed's Roman Kitchen.

The **Colors and Flavors of the Mediterranean** cooking classes are housed at Diane's favorite hotel, Il Melograno, a converted sixteenth-century fortified farmhouse amid ancient olive groves and walled citrus gardens in Puglia, on the coast of the Adriatic in the "heel" of Italy.

Guests participate in hands-on cooking lessons, learning to prepare the cuisine of Puglia using the finest local ingredients. Excursions include visits to see food artisans making cheese and the local *orecchiette* pasta, a lesson on traditionally preserved vegetables in olive oil, and tours of the medieval white hilltop town of Ostuni, the old town of Monopoli (with dinner at a local fish trattoria), the *turlli* houses of Alberobello, and the Baroque city of Lecce to shop for local pottery, crafts, and foods. During free time, guests can enjoy an outdoor pool framed by citrus and pomegranate trees, the tennis courts, and a private beach which includes a fish trap dating back to Roman times.

Diane's **Roman Kitchen** class takes place in her home in the *Doria Pamphili* Palace in the center of Rome. The class begins on Sunday evening with a welcome dinner. Lessons take place Monday through Thursday morning, and focus on authentic Italian food from many regions. Guests then enjoy a lunch of food prepared in class, along with assorted local specialties and wine. Friday's class begins in the evening and is followed by a gala farewell dinner. Once a week there are optional visits to food markets and local specialty shops before class.

"Bologna is a culinary paradise," says Judy Ebrey. "And every Bolognese is sure that the best way to live longer and laugh more is to eat the traditional Bolognese way, with such foods as Parma ham, *Mortadella*, *Sampone*, *Cotencino*, *Salami*, balsamic vinegar, Parmigiano-Reggiano cheese—the king of cheeses!—local wines, and Bologna's most famous dish, tortellini, which is meant to be shaped like Venus's navel."

La Settimana della Cucina offers a culinary experience in Bologna, where guests learn to prepare many of the best Italian and Bolognese dishes. Classes are taught by noted local chefs and are held at one of the most famous and oldest restaurants in Bologna, *I Notai*. There are also guided tours of factories where Parmigiano, balsamic vinegar, and salami are produced, excursions to a ceramic factory and to Dozza, a charming small town, and a dinner at the elegant restaurant, *San Domenico in Imola*, where Chef Valentino Marcattili will demonstrate the preparation of one of his special recipes.

THE DETAILS: Villa Crocialoni runs six days; Colors and Flavors of the Mediterranean runs one week; Roman Kitchen runs five days; and *La Settimana della Cucina* runs eight days. The group sizes range from eight to twelve. The costs include accommodations, all meals, cooking lessons, and excursions, except for Roman Kitchen, which only includes lunches and does not include accommodations (call Judy for housing suggestions).

Villa Crocialoni: $2,100
Colors and Flavors of the Mediterranean: $2,600
Roman Kitchen: $900
La Settimana della Cucina: $2,450
Single Supplements: $300–$400

Contact:
Judy Ebrey
Cuisine International
PO Box 25228
Dallas, Texas 75225
Phone: 214-373-1161
Fax: 214-373-1162
E-mail: CuisineInt@aol.com
Web site: www.cuisineinternational.com

• THE INTERNATIONAL KITCHEN •

In addition to her French cooking vacations (see page 73), Karen Herbst, owner of The International Kitchen, offers about a dozen culinary holidays in Italy, ranging from informal agriturismo vacations to elegant country house holidays to spa resort cooking trips. The following is a brief selection of some of her Italian programs not mentioned elsewhere in this section.

The **Classic Tuscany** program begins in the medieval town of Filgine Valdarno, located in the triangle formed by the cities of Florence, Arezzo, and Siena. Your home is the thirteenth-century palazzo, *Villa Casagrande*, which has offered hospitality to Pope Leo X, King Charles VII of Bourbon, King Charles V of Spain, and, more recently, Prince Umberto of Savoy and his wife, Princess Maria Jose.

Cooking lessons are held at the nearby restaurant, *Torre Guelfa*, where Chef Claudio Piantini will teach you classic dishes such as *ribollita, crostini*, gnocchi *al ragu, quaglia alla fiorentina, sciacciata all'uva* (Tuscan cake with grapes), *crostini di fegatini* and *porrata* (toast with liver sauce and leek souffle), *cenci* (Tuscan fried pastry), and *castagnaccio* (cake with chestnuts, pine nuts, and rosemary). When not cooking, you'll go on excursions to Siena, San Gimignano, Greve in Chianti, Montefioralle, and Volpaia. You attend wine tastings and will have a chance to enjoy the pool, sauna, and fitness room, or just wander through the Renaissance garden.

You then travel to Florence, where you'll stay in a centrally located, four star hotel. You'll go sightseeing and shopping, will visit classic Florentine restaurants such as *Il Latini* or *Cocolezzone*, and will have an afternoon excursion to Fiesole, in the hills above Florence, and dinner in a typical Fiesole restaurant such as *La Reggia*.

The **Flavors of the Amalfi Coast** begins with your arrival at

Hotel *Bacco*, a three-star, family-run hotel on a cliff overlooking the sea in the small Amalfian town of Furore. You'll be welcomed with get-acquainted aperitifs and dinner, and will then spend your first evening in Amalfi relaxing and recovering from your trip.

Over the next few days, you'll have a walking tour of Amalfi, enjoy lunch in a local trattoria by a fresh spring water fountain, travel down the coast to the town of Atrani for sightseeing and a cappuccino in the piazza, attend cooking classes, explore the ruins at Pompeii, and have lunch in a famed pizzeria in Vico Equense where you order brick oven pizza by metric length.

You can also take a boat trip to Capri, see Naples and Ravello, visit a farmhouse for a cooking lesson and dinner, go wine tasting, enjoy meals in a variety of local restaurants, and have time to just relax and enjoy the coast.

Italian Cooking at Villa d'Este brings you to the Lake Como area. The villa, which was originally built in the sixteenth century for a cardinal, has hosted royalty from Napoleon to the Duchess of Windsor, and was converted into a hotel in 1873. It still offers a peek into a time when royalty used the villa as a summer residence—with lavish gardens and spectacular views of Lake Como and the snow-capped mountains beyond.

Cooking classes are taught by Chef Luciano Parolari, the Villa's executive chef, who has presided over the kitchen for twenty years. During one class, Chef Luciano will introduce you to typical northern Italian food, which you'll then enjoy for lunch with accompanying wines. Another class may cover fish cookery, followed by a boat trip to the lakeside town of Bellagio and lunch at a favorite local restaurant such as *Isola Comacina*. Or you may have a full day excursion to Pavia to explore the historic town and the famous Certosa Abbey, before visiting *Frecciarossa* wineries for a wine tasting and lunch.

Italian Home Cooking at Villa Vallerosa is located in Selci, a small village in the Sabine hills that rise above the valley of the

Tiber to the north of Rome. *Villa Vallerosa* is a working farm where wine, oil, and fruit are produced, and thoroughbred horses are raised. And where, of course, cooking classes are offered.

The cooking classes are taught by the local women of northern Lazio, who will share recipes and skills that have been passed down through generations. You'll learn how to make the local specialty, *falloni*, discover the secrets of wood-burning oven cooking, and visit a traditional cheese maker where ricotta and *pecorino* are produced. The week ends with a trip to the Eternal City, where you learn to cook typical Roman dishes and enjoy a farewell dinner at a local trattoria.

The **Spa and Cooking in the Veneto** program starts with a spa checkup and a *fango* body wrap or mud treatment and a massage. Having checked into the four-star Hotel Ritz the night before, you spend your first morning at the *Abano Terme*, a spa resort known for its pristine waters and mineral rich muds in the foothills of the Euganean Hills in northeast Italy.

In the afternoon, you'll meet Chef Sergio Torresini, who will take you to the market to buy fresh ingredients for your cooking lessons on *cucina Mediterranea*. You'll visit the city of Verona (literary home of Romeo and Juliet) on the banks of the Adige River, travel to the town of Bassano del Grappa to meet a *grappa* maker and taste his wares, and spend a full day in Venice, which ends with a cruise on board the *Bragasso*, a renovated sailing ship used during the time of the Republic of Venice for fishing in the lagoon and the sea.

On your first day at **A Taste of Umbria**, you arrive in Montefalco, a quiet hilltop village known as "Umbria's balcony" due to its position overlooking the old Roman Via Flaminia, and settle into *Villa Pambuffetti*, a restored former country home which overlooks the valley.

Cooking classes are taught by Alessandra Angelucci, a professionally trained chef who frequently appears on Italian culinary television programs. Classes focus on the Umbrian cuisine, from the black truffles of Norcia to the handmade pasta of Spoleto—you'll learn to make dishes such as *minestra di frascarelli*, spaghetti *alla Norcina*, and *porchetta*.

Excursions include visiting the Torgiano wine museum and the famous pottery town of Deruta, attending a handful of wine tastings, and touring the hill towns of Spello and Assisi (where you'll see the remarkable Basilica of St. Francis). You'll also visit Perugia to see the national gallery and have a *passeggiata* down the city's main street, Todi to see the gothic palaces and the medieval cathedral in the central Piazza del Popolo, and Orvieto, a town with an almost perfect medieval character and delicious white wines.

La Bottega del 30, in addition to being the only restaurant in Chianti to receive a Michelin star, offers a Tuscan cooking vacation that teaches guests the ancient culinary techniques of the women of Chianti. The school and restaurant are part of a complex of field-stone and stucco buildings in Villa a Sesta, a small village perched on a hill fifteen miles northeast of Siena. The chef, Helene Stoquelet, offers lessons in a traditional Tuscan kitchen (complete with wood-burning oven), teaching guests how to cook *antipasti*, Tuscan soups, fresh pasta, main courses, and *dolci*. You'll have dinner and wine tastings at local restaurants and wineries, and you can also explore the countryside both on your own and with a guide, or hike through the vineyards, or just relax under the shade of an olive tree or next to the pool.

The Umbrian Table offers the opportunity to live in the historic center of Spoleto, in the *Palazzo Dragoni*, a four-star hotel which was built as a private residence in the fourteenth century, and discover the varied cuisine of Umbria through a series of classes around the region.

You'll attend your first cooking class in Spoleto, possibly taught by Simone Ciccotti of the Michelin-starred *Osteria del Bartolo*. You'll visit Norcia, the birthplace of St. Benedict (famous for its cheese and salami, and the mountain lentils of Castelluccio) where, after sampling local produce and exploring the shops, you'll have another class in the friendly atmosphere of a traditional, family-run trattoria. You'll taste *torciglione* and *torcolo di San Costanzo* (made of sweet bread dough with sultanas and candied fruit) at Perugia's leading pasticceria, and will then have a third class devoted to handmade pasta in the kitchen of the *Palazzo Dragoni*.

You'll also drive to the mountain town of Patrico, where a local family will treat you to dinner and a class in traditional country-style cooking and, depending on the season, wild asparagus picking or truffle hunting. You may also explore the wooded slopes of Monteluco, follow an ancient pathway through the forest to reach a convent founded by St. Francis in 1218, see the frescoes of Giotto, Lorenzetti, Martini, and Cimabue, and visit the Temple of Minerva and the church of Santa Chiara.

Villa la Massa is a Renaissance villa on the banks of the Arno River, just a stone's throw from Florence. It has been home to several aristocratic families over the centuries and is now an elegant hotel (and its restaurant, *Il Verrocchio*, was named one of the top fifty restaurants in the world by *Condé Nast* magazine).

You can spend a culinary week in early autumn at *Villa La Massa*, learning how to cook regional specialties such as *crostini*, *ribollita*, and *fagioli*. On the first evening, you'll be greeted with a welcome cocktail party on the terrace overlooking the Arno, and over the following week you'll taste local olive oils and wines, followed by lunch featuring Tuscan specialties in the restaurant. You'll also go on a full day trip to Siena and a walking tour of Florence. In your free time you can relax by the pool, or take the short shuttle ride to Florence for shopping or sightseeing.

Tuscan Cooking at *Palazzo Mannaioni* is based in a palace built at the end of the sixteenth century; today it's a country house hotel, with gardens, lemon groves, stables, and an olive mill—and a swimming pool, jacuzzi, and tennis court. Its restaurant is housed within the former cellars of the building, and is presided over by Chef Vincenzo Carlucci, who has worked at the Plaza in New York and the Ritz in Paris. Chef Vincenzo leads your hands-on cooking lessons in Tuscan cuisine. You learn to cook Tuscan breads, homemade pastas, soups, and main courses, and will enjoy local specialties such as mushrooms and the white truffle from Montaine.

The *Palazzo Mannaioni* lies in the center of the town of Montaione, a pristine medieval village near San Gimignano, Florence, and Pisa. You'll have the opportunity to go on excursions to *Fattoria di Sonnino* and *Fattoria Poggio Capponi* for wine tastings, and to the towns of Certaldo and San Gimignano for sightseeing and dining.

THE DETAILS: The programs all run one week (although the Classic Tuscany program can be taken for four days only). The costs include accommodations, all meals with wine, cooking lessons, and excursions.

The Cost: $1,850–$2,550

Contact:
The International Kitchen
1209 N. Astor #11-N
Chicago, IL 60610
Phone: 800-945-8606
Fax: 312-654-8446
E-mail: info@intl-kitchen.com
Web site: www.intl-kitchen.com

·3·

ASIA
(INCLUDING INDIA
AND AUSTRALIA)

THE PROGRAMS in this section do more than introduce you to Asian culture and cuisine. They make the experience of cooking Asian meals—based on cuisines as diverse as Indian, Cambodian, Balinese, and Thai—in your own kitchen not only possible, but pleasurable. You'll learn how to cook Chinese dim sum, Indian curries, Japanese sushi, Thai soups and sauces, Asian-Mediterranean appetizers, Vietnamese fish dishes, contemporary Australian cuisine, and more: You'll learn how to recreate these dishes with readily available ingredients in your own home.

You may decide to stay in a willow-lined valley in Australia's Victorian Alps. Or you might enjoy discovering the influence of Arab/Jewish/Syrian cuisine in the dishes of Kerala in southern India. Maybe you'll opt to stay and study at a small, serene resort in eastern Bali. Or you may be interested in day classes in Thailand, Japan, Singapore, or Hong Kong. And in addition to the specific programs, two organizations in this section—Absolute Asia and Asian Transpacific Journeys—offer customized vacations to almost any destination in Asia, Australasia, and the Pacific Islands. You can cook and feast in any of dozens of locations.

You can also travel and explore. You can visit the Po Lin Monastery on Lantau Island (Hong Kong) for a vegetarian lunch, meet His Excellency, the current Nawab of Awadh in northern India, or enjoy the services of a luxury spa in Thailand. You can go on an evening boat ride on the Mekong River in Cambodia, shop at village markets on Bali, have a rickshaw tour of the Old Quarter in Hanoi, or fly by helicopter to a lavish resort on New Zealand. And you can snorkel and kayak, hike through jungles to remote waterfalls, attend language classes, and enjoy rounds of golf on world-class courses.

Asian culture and cuisine is rich, deep, and incredibly diverse. The following cooking vacations guide you down the path of discovery—of fascinating traditions, cultures, and cuisines.

· ABSOLUTE ASIA ·

Asia

Imagine the sights and sounds—and the regional cuisines—of Vietnam, China, Cambodia, and Laos. Of Thailand, Java and Bali, Hong Kong, Korea, and Malaysia. Of Taiwan, Myanmar, Singapore, Japan, India, the South Pacific Islands, Papua New Guinea, Australia, and New Zealand. And of others—Sri Lanka, Bhutan, Nepal, Borneo,

Mongolia, and more. Absolute Asia's privately guided cooking tours—from formal cooking schools in deluxe resorts to "hands-on" family-style classes in local villages—provide customized travel to all the above countries and the rest of Asia and Australasia.

"Each itinerary is customized to the individual's or family's schedule, needs, and interests," says Ashley Isaacs, the Director of Special Interest Travel. "We can provide instructors who are well-known chefs or local village housewives—or both. Guests stay in deluxe hotels and resorts, but they also have the opportunity to eat in family homes, and explore the culture of a region through visits to ancient temples, modern markets, and local artisans. We also provide extensive touring and activity options for guests, spouses, and children."

Each of Absolute Asia's travel programs is different. Here's a sample tour they organized for a chef who visited—and cooked in— eight countries during a one month vacation:

Three days in Hong Kong: Touring the city, riding a sampan to a fishing village, visiting Bird Street, the Jade Market, and an open-air food market, and attending Chinese cooking classes.

A week in Vietnam: Attending the Water Puppet Theater, visiting the five-hundred-year-old pottery village of Bat Trang, wandering through bazaars, accompanying the chef of the Metropole Hotel (where the guest stayed) on a trip to the local market, visiting the tombs of Khai Dinh and Tu Duc (set among lotus ponds and frangipani trees), cruising the Perfume River, having a cooking class and dinner at *An Dinh Cung* Restaurant, traversing the *Hai Van Pass* (Pass of the Ocean Clouds), visiting art galleries, museums, and silk markets (where he had clothes tailor-made), and traveling to Saigon for sightseeing and a private South Vietnamese cooking class with an instructor whose weekly cooking show airs on international television, followed by dinner at her home.

Three days in Cambodia: An evening boat ride on the Mekong River, a private class with a local Khmer chef, a tour of Phnom Penh (including visits to the Royal Palace and the National Museum), and visits to Angkor Wat and Angkor Thom (an ancient royal city which covers four square miles).

A week in Thailand: Touring Chiang Mai (visiting the original home of the Emerald Buddha, a temple on the summit of Doi Suthep Mountain, and the festive night bazaar), dining in a northern Thai-style Kantoke restaurant while watching performances of northern and hilltribe dances, and attending Thai cooking classes. The guest also traveled to Bangkok for a cruise along the Chao Phraya River to the Grand Palace, visited the Prasart Museum and botanical garden, and attended two more days of private cooking classes. (A spouse or travel partner, if not interested in the cooking classes, could opt to go on a guided excursion to the ancient capital of Ayuthaya or visit the famous floating market of Bamnoen Saduak.)

A week in Indonesia: Staying in the Amandari (one of the top rated resorts in the world) and receiving cooking instruction from the executive chef, going on a private tour of Bali—passing through rice terraces to Bali's holiest temple, *Pura Besakih,* perched on the slopes of a sacred volcano—visiting *Boa Lawa,* an old temple filled with bats and snakes, attending a Balinese cooking class, and shopping in the local market. The guest also stayed at a luxury resort (at which the chef was "eager to welcome [the guest] to his 'cooking brigade,' " and accompanied him to local food markets and Javanese restaurants) and visited volcanoes, rainforests, temples, villages, *Borobodur* (a magnificent Buddhist temple), and the ancient Javanese capital of Surakarta.

Three days in Singapore: Visiting the botanical gardens and Mandai Orchid Farm, attending cooking classes at the Raffles Culinary Academy (see page 200), walking through the spice garden at Fort Canning Park, visiting a typical Peranakan house, wandering the narrow streets of Little India, visiting an herbalist in Chinatown, and cruising on an authentic Chinese junk through the harbor and on to Kusu Island.

Three days in New Zealand: Traveling by helicopter to *Wharekauhau,* a working farm and luxurious resort situated above the sweeping immensity of Palliser Bay, with black volcanic sand beaches, rolling pastureland, ancient forests, and mountain peaks for days of trekking, horseback riding, fishing, swimming, wine tasting, and cooking in the resort's kitchen.

Three days in Fiji: Relaxing on the beach, participating in all the resort activities, and—if the guest could pry himself away from the beach—attending cooking classes in the resort's kitchen.

Some specific dishes the guest learned to make (in Thailand and Vietnam) included Chicken in Coconut Milk Soup, Papaya Salad and Sticky Rice, Prawn Salad with Crisp Lotus Stems, Fried Mixed Mushrooms with Baby Corn, Crispy Pancakes with Peanut and Sesame Sauce, and Steamed Banana Cake.

Noncooking travel partners and children are very welcome. Absolute Asia recently partnered with Ms. Kiyoko Konishi, one of Japan's leading cookbook authors, and now offers specialized cooking vacations in Japan.

THE DETAILS: Details for Absolute Asia's trips vary. Tours can last several days, several weeks, or several months, and can be designed for as few as one to as many as fifteen people. Absolute Asia also occasionally organizes a standardized group trip. In general costs include accommodations, all meals, cooking lessons, and excursions.

The Cost: Costs range widely, based on the length of the program, itinerary, and lodging choices. For example, an individually designed two-week trip to Vietnam costs about $4,200, and a two-week group trip to China costs about $3,800 (with a $1,620 single supplement).

Contact:
Absolute Asia
180 Varick Street, 16th Floor
New York, NY 10014
Phone: 800-736-8187; 888-285-6094
Phone: 212-627-1950; 212-627-8285
Fax: 212-627-4090
Web site: www.absoluteasia.com
E-mail: info@absoluteasia.com

• ASIA TRANSPACIFIC JOURNEYS •

Asia

Asia Transpacific Journeys offers group and customized vacations to Australia, Burma, Cambodia, Fiji, Indonesia, Laos, Malaysia, Micronesia, New Zealand, Papua New Guinea, Philippines, Thailand, the South Pacific, and Vietnam. In addition to preplanned tours of two or three weeks—during which guests might trek in Burma, go island hopping via kayak in Australia, and see Komodo dragons in Indonesia—they offer theme vacations such as golf vacations, art and craft collecting tours, women's celebration tours, and, of course, culinary tours.

The culinary tours most commonly depart for Thailand and Cambodia, although programs in Bali, Singapore, Australia, and New Zealand are becoming more common. As Marilyn Staff, the cofounder of Asia Transpacific, says, "The bottom line is that we can include cooking instruction and design 'foodie' tours to any of our destinations. We've designed programs focusing on Laotian, Vietnamese, and Cambodian cooking, and have offered programs in Indonesia that included cooking in Yogyakarta, Bali, and Jakarta."

A sample itinerary of a cooking tour to Thailand and Vietnam begins with your arrival in Bangkok. You'll be driven to the Thai House homestay (page 215) where you'll spend several days relaxing, cooking, and sightseeing. You may take a boat to the Banglumpoo area for some night shopping, sample the food in the many cafés and bars, explore the markets and temples of Bangkok, or watch a Thai kickboxing match.

During your cooking classes, you'll learn to prepare dishes such as *larb moo* (spicy Thai port salad), *pad thai, tom yam kung, kaeng kari kai* (yellow chicken curry), and *Panang neua* (coconut beef curry). You'll go on escorted trips to local markets to select ingredients for the day's menus, and will enjoy lunches of the dishes you prepared.

On the third day of this itinerary, guests depart from the Thai House by boat, to visit *Wat Arun* (Temple of Dawn), the Royal Barges, the Royal Palace, and *Wat Phra Kheo*, where you'll see Thailand's most sacred relic, the Emerald Buddha. You then spend several days in Bangkok—shopping, exploring, dining, relaxing, or going on optional excursions: a day trip to Ayuthaya, the capital of Siam from the fifteenth to the eighteenth century, and *Bang Pa-in*, the old Royal Summer Residence; an afternoon aboard the *Horizon* luxury cruiser; a visit to *Damnern Saduak* Floating Market; or a massage at the Bangkok School of Traditional Massage.

Toward the end of your first week in Thailand, you'll fly to Chiang Mai, a thirteenth-century town that is currently a flourishing cultural and economic center, for cooking lessons at the Chiang Mai Thai Cookery School. The owners of the school, Somphon and Elizabeth Nabnian, will teach you to prepare Northern-style dishes such as Chiang Mai curry, Panang curry pork, chicken in coconut milk soup, and fried mixed mushrooms with baby corn.

You'll also dine, shop, and explore Chiang Mai's famous Night

Bazaar (the legacy of the original Yunnanese trading caravans that stopped here along the ancient trade route between China and the Burmese coast). You'll spend a day at Lampang, where you'll see some of Siam's finest architectural history in the last Thai town where horsecarts are still used as public transport.

On your final full day in Chiang Mai, you'll travel to Mae Sa Valley, where you'll ride elephantback through a forest, past ethnic Samoeng villages, and then have lunch at the Regent Resort before traveling to the isolated *Wat Doi Kham* temple. And on your way back to the hotel, you'll stop off at the wood-carving and ceramic making village of Hang Dong.

The next day you fly to Vietnam. Your Vietnamese vacation begins in Hanoi, a serene city of lakes, shaded boulevards, green parks, and grand French architecture. You'll have a *cyclo* (pedal rickshaw) tour of the Old Quarter, where you'll find each colorful street devoted to a particular craft or ware. You'll be pedaled among the quaint French buildings along Shoe Street, Silk Street and Banner Street (to name just a few) and walk through small local outdoor markets that sell everything from fish to flowers.

The next morning you travel to Hoi An, arriving in time for a late morning walking tour of this former Cham seaport. You'll stroll past its active riverside market, neighborhood pagodas, and major historical landmark—the Japanese covered bridge. Due to its history as a port and trade town, Hoi An exhibits cultural and culinary influences from many nations, including India, China, Japan, France, and even Spain.

That afternoon, you'll attend the first of several Vietnamese cooking classes at the *Nhu Y* restaurant. Each lesson will begin with the purchase of various ingredients at the nearby riverside market. You'll learn to make dishes such as curry vegetable soup, grilled tuna with saffron in banana leaf, green papaya salad, stuffed squid, and grilled eggplant.

When not in class, you'll have free time to relax and explore Hoi

And on your own—to stroll through the old French quarter, shop for handicrafts, or rent a bike for a beautiful three-mile ride to the beach. There's also an optional sunset boat excursion along the local river.

Finally, you return to Hanoi for two more days of sightseeing, dining, and relaxation. You may visit Ho Chi Minh mausoleum, house, and museum, the One-Pillar Pagoda, the Temple of Literature (Vietnam's first university), or can go shopping for silk in the mazelike Old Quarter.

THE DETAILS: The details for Asia Transpacific journeys vary. The programs can last several days to many weeks, and are offered year-round. They can arrange programs for one to sixteen people (although two people is generally the minimum size). The cost generally includes accommodations, most meals, cooking lessons, excursions, and all transportation.

The Cost: Costs range widely, based on itinerary and lodging choices. A typical vacation, however, costs approximately $175–$200 per person per day.

Contact:
Asia Transpacific Journeys
PO Box 1279
Boulder, CO 80306
Phone: 800-642-2742
Fax: 303-443-7078
E-mail: travel@southeastasia.com
Web site: www.southeastasia.com

• HOWQUA DALE GOURMET RETREAT •

Australia

Howqua Dale is located in the willow-lined Howqua Valley, on forty acres in the Victorian Alps. It's one of Australia's leading country house hotels; it provides easy access to rivers for canoeing, fly-fishing, and kayaking, to bush for walking and horseback riding, to unspoiled mountains for summer trekking and winter skiing, and to tennis, golfing, windsurfing, and swimming (in a saltwater pool and in the river).

Several times a year, Marieke Brugman, co-owner and chef of the *Howqua Dale* Gourmet Retreat, offers cooking vacations. The cuisine taught in the classes begins with the classical techniques of Europe, but also includes an array of multicultural influences of the Mediterranean, California, Asia, and the Middle East. All of which is then combined with personal inspiration and created with the use of the abundant local Australian produce.

Menus are designed around the seasons and the interests of the guests. Some dishes you may learn include Roast Beetroot Ravioli with Citrus Sauce and Salmon Caviar; Tomato *Tarte Tatin*; Crispy Spiced Wild *Barramundi* (lungfish) with Black Rice Pilaf and Orange, Mussel, and Saffron Sauce; Blue Swimmer Crab Consomme with Crab Wontons; Roast Squab served with Celeriac Fondue, Wild Mushrooms and Verjus Sauce; and Caramelized Pineapple and Banana Tarte with Passionfruit Sauce and Coconut Sorbet.

Howqua Dale also offers Celebrity Chef weekend schools. They invite celebrity chefs—some past chefs have been Jacques Reymond, Cheong Liew, Maggie Beer, Stephanie Alexander, and Janni Kyritsis—to introduce guests to their specialties. One weekend might focus on pastry, one on Asian-inspired cuisine, one on food-and-wine matching, and one on preparing contemporary dishes suited to increasingly busy lifestyles.

Other programs offered by *Howqua Dale* include gourmet cycling and walking tours all around Australia, gourmet tours abroad, and wine and food weekends. *Howqua Dale* also offers guided adventure tours: all-day and overnight bushwalks, ballooning, bird watching walks, trout fishing expeditions, and more.

Howqua Dale also offers a program in Bali, Indonesia (see page 196 for more information).

THE DETAILS: Programs run for two or four days and are offered year-round. Group size is limited to twelve. The cost includes accommodations, all meals with wine, and cooking lessons.

Two Days: AUS$750 (approx. US$490)
Four Days: AUS$1,400 (approx. US$910)

Contact:
Howqua Dale Gourmet Retreat
PO Box 379
Mansfield, Victoria
3722 AUSTRALIA
Phone: 61-57 773 503
Fax: 61-57 773 896
E-mail: howqua@mansfield.net.au

• CHOPSTICKS COOKING CENTRE •

Hong Kong, China

The Chopsticks Centre **Gourmet Tour** offers an authentic Chinese cooking experience. The founder of the center, Cecilia Jennie Au-Yang, has been teaching students the secrets of Chinese cuisine since 1971, and has created a gastronomic tour of the best of Hong Kong cooking.

The trip begins on the evening of your arrival with a tour of the kitchen and dinner at a seafood restaurant. The next morning is reserved for a cooking demonstration from Cecilia or one of her staff during which you'll learn to make two main dishes and one dessert. Then, following a dim sum lunch at a Cantonese restaurant, you'll visit Hong Kong markets, including both a fresh and a "dried" seafood market. Then you'll tour the kitchen of a restaurant specializing in regional Chinese cuisine, followed by dinner.

Day three includes a tour of the *Po Lin* Monastery on Lantau Island, where you'll be treated to a vegetarian lunch, and then dinner and kitchen tour of another restaurant. On the final day of the course, you'll be free to explore on your own after breakfasting with the group at the hotel.

In addition to the Gourmet Tour, Chopsticks also offers **One Day** and **One Week Intensive** classes in Chinese regional cuisine. A one day intensive might teach students how to prepare a twelve-course Chinese banquet, with individual classes teaching students how to make dim sum, Chinese roast, cakes and pastries, and breads. The one week intensive covers fifteen main courses (such as sweet and sour pork, bean curd *ma po*, Szechwan prawns, and chicken in *yunan* pot); six dim sums (such as pot stickers, *shiu my*, and spring rolls); four Chinese roasts (such as barbecued pork and soy sauce chicken), and includes a seafood market visit, and an introduction to Chinese ingredients, utensils, and banquet and table settings. The one day and one week intensives do not include accommodations.

Cecilia has published more than thirty Chinese cookbooks and has been a consultant to several food manufacturers—training their staff and creating new recipes for them.

THE DETAILS: Chopsticks Gourmet Tour runs four days. The tour size ranges from twelve to twenty-four. The cost includes accommodations, all meals, cooking lessons, excursions, interpreter, and airport transfers. The costs for the One Day and One Week Intensives include only cooking lessons, some meals, and some excursions. Tours and other classes are offered March through June and September through December.

Chopsticks Gourmet Tour: US$1,200–1,800 (seasonal rates vary)
Single Supplement: US$200–$250 per night
One Day Class (from one-hour to all-day): US$90–$750
One Week Intensive: US$1,400

Contact:
Chopsticks Cooking Centre
8A Soares Avenue, G/F, Kowloon
Hong Kong, CHINA
Hong Kong Phone: 852-23-36-8433
Hong Kong Fax: 852-23-38-1462
E-mail: cauyeung@netvigator.com

• PENINSULA ACADEMY AT THE • PENINSULA HONG KONG HOTEL

Hong Kong, China

The Peninsula Academy offers two learning vacation programs with culinary components: the Chinese Cultural Experience and the Chinese Culinary Experience.

As you'd expect, the four-day **Chinese Cultural Experience** offers a wide range of activities. Guests start the morning with tai chi exercises on the garden terrace, and then, after breakfast, one of the Peninsula's chefs gives them a tour of the kitchen. Over the next few days, guests are taught about ancient Chinese tea-drinking procedures and brush painting (learning to brush-write their

Chinese names), and visit a chaotic, off-the-beaten-path local food market. They attend a kitchen and dim sum making tour at the historic *Luk Yu* Teahouse, a traditional Chinese medicine practitioner will explain the philosophy of Chinese herbal medicine, and they are introduced to feng shui, examining a home interior plan with bad feng shui and learning simple ways to improve it (you're encouraged to bring your own home plan to discuss).

The **Culinary Experience** allows guests to participate in one to four days of cookery classes. Small, hands-on lessons focus on Cantonese food, Eurasian cuisine, pastries and desserts, and other topics. Guests learn tools and techniques, traditional and cutting-edge preparation methods, and artistic display as the chefs walk them through all the steps required for cooking and serving a gourmet dish such as Chinese Barbecued Duck Triangles with Tomato Basil Coulis and Papaya Relish. Other activities include helicopter and antique tours, hiking, biking, and sightseeing trips.

THE DETAILS: The programs last one to four days, The cost includes accommodations, some meals, cooking lessons, and excursions. The Peninsula Group also occasionally offers cooking events at its other hotels: in Beijing, Manila, Bangkok, Carmel, Beverly Hills, and New York.

The Cost: Approximately $500 per day

Contact:
The Peninsula Academy
Salisbury Road, Tsimshatsui, Kowloon, HONG KONG
Phone: 800-223-6800
E-mail: academy@peninsula.com
Web site: www.peninsula.com/hotels/hk/academy.html

• THE SPICE GARDENS OF KERALA, •
INDIA, AND THE FABLED KITCHENS
OF THE NAWABS OF AWADH

Indus Tours
North and South India

"Indian cuisine is amazingly diverse, from jumbo prawns in Cochin, simply grilled with a hint of masala, to the complexity of the Awadh cuisine in Lucknow, so rich and aromatic, they say some dishes can take years to prepare," says Deborah Ratcliffe, who organizes Indus Tours' culinary vacations to India. "One trip wasn't enough to give guests a real taste of India, so I decided to organize two. One in Kerala, in the south, where the fragrant cuisine is dominated by the ever-present coconut, fresh fruits and vegetables, and abundant seafood. And the second in the north, with the cuisine of the Nawabs, the subtle dishes of Agra, and the traditional Rajasthan food of Jaipur."

The trip to the south of India—the Spice Gardens of Kerala—begins with an afternoon of sightseeing in Madras. Then you'll go to Periyar, to stay in the Spice Village, where you'll spend several days. You'll attend talks on Indian spices, visit a spice plantation and a cardamom auction house, and attend hands-on and demonstration classes.

The classes teach the use of spices in Keralan cooking, including the preparation of masala and curry, the fundamentals of Keralan culinary techniques and utensils, and the use of coconut in Keralan cuisine. You'll also visit Periyar Lake, where, if you're lucky, you'll catch sight of tigers, elephants, antelopes, and exotic birds. And there's still time for leisure: dozing by the hotel pool, going souvenir hunting, and relaxing in the Ayurveda Center.

Then, after an optional dawn jungle walk, you'll travel by boat to Kumarakom where you'll attend a lecture and cooking demonstration on the culinary influence of the Europeans following the Spice Route, and the Arab/Jewish/Syrian heritage of southern Indian cuisine. Other courses and activities include an evening boat cruise, a food demonstration covering Syrian Christian food, a boat trip to visit a traditional lagoon farm, Ayurvedic massages, and classes on Keralan seafood. You'll also travel to Cochin to visit the Fish Landing Harbor, the spice markets, and to see traditional Kathakali dances. And, following a visit to an old Hindu family for a demonstration of Hindu vegetarian cooking, you'll go to the Marari Beach resort at Mararikulan, a picturesque fishing village on the coast of Kerala, where you'll spend three days relaxing on the beach.

The trip to the north of India—**the Fabled Kitchens of the Nawabs of Awadh and a Taste of Rajasthan**—begins (after arriving in Delhi) in Lucknow. After a morning talk about Awadhi breakfasts, you'll visit the Chowk vegetable market, go sightseeing at Bara and Chota Iamambara, and then return to the hotel for an Awadhi dinner.

Lectures and cooking classes cover milk-based dishes, Lucknow kebabs, traditional breakfast specialties, and the history of Rajasthan cuisine. Other activities include a cultural tour of La Martinire, a visit to spice markets, a meeting with His Excellency, the current Nawab of Awadh, a walk through the colorful bazaars of the Pink City, a sightseeing trip to the Taj Mahal (or a dawn visit by rickshaw), an elephant ride, many meals (such as a Mughal dinner and a traditional rustic Rajasthan meal with dancers and music), and, of course, time for leisure and relaxation.

Deborah Ratcliffe, a professional food writer and Scottish Masterchef Finalist, has been a food enthusiast all her life. Memories of the food from her childhood in Asia left her with a passion for the exotic spices and intricate flavors of the region. "I'm an enthusiast rather than an expert," she says. "As with all things in life, we continually learn and grow. And with Indian food, this is especially true—as chefs are now using traditional ingredients with a thoroughly modern twist."

Kids and noncooking travel partners are very welcome: Yasin Zargar, the director of Indus tours and a native of Kashmir, says, "There are many options for children and noncooking travelers— cultural activities, shopping, relaxing by the swimming pools, and plenty of sightseeing in wonderful cities. Tours are not for cooks only, anyone can join. But having a passion for food will add to the delight of the travelers."

THE DETAILS: The courses run two weeks and are offered in February. Group sizes range from fifteen to twenty. The costs include accommodations on half board basis (including themed dinners), all transport inside India, cooking lessons, and excursions with services of an English-speaking guide.

Spice Gardens of Kerala: £1,434 (approx. $2,360)
Single Supplement: £375 (approx. $620)

Nawabs of Awadh: £1,480 (approx. $2,440)
Single Supplement: £382 (approx. $630)

Contact:
Indus Tours and Travel Limited
Premier House
2 Gayton Road
Harrow, Middlesex
HA1 2XU
ENGLAND
Phone: 44-181-901 7320
Fax: 44-181-901 7321
E-mail: indus@btinternet.com

From the kitchen of Indus Travel

❂

FISH MOILEE

A traditional *Keralan* (southern Indian) dish.

2 teaspoons sunflower oil	1 teaspoon turmeric powder
1 teaspoon crushed garlic	1 teaspoon freshly ground
1 teaspoon ginger cut into a	black pepper
fine julienne	$1/2$ pound of any firm white
2 green chilies, cut in half	fish fillets, cut into
lengthwise	cubes
1 cup onion, finely sliced	10 to 15 curry leaves
1 cup water	2 teaspoons lime juice
1 teaspoon salt	1 cup coconut milk

In a heavy pan sauté the garlic in the sunflower oil for 2 minutes. Add the ginger, chilies, and onion and sauté for another 2 minutes, stirring constantly. Then add the rest of the ingredients except the coconut milk.

Stir occasionally, cover the pan, and cook the fish until tender (the exact time will depend upon the size of your fish cubes). Add the coconut milk and gently heat through to avoid curdling.

Serve immediately garnished with slices of tomato.

• HOWQUA DALE GOURMET RETREAT •

Bali, Indonesia

Howqua Dale offers many programs in Australia (see page 188) as well as this trip to Bali, based at the *Serai* Hotel. The *Serai* is a tranquil property located on the beach near Candi Dasa (in eastern

Bali)—set amidst swaying palms, the hotel boasts genuine Balinese hospitality and service, gorgeous open pavilion architecture, and delicious food.

"This is the favorite hotel of many Bali connoisseurs," says Marieke of *Howqua Dale*. "It outranks the more swanky and expensive resorts for its soothing and relaxing calm and unparalleled attention to detail."

Each morning, guests attend classes dedicated to rice dishes, *sambals* and spices, classic Balinese dishes, the Thai influence, and Asian sweets. Cooking is hands-on and predominantly about mastering the wok.

The program also includes excursions to rice terrace villages, fishing and salt making villages, and to the vibrant and colorful market of Klungkung, where you'll buy produce to bring home to the hotel for preparation and tasting. Other trips include snorkeling with fishermen and a dinner banquet at the Palace of Amlapura, the ancient kingship and regency of Karangasem.

Or you can go fishing, diving, rafting, trekking, or play tennis, or just wander around, discovering the "real" Bali beneath the surface of the tourist hustle and bustle.

The cooking courses are taught by Steve Baker, who was trained in Australia, and has worked in London, Switzerland, and Bermuda. "Steve emphasizes a style of cooking that is absolutely of the moment," Marieke says. "It's full of fabulous techniques, remarkable flavors, and deeply satisfying combinations."

Noncooking partners are welcome and can join all the meals and excursions, and children are welcome, although the resort is small and not particularly child-oriented.

THE DETAILS: The program runs seven days and is offered in July, August, or September. Group size is limited to twelve. The cost includes accommodations, most meals, cooking lessons, and excursions.

The Cost: AUS$2,350 (approx. US$1,525)
Single Supplement: AUS$900 (approx. US$590)
Noncooking Guest: AUS$1,500 (approx. US$975)

Contact:
Howqua Dale Gourmet Retreat
PO Box 379
Mansfield, Victoria
3722 AUSTRALIA
Phone: 61-57 773 503
Fax: 61-57 773 896
E-mail: howqua@mansfield.net.au

• A TASTE OF CULTURE •

Tokyo, Japan

A Taste of Culture offers cooking classes, tasting programs, market visits, and field trips that combine practical lessons on how to prepare Japanese food with spicy tidbits of indigenous food folklore. The cooking classes, based in Tokyo, can either be one-day themed classes or multiple-day intensives.

The **themed cooking classes** emphasize mastering basic Japanese kitchen skills. You might take a class on temple-style vegetarian (*Shoujin Ryouri*) cooking, in which you make simmered root vegetables with tofu dumplings, classic sesame-dressed leafy greens, nourishing miso-thickened mushroom soup, chestnuts and rice garnished with black sesame, and assorted pickles. Or you might take the class on fish, in which you make dishes such as *shigure ni* (ginger and soy simmered rockfish), *saikyo yaki* (miso-marinated and grilled swordfish), and miso-thickened clam chowder. Or you could study *Obento*, learning how to create both poetic and kitschy-cute styles of boxed lunch, such as "Autumnal Stroll" (a dramatic pilaf of wild mushrooms garnished with "maple leaf" carrots and "pine needle" string beans), sunny-rolled omelettes, and *kimpira gobo* ("golden haystack" of shredded burdock root sautéed with a blend of seven spices).

The **three to five day intensive** classes are designed for small groups of highly motivated students interested in rapidly acquiring an in-depth knowledge of traditional Japanese foods and kitchen skills. The curriculum of the intensive courses is tailored to the needs of each group. It typically includes kitchen and class time, field trips, restaurant meals, and market tours.

The **tasting programs** are demonstration classes that include generous samples and focus on the traditional Japanese pantry. Programs include A Taste of Tofu, Foods from the Sea, A Taste of Miso, and A Taste of the New Year. You can learn how to cook with grilled *yaki-dofu*, silky *kinugoshi*, sea vegetables, smoked fish, dozens of miso pastes (focusing on soups and sauces), and will learn how the Japanese celebrate *Oshogatsu* (the New Year holidays) and sample a range of traditional *Osechi Ryouri* (New Year dishes).

All lessons are taught in a spacious home-style kitchen, fully equipped for teaching traditional Japanese cooking. Tables and chairs provide comfortable seating during classes; *tatami*-matted seating is also available.

Your teacher is Elizabeth Andoh, who was born and raised in America, received her formal culinary training at the Yanagihara Kinsaryu School of Traditional Japanese Cuisine in Tokyo. She has been the director and instructor at a culinary arts center in Tokyo and has taught Japanese cooking at the Culinary Center of New York for ten years. She is the Japan representative for the International Association of Culinary Professionals and the author of several cookbooks and numerous magazine and newspaper articles.

THE DETAILS: The themed cooking classes are limited to six students; the three- to five-day intensives range from one to six; and the tasting programs are limited to sixteen. The costs include cooking lessons, excursions, and restaurant meals. Accommodations are not included.

Themed Cooking Classes: $70 per class
Three-to-Five-Day Intensives: $1,000 per day for one to three students; $1,500 per day for four to six students.
Tasting Programs: $55 per class

Contact:
Elizabeth Andoh
A Taste of Culture
1-22-18-401 Seta
Setagaya-ku, Tokyo 158-0095
JAPAN
Phone/Fax: 81-3-5716-5751
E-mail: aeli@gol.com

In the US:
Elizabeth Andoh
c/o SAXE
50 Sutton Place South
New York, NY 10022
E-mail: aeli@gol.com

• RAFFLES CULINARY ACADEMY •

Singapore

Singapore is one of the few states to have four national languages—English, Chinese, Malaysian, and Hindi—and it has the diverse, multiethnic cuisine to match. Each of its ethnic neighborhoods offers its own cuisine, shopping opportunities, and cultural events.

The Raffles Culinary Academy, influenced by the wealth of cultures and cuisines that surround it, offers day classes that cover many specialties. You can study, for example, Ethnic Malay Cooking, Cantonese Dim Sum Recipes, Chinese Vegetarian Cooking, North Indian Curries, Desserts and Pastries, Tandoori Cooking for the Home Oven, and even classic French or Spanish cuisine.

Raffles also offers instruction in local specialties: *Hainanese* Chicken Rice, *Nasi Lemak*, *Peranakan* Cooking, Indian *Pulaos* and *Daal*, and featured recipes from local restaurants.

The classes are primarily demonstration, although students are encouraged to interact and participate with the chefs to some degree. Each class concludes with a meal, and detailed recipes are provided.

The Raffles Hotel is a grand old hotel, which has been visited by such famous literary figures as Noel Coward, Somerset Maugham, and Rudyard Kipling. Most rooms at the hotel are suites filled with comfortable furniture and antiques. You do not need to be a guest at the hotel in order to take the cooking classes.

THE DETAILS: Programs run one day and are offered year-round. Group sizes are limited to twenty-four. The costs include cooking demonstration and one meal.

The Cost: SG$60–$100 (US$35–$60)
Accommodations at Raffles: SG$550–$4,000 (US$325–$2,380)

Contact:
Raffles Culinary Academy
Raffles Hotel
1 Beach Road
SINGAPORE 189673
Phone: 65-337-1886
Fax: 65-339-7013
E-mail: raffles@raffles.com
Web site: www.raffles.com

• THE BAAN KATA CENTER •

Phuket Island, Thailand

After several hours off-road traveling through forest and jungle, Harvard-educated architect Mom Tri Devakul arrived at a remote beach on Thailand's Phuket Island, with stunning views over the Andaman Sea—and decided it was the perfect site to build a home. Since that time, the clifftop family house has evolved into *Baan Kata*, a center for food and culture, with fine dining, upscale shopping, luxury villas and apartments, private and shared swimming pools, and, of course, a cooking school.

The original house, surrounded by lush tropical garden, is now the hub of the estate, which includes the Gallery Grill, an innovative Asian-Mediterranean restaurant, where cooking classes and wine workshops take place.

The center offers four participation-based classes—Basic Thai, Seafood Dishes of Southern Thailand, Curries of Thailand and Southeast Asia, and the Asian Grill, each of which lasts two or three days—and a variety of demonstration classes featuring guest chefs.

During the Basic Thai course, for example, you'll learn how to make Thai-style spicy glass noodle salad, coconut soup, curried pork, and steamed fish mousse. You'll study curry, Thai sauces, and marinades, learning to balance the three key flavors of Thai food—salty, sour, and sweet—while being introduced to ingredients rarely found outside Southeast Asia.

The island of Phuket, famous for its powdery white beaches fringed by palm trees, is also a culinary melting pot. Beachside cafés, street stalls, exclusive cliffside restaurants, and posh hotels offer various versions of Thai, Chinese, and Malay food. Fresh and abundant seafood and locally grown produce can be found at seaside fishing stalls and in Phuket's daily markets.

As you would expect from a tropical island, water sports are ubiquitous: sailing, diving, windsurfing, snorkeling, and fishing are the most common. If you're more nautically minded, you can charter a yacht to any of a number of remote islands with some of the best diving in Southeast Asia. Another possibility is an eco-friendly sea-canoeing trip in Phang-nga Bay to see the remarkable limestone formations (including those filmed in the James Bond movie *The Man with the Golden Gun*) and sunken caves.

If you're interested in hiking, the interior of the island is covered with plantations, rice paddies, and forests offering waterfalls, jungle hills, and tropical seclusion. You can also enjoy golf (Phuket has several excellent courses), traditional Thai massage, Thai language classes, bowling, mini-golf, and, of course, shopping (particularly for silk, teak furniture, gems, gold, and ceramics). There's also Phuket Town, where you can observe the bustle of a small Thai town and see Sino-Portugese architecture and highly decorated Buddhist temples.

Cooking classes at *Baan Kata* are team-taught by Chefs Sue Farley, also the course director, and Teeranate Rochnarat, who has worked in Thai restaurants in Bangkok, New Zealand, Australia, and Singapore. Sue has worked with many renowned chefs (including Marcella Hazan, Ken Hom, Jeremiah Tower, Alice Waters, Julia Child, and Madeleine Kamman), and, before arriving in Thailand in 1997, was the director of the Napa Valley Cooking School.

Baan Kata does not have facilities for overnight stays, but they can make reservations to suit all pockets and requirements—from luxurious five-star hotels to basic beach bungalows—all within walking distance.

Spouses and children will have no trouble amusing themselves around Phuket while you're busily preparing a *tom ka gai* or *haw moke*. (And, in fact, several of the nearby hotels have programs for children.)

THE DETAILS: Programs run two to three days and are offered year-round. Group size is limited from twelve to twenty-five. The cost includes cooking lessons, lunch with wine, and some field trips.

The Cost: $50–$100

Contact:
Sue Farley
Baan Kata Center
3/2 Moo 2
Patak Road
Kata Beach, Phuket 83100
THAILAND
Phone: 66-76 330123
Fax: 66-76 330482
E-mail: sue@baankata.com
E-mail: info@baankata.com
Web site: www.baankata.com

From the kitchen of the Baan Kata Center

ə

CHILLED LEMONGRASS AND CORIANDER SOUP WITH LIME OIL

SERVES 4

A Thai version of the classic vichyssoise, the unexpected lemongrass and lime oil flavors make this a wonderful starter when the evenings are hot and steamy.

¼ cup fresh coriander
(cilantro) leaves
4 thick stems lemongrass
3 cups water
¼ cup butter
2 medium onions, chopped
1¼ cups new potatoes,
chopped small
5 ounces (½ cup plus 2 tablespoons) milk
Salt and pepper

LIME OIL AND GARNISH:
2 limes—preferably kaffir limes
½ cup vegetable oil
½ cup olive oil
4 spring onions or scallions,
finely chopped

Pick the coriander leaves from the stalks and prepare the lemon-grass by removing the hard outer leaves and chopping finely. Save the trimmings from the coriander and the lemongrass and make stock—add 3 cups water and salt to taste, and simmer for about 30 minutes.

Meanwhile, melt the butter in a large saucepan and add the lemongrass, onion, and potatoes. Cover the pan and let the vegetables sweat on a low heat for about 10 minutes. Pour the stock through a strainer, then add the milk and coriander leaves, reserving a few for garnish. Season with salt and pepper, and simmer gently for about 25 minutes.

Allow the soup to cool a bit, then purée in a blender. Pour the purée through a strainer into a bowl. After it cools, cover it and put it in the refrigerator to chill.

To make the lime oil, add the juice of the two limes to the vegetable and the olive oil and mix well.

When you're ready to serve the soup, garnish it with green onions and the coriander you reserved, and drizzle it with spots of lime oil.

• THE ROYAL THAI SCHOOL •
OF CULINARY ARTS

Bang Saen, Thailand

The Royal Thai School school offers three regional Thai cooking programs: Northern Thai Cooking, which is inspired by the cuisine of the ancient kingdom of Lanna; Northeastern Thai Cooking, for "seriously hot" chili addicts; and Southern Cooking, which is largely inspired by the Muslim-Indian influence in Thailand.

The school also offers "Thai fusion" cooking classes. The head chef, Chris Kridakorn-Odbratt, explains that "fusion cooking has always been around, such as the influx of chilies from Latin and South America to Asia, tomatoes from the Americas to Europe, and so on. Today it's a way of 'fusing' classic French and Mediterranean cooking with Caribbean, Mexican, Latin, South American, and Asian. And here at the school we merge French and Mediterranean classical cuisine with Asian flavors." And, if you'd like to expand your culinary skills beyond the Thai border, there is also a South-east Asian cooking class that will introduce you to Thai, Burmese, Malaysian, and Laotian cooking.

Classes meet every day in the school's professional kitchen for three to four hours. Lessons vary during the week, sometimes you'll have a morning class where you'll learn to make lunch specialties, other times the class is in the afternoon for preparing dinner.

The school is located on a private beach in the seaside resort of Bang Saen, a very popular vacation spot for Thais, but largely unknown to foreign tourists. You'll stay at a three-star hotel with views of the sea from your room and many noncooking activities: swimming, visiting the Marine Research Center, playing golf, fishing, or jet skiing, scuba diving, or enjoying any other water sport. And at night, you can visit any of the many Thai pubs (which also offer live music) or great seafood restaurants in the area.

THE DETAILS: The programs run one week and are offered December through March. Group size is limited to eight. The costs for each program include accommodations, all meals, and cooking lessons.

Regional Northern Thai Cooking: $1,865
Regional Northeastern: $1,695
Regional Southern Cooking: $1,845
Fusion Cooking: $1,995
Southeast Asian Cooking: $1,945

Contact:
Chris Kridakorn-Odbratt, Exec. Head Chef
The Royal Thai School of Culinary Arts
Bahn Pratabjai
411 Moh 13 Thanon Rob Kau Sammuk, Bang Saen
Thamboon Saen Suk
Amphoe Muang
Chonburi 20130 THAILAND
Phone: 66-38-748 404
Fax: 66-38-748 405
US Fax: 508-629-8121
E-mail: info@rtsca.com
Web site: www.rtsca.com

From the kitchen of the
Royal Thai School of Culinary Arts

●

PAD THAI

SERVES 4

One of Thailand's best known dishes. If you can't find the banana blossom just omit it; the other ingredients you can find in an Asian supermarket.

1 cup small rice noodles
 (*sen lek*)
3 tablespoons unflavored oil
3 cloves of garlic, minced
1/4 cup dried shrimp
1/4 cup fish sauce (*nam pla*)
1/4 cup sugar
2 tablespoons tamarind juice
 (or pulp, soaked in a little
 hot water)
1 tablespoon paprika
1/2 cup tofu, cubed small, fried
 in a little oil till golden
2 tablespoons turnips,
 unsalted, dried, cut into
 small pieces

1 egg, beaten
1/4 cup chives, cut into 1-inch
 pieces
1/4 cup peanuts, roasted and
 ground
1 cup bean sprouts, fresh

GARNISH:
1/2 cup fresh bean sprouts
1/2 cup chives, cut into
 1-inch pieces
1/4 banana blossom, fresh,
 cut into strips
1 lime, cut into wedges

Soak the noodles in cold water for a half hour, until soft. Drain and reserve. Heat a wok or large skillet, add the oil. Add the garlic and dried shrimp, constantly stirring. Add noodles and stir until translucent. Reduce the heat if the noodles start to stick together.

Add the fish sauce, sugar, tamarind juice, and paprika. Stir-fry until thoroughly mixed. Add the fried tofu, turnip, and the egg. Turn the heat to high, stirring gently until the egg is done (about 2 to 3 minutes) and the liquid is mostly evaporated.

Mix in the chives, peanuts, and bean sprouts. Put the Pad Thai on a serving platter, arrange the garnish on top, and serve.

· SOMPET THAI COOKERY SCHOOL ·

Chiang Mai, Thailand

Sompet Thai offers short-term classes in traditional and vegetarian Thai cooking. Busara Sarerak, co-owner and chef, teaches guests special cooking techniques and traditional recipes that have been passed down for generations. The classes emphasize participation, and each guest is assigned their own wok and burner, and mortar and pestle for making curry paste.

Your day begins with a drive to Mrs. Busara's spacious traditional Thai home on stilts by the river. You'll tour the garden, picking herbs and spices for cooking along the way, and then settle into the kitchen. After class, you dine on the spacious tree-shaded verandah in the Northern Thai style, with piles of cushions and low tables.

Sompet Thai offers four courses—although they emphasize that for vegetarians and others with special dietary needs, Thai cooking is infinitely adaptable. If you take the first course, you'll learn how to make green curry paste, hot and sour prawn soup, fried Thai-style noodles, chicken in pandanus leaf, papaya salad, sweet and sour stir-fried vegetables, and a handful of other dishes.

The second class covers recipes for red curry with chicken or tofu, Chiang Mai curry with pork, Thai-style barbecue, deep fried spring rolls, noodles with pork sauce, peanut sauce with cucumber salad, and dessert.

In the third class, you learn how to make chicken curry puffs, crispy fried whole fish with sour peppers, Panang chicken, Tom Yam curry paste, tamarind sauce, chili fish sauce, and squid and glass noodle salad.

And the fourth course is a specialized course on fruit and vegetable carving.

THE DETAILS: The courses run from one to three days. Group size is limited from two to fourteen. The cost includes cooking lessons and

meals. Accommodations are not included. This program often provides a culinary adventure for people already traveling in Thailand.

The Cost: 800–1,600 baht (US$20–$40)

Contact:
Sompet Thai Cookery School
101/1 Chiang Inn Plaza
Opposite the Entrance of Chiang Inn Hotel
Nightmarket Area, Ground Floor
Chiang Mai
THAILAND
Phone: 66-53 280-901
Cell Phone: 66-531 671 3190
Fax: 66-53 280 902

School Location:
56 Patan Road
Chiang Mai 50300
THAILAND
Phone: 66-53 872 729
E-mail: sompet67@hotmail.com

• TASTING PLACES •

Koh Samui Island, Thailand

Tasting Places initially offered culinary vacations only to Italy (see
page 140). But when Sarah Robson, the co-owner of Tasting Places,
visited the island of Koh Samui in 1997, on a trip to Thailand, she
fell in love with the island. She convinced the manager of the *Laem
Set* Inn to build an outdoor, shaded kitchen just yards from the
ocean for the sole purpose of hosting Thai cooking classes.

While Koh Samui Island is one of the more popular destinations of Thailand, the coast around the *Laem Set* Inn remains relatively undiscovered. All of the rooms at the Inn have views of the ocean, and many evenings are spent watching the sunset while drinking in the tropical night air and exotic Thai cocktails.

The days are spent relaxing, sightseeing, and cooking. You'll learn to make chicken coconut cream and galangal soup; sweet corn cakes with cucumber pickle sauce; spicy fish and prawn cakes with cucumber and shallot dressing; green curry of prawns and eggplant with fresh basil; hot and sour barbecued beef salad with fresh herbs and chili lime dressing; noodles with beef and black bean sauce; sweet sticky rice with mango and coconut milk; and fried bananas with sesame seeds. And that's just for starters—at the end of the class, you'll get a recipe booklet containing about sixty dishes.

You'll also have plenty of free time to explore the island. You'll visit local tropical fruit, vegetable and fish markets, traditional Thai restaurants, and neighboring islands for shopping, picnics and snorkeling excursions. Spouses and children are welcome and sightseeing, scuba diving, sailing, and swimming are just some of the activities available to keep them happily occupied.

The cooking school teachers in Thailand are Paul Blain, owner of the Chili Jam café, in Queensland, Australia, and Peter Gordon, head chef of the Sugar Club restaurants in New Zealand and author of the *Sugar Club Cookbook.*

THE DETAILS: The program runs one week and is offered in May and September. Group size is limited to twelve. The cost includes accommodations, meals with wine, cooking lessons, excursions, and transfers to and from recommended flights. Prices for noncooking partners are reduced by £100 (approx. $165).

The Cost (ranges from beach bungalow to air-conditioned suite):
   £1,200–£1,650 (approx. $1,980–$2,725)

Contact:
Tasting Places Limited
Unit 40, Buspace Studios
Conlan Street
London W10 5AP, ENGLAND
Phone: 44-171 460 0077
Fax: 44-171 460 0029
E-mail: ss@tastingplaces.com
Web site: www.tastingplaces.com

From the kitchen of Tasting Places

⦿

TOM GOONG GATI
(PRAWN AND COCONUT SOUP)

1 teaspoon white peppercorns
1 medium coriander
    (cilantro) root
4 to 5 cups of coconut milk,
    medium thickness
4 to 5 small dried chilies,
    crushed
3 lemongrass stalks, sliced
4 slices galangal (substitute
    fresh ginger)

4 to 5 kaffir lime leaves
4 to 6 large prawns, shelled
    and deveined, cut or whole
3 to 4 tablespoons lime
    juice
2 to 3 tablespoons fish sauce
Roasted garlic
Coriander leaves

Pound the peppercorns and coriander root to a paste.

Bring 3 cups of coconut milk to the boil and add the paste. Continue to simmer adding the chilies, lemongrass, galangal, and lime leaves. Allow to infuse. Add the prawns and simmer until tender.

Season with lime juice and fish sauce. Serve garnished with roasted garlic and coriander leaves.

· THE THAI COOKING SCHOOL ·
AT THE ORIENTAL HOTEL

Bangkok, Thailand

Upon your arrival at the Oriental Hotel, you'll recieve a comple-
mentary "jet lag" massage and a welcome dinner at the *Sala Rim
Naam* Restaurant. Then you can settle in or explore the hotel and
its surroundings before resting up for the cooking classes that begin
the next morning.

The Thai Cooking School is located just across the river from
the Oriental Hotel—you'll hop on the shuttle boat at the hotel pier
to be ferried to the school. The school has been teaching novice
and professional cooks about the major elements of Thai cuisine for

more than fifteen years, with a curriculum that emphasizes demonstration classes, but also includes some hands-on participation. The classes also cover the practical application of recipes outside of Thailand: The chefs will introduce you to alternative ingredients and will focus on easy-to-prepare methods.

Monday is spent on an introduction to Thai cuisine—you learn the history, origin, and ingredients of traditional dishes, as well as commonly used herbs and spices. The class ends with the creation of a few recipes for *khong waang* (snacks and hors d'oeuvres) and *yaam andpla* (herbed and spiced salads). On Tuesday, you learn *tom* and *gaeng* (soups), *khong waan* (desserts), and how to carve fruits and vegetables into traditional Thai designs. The next day you study *krueang gaeng* and *krueang kiang* (curries, condiments, and side dishes), and Thursday is reserved for exploring various Thai cooking methods: *nueng, paad, thod,* and *yaang* (steaming, stir-frying, frying, and grilling). Finally, your last class covers menu preparation and selection, and how to order in Thai restaurants.

Students of the cooking school are not obligated to stay at the Oriental Hotel (prices for cooking classes only are listed below). But those who do can take advantage of its luxury spa, excellent restaurants, gardens, pools, and wonderful riverside activities.

THE DETAILS: Classes run five days and are offered all year round. Group size is limited to fifteen. The cost includes accommodations, most meals, cooking lessons, airport transfers, and a "Jet Lag Massage" at the Oriental Spa.

The Cost: $1,790
Noncooking guests: $1,140
Single Supplement: $700
Additional nights at the hotel: $250
Cooking lessons only: $120 per day

Contact:
The Oriental
48 Oriental Avenue
Bangkok 10500 THAILAND
Phone: 66-2 236 0400
Fax: 66-2 439 7587

• THE THAI HOUSE •

Nontaburi, Thailand

The Thai House is a homestay built of teak in the style of Ayut-
thaya temple buildings, in which the distinctive "wing-shaped"
rooftops are thought to help guests reach heaven. The house is surrounded by three hundred and fifty fruit trees on five acres of
orchard and gardens. Twenty-five craftsmen lived and worked on
the premises for one year to create the traditional building—with
wood carvings, tile floors, and open patios.

Cooking classes meet in the "open-air" kitchen, where you'll
learn how to blend fresh herbs and spices, use traditional utensils
such as the mortar and pestle and coconut grinder, and discover the
traditional skills and authentic recipes of Thailand.

On the first day, you'll learn about herbs and spices. You'll prepare spicy Thai pork salad as a appetizer, with Thai fried noodles as
a main dish, and hot and sour prawn soup or coconut and galangal
soup as a side.

The next day you'll visit the market and learn how to identify,
select, and buy the ingredients you'll be using that day when you
cook beef curry in sweet peanut sauce, yellow chicken curry,
chicken in red curry with bamboo shoots, and green beef curry.

On the third and fourth days, you'll learn dishes such as savory
stir-fried chicken with ginger, sweet and sour pork, pork and tomato
chili dip, and clear melon soup.

You'll also have free time to go bicycling or walking to the local temple and village, paddle along the nearby *klong* (canal), visit the nearby horticultural garden, or take a shopping trip to Bangkok by boat.

Most guests of the Thai House cooking school enjoy it as a vacation-within-a-vacation: they take one, two, or four days off from their travels within Thailand for a peaceful, friendly, and delicious culinary interval. But it is rare for guests to travel to Thailand exclusively for the school.

THE DETAILS: The program runs one, two, or four days and is offered year-round. Group size is limited to ten. The cost includes accommodations, all meals, cooking lessons, some excursions, and transfers to and from Bangkok.

One day: $100
Two days: $225
Four days: $530
Single Supplement: $20

Contact:
Thai House Reservation Office
22 Par-Athit Road
Bangkok 10200
THAILAND
Phone: 66-2 280 0740
Fax: 66-2 280 0741

Thai House
32/4 Moo 8
Tambol, Bangmaung
Ampur, Bangya
Nontaburi
THAILAND
Phone: 66-903-9611
Fax: 66-903-9355

From the kitchen of the Thai House

ə

KAENG KA-RI KAI (CURRIED CHICKEN)

SERVES 4

2 cups coconut cream
2 tablespoons red curry paste
1 tablespoon curry powder
1 pound chicken, cut into 2-
inch squares
2 cups coconut milk

1 cup of potato, in bite-sized
chunks
$^1/_2$ cup onion, chopped
3 tablespoons fish sauce
1 tablespoon sugar

Pour one cup of the coconut cream into a wok on a medium burner. Stir in the curry paste and curry powder, and slowly bring to a boil, adding the remaining coconut cream a little at a time. Stir until the coconut cream has an oily sheen.

Add the chicken and cook until heated through. Then pour the curry mixture into a pot. Add the coconut milk, potato, onion, fish sauce, and sugar, and bring slowly to a rolling boil. Cook until done.

·4·

THE UNITED STATES
AND CANADA

 YOU DON'T NEED to cross a handful of time zones to find beautiful sights, authoritative teachers, and delicious food; the best vacation may be the closest to home. You can study under celebrity chefs—from Marcella Hazan to Julia Child to Roy Yamaguchi to Michel Richard—at a beautiful winery in California's Napa Valley. You can bike the backroads of Nantucket, stopping along the way for a traditional Nantucket clambake. You can cook and relax in a French château just miles from Yosemite Park in the Sierra Nevada foothills, where the owner's favorite saying is: "When one of my guests wants something, the answer is yes. The answer is always yes."

Or you can sea-kayak, tide-pool, and cook with indigenous plants and herbs on Vancouver Island; hike, fish, and feast at a country inn–style program in rural Pennsylvania; study southwestern cooking while at the Santa Fe estate where Georgia O'Keeffe lived for two years; or unlock the secrets of Napa Valley cuisine with best-selling cookbook author and chef Hugh Carpenter. You can cook in luxury (and under the direction of internationally known chefs) at the extremely elegant Greenbrier resort in the Allegheny Moutains of West Virginia; stay at a country inn near Okemo Mountain in Vermont; enjoy the hot springs of Calistoga; explore Boulder, Colorado, from your base at the foothills of the Rocky Mountains; or cook under the charming direction of two chefs who will custom-design lessons for you at their bed-and-breakfast in Stratford, Ontario.

These cooking vacations help you rediscover the treasures of home: a delicious and diverse melting pot of culture and cuisine.

· Camp Napa Culinary · with Hugh Carpenter

Hugh Carpenter, who estimates that he's taught more than eighty-five thousand students at cooking schools across the country, founded his own school, Camp Napa Culinary, in 1990. He is the author of eleven cookbooks, including *Pacific Flavors* (which won the "Best Asian Cookbook" award from the International Association of Cooking Professionals), and the best-selling "Hot" series: *Hot Wok*, *Hot Chicken*, *Hot Pasta*, and *Hot Barbecue*.

Camp Napa Culinary offers a balance between cooking lessons, wine tastings, and free time to explore the delights of the Napa Valley: hot-air balloon rides, the Calistoga Spa, and the many fine restaurants. And, as one recent guest said, "Hugh is the ultimate host and teacher. He opens you to the heart of the Napa Valley and to food and wine in a way you will never forget. You will not want the week to end."

You arrive on Sunday, just in time for a welcome reception hosted by Hugh and his wife, Teri, at their home, where Hugh will prepare Asian-Californian appetizers accompanied by local Napa Valley wines. Later, after settling in, you'll head to a local restaurant for dinner made by a well-known chef from Oaxaca, Mexico.

On Monday, you'll have your first cooking lesson. The class

meets at the Cakebread Cellars, a professional quality family kitchen that has hosted many of the country's top chefs. Hugh's lessons are hands-on and include many of the recipes from his cookbooks. You have lunch with the Cakebread family before spending a few hours exploring the wine region on your own. In the late afternoon, you'll meet up with the group at Meadowood Resort for a croquet wine party—complete with a croquet pro who'll offer pointers on the resort's championship green.

The next day your cooking class will meet in the outdoor kitchen at Cakebread Cellars, and you'll have lunch in the garden. Your afternoon is free, and in the evening you'll tour the Chappellet Winery. You'll taste some older wines accompanied by appetizers while enjoying the winery's view of Napa Valley.

On Wednesday, you'll spend the morning at the Robert Mondavi Winery (see page 234) for a special presentation about the history of wine and and a lunch created by the winery's chefs. You'll spend the afternoon on your own, and will then meet at the Duckhorn Winery for wine tasting and appetizers from Hugh's appetizer cookbook.

Thursday begins with a visit to the Beaulieu Vineyards, established in 1899 and almost never open to the public. You'll tour the winery, have a cooking lesson in the estate's kitchen, and enjoy lunch in the beautiful garden. Another winery trip is made in the late afternoon for appetizers and a tasting, this time to the Pine Ridge Winery.

Your final morning is spent touring Opus One, a small winery known for its premium Bordeaux style wine, co-owned by Baron Philippe Rothschild and Robert Mondavi. You'll have lunch in the courtyard of the famous Tra Vigne restaurant, the afternoon free, and will then meet for your final cooking lesson and dinner at Cakebread Cellars.

DETAILS: The program runs five days and is offered once per month, June through October. The cost includes cooking lessons, meals noted in the itinerary, and private tours of wineries. Accommodations are not included, but Hugh will be happy to make recommendations.

The Cost: $1,530

Contact:
Hugh Carpenter
Camp Napa Culinary
P.O. Box 114
Oakville, CA 94562
Phone: 888-999-4844; 707-944-9112
Fax: 707-944-2221
E-mail: hugh@hughcarpenter.com
Web site: www.hughcarpenter.com

*From the kitchen of Camp Napa Culinary
with Hugh Carpenter*

●

RIBS IN CHINESE BARBECUE SAUCE

SERVES 12 AS AN APPETIZER, OR 4 AS AN ENTRÉE.

2 slabs pork baby back ribs
2 cups wood chips

BARBECUE SAUCE:
1 tablespoon garlic, chopped
1 tablespoon ginger, finely
 minced
1/4 cup green onions, minced
1/4 cup cilantro sprigs, minced
2 teaspoons orange zest,
 grated or finely minced

1/2 cup hoisin sauce
1/3 cup plum sauce
2 tablespoons dark sesame oil
2 tablespoons distilled white
 vinegar
2 tablespoons oyster sauce
2 tablespoons dark soy sauce
2 tablespoons honey
2 tablespoons Chinese rice
 wine or dry sherry
2 teaspoons Asian chili sauce

Advance preparation: On the underside of the ribs is a tough white membrane; using your fingernail or a sharp pointed knife, loosen the membrane along the bone at one edge and then, gripping the membrane with a paper towel, pull it away.

In a bowl, combine all the barbecue sauce ingredients and stir well. Yields 1^1/$_2$ cups. You can complete to this point up to 8 hours in advance of last-minute cooking.

Last-minute Cooking: Soak the wood chips in water for 30 minutes before using. Rub the ribs with barbecue sauce and marinate no more than 30 minutes. If using a gas barbecue, preheat to medium (350°F). If using charcoal or wood, prepare a fire.

When the coals or wood are ash covered, drain the chips and place on a 6-inch square of aluminum directly on the coals. When the chips begin to smoke, brush the rack with oil, lay the ribs on, and cover the barbecue.

Cook at medium temperature until the meat begins to shrink away from the ends of the rib bones, about 45 to 60 minutes. Brush the ribs with more barbecue sauce halfway through cooking.

Or, if you prefer to roast the ribs, place the ribs meaty side up on a flat elevated rack on a baking sheet, place in a preheated 350 degree oven, and roast until the meat begins to shrink from the ends of the bones, about 1 hour.

Serve hot or at room temperature. If eating these as an appetizer, cut into individual ribs before serving them.

• CHEZ SOLEIL COOKING SCHOOL •

Cathy Lynn Grossman, who spent seven years as a travel writer for *USA Today*, mentioned Chez Soleil as one of her most favorite destinations in the world: "The funky fantasy of an Italian farmhouse kitchen at Chez Soleil [offers] cooking school vacations in which spirited lessons in life are included." She mentioned it as one of the two places she'd like to visit again.

Chez Soleil is a bed-and-breakfast owned by Liz Mountain and Janet Sinclair. You wake up the first morning in an eccentric, charming room in their English Tudor–style cottage. (Janet used to be an interior designer, and she has created theme rooms at the small bed-and-breakfast.) Then you wander downstairs to a breakfast prepared by Janet and Liz. In addition to homemade breads, scones, chutneys, and fruit butters, breakfast may include more exotic treats: poached eggs on artichoke-saffron risotto or a quiche of grilled vegetables with asiago cheese in a sweet-potato pastry. Then you're ready to start your cooking class.

When booking the course, Liz and Janet ask guests what kind of food they'd like to cook. They are willing to delve into any food theme of your choice, and will spend hours preparing for the course, researching and testing new recipes, and customizing lessons. Past courses have centered around themes such as French bistro, Chinese regional cuisine, Tuscan spring, Bordeaux fall, Indian vegetarian, and Malayan and Tunisian cuisine. They've also conducted courses just on soups and breads, and "fast" foods from around the world, such as tapas, *merienda, meze,* and dim sum. Another offering is Comfort Food Therapy—which they describe as "what we all need during the hard winter months—nourishment which feeds body and soul." This course includes recipes for chicken pot pie, crème brûlée, macaroni and cheese, and fruit grunts.

You'll spend five hours in the kitchen with Liz and Janet, learning recipes, cooking techniques, and how to create a plan of action based on the recipes, preparation time, and cooking methods. You break for lunch in the middle of the day, and then relax in the afternoon before helping Liz and Janet put the finishing touches on the meal to be served for dinner.

Some dishes you might learn to make are Vietnamese noodle soup, sticky buns, braised lamb shanks, *tarte tatin,* ratatouille, magnolia hot pot, potstickers, spanikopita, empañadas, schnitzels, cock-a-leekie, pierogis, fresh pasta, eggplant and basil mousse, fennel-stuffed pumpkin, brandade of leek, jambalaya, tequila lime pie, and jalapeno corn pones.

Also in the works at Chez Soleil is a Master's Cooking Week that will take place in September. The course will involve a wide range of hands-on instruction, cooking, recipe development, food styling, menu planning, and market tours, as well additional instruction in resources, kitchen organization and equipment, and organic gardening. Check with Janet or Liz for further details if you're interested.

THE DETAILS: The program runs three days and is offered year-round. Group size is limited to six. The cost includes two nights bed and breakfast, a full day of cooking instruction, and dinner based on the cooking day's achievements.

The Cost: CA$350 (Approx. US$235)

Contact:
Janet Sinclair or Liz Mountain
Chez Soleil Cooking School
120 Brunswick Street
Stratford, Ontario N5A 3M1
CANADA
Phone: 519-271-7404

From the kitchen of Chez Soleil

◦

POACHED EGGS ON SAF-FRON AND ARTICHOKE RISOTTO

SERVES 4

Janet and Liz like to serve this for breakfast at Chez Soleil

1 tablespoon olive oil
1/4 cup sweet red onion, chopped
2 teaspoons garlic, minced
4 large artichoke hearts, fresh or frozen
1/2 cup water
1/4 teaspoon saffron
1/8 teaspoon salt

4 cups chicken or vegetable stock
1 cup arborio rice
1/4 cup flat-leaf parsley, chopped
4 tablespoons sweet butter
1/3 cup freshly grated Parmesan cheese
4 eggs, poached

Heat oil in a heavy-bottomed saucepan over medium-high heat. Add onion and cook until translucent, about 5 minutes. Add garlic and very thinly sliced artichoke hearts. Cook 3 minutes. Add water, saffron, and salt.

Turn heat to low and cook, covered, 20 to 30 minutes, until soft. Add more water if needed to prevent sticking. Stir occasionally. Meanwhile, bring stock to a simmer.

When artichokes are soft, turn heat to medium-high, and when hot, stir in rice. Once coated, gradually add stock a half cup at a time, stirring constantly. Allow each addition to be absorbed before adding more. Continue to stir constantly. When all stock has been absorbed the rice should be tender but firm. Remove pan from heat, stir in parsley, butter, and cheese.

To poach eggs, have poaching liquid on heat and add eggs just before the last addition of stock to risotto. Serve on top of risotto.

• COOKING SCHOOL •
OF THE ROCKIES

The Cooking School of the Rockies offers many cooking classes throughout the year and cooking vacation programs in the summer. The cooking vacations include four Basic Techniques programs, which focus on American, French, Mediterranean, and World Cuisine, an Asian Techniques Course, and a Pastry Course.

The most popular cooking vacation is **Basic Techniques I**, in which you learn fundamental cooking techniques such as working with knives, making basic sauces, omelets, soups, and stock, and the best approach to grilling, poaching, roasting, and sautéing. The culinary focus is on Country French, Contemporary American, and Mediterranean cuisine. You'll learn to make French dishes such as Niçoise salad, Grilled Tuna with Orange Basil *Beurre Blanc* Sauce, and Poached Pears in Spiced Red Wine Sauce; American dishes such as Puréed Jerusalem Artichoke Soup with Orange-hazelnut Compound Butter, Pan-Seared Colorado Beef Tenderloin with a Zinfandel Glaze, and Spiced Apples with Nutmeg Cream and Cranberry Coulis; and Mediterranean dishes such as Savory Vegetable Soup with Basil and Mint Pesto, Omelets with Wilted Arugula, Gorgonzola, and Roasted Red Pepper; and Caramel Flan with Seasonal Fruits Macerated in Sherry.

Basic Techniques, II, III, and IV each build on the techniques learned in the previous class. **Basic Techniques II** focuses on additional country French sauces, soups, main dishes, and desserts. **Basic Techniques III** explores world cuisines, with each day offering recipes from a new region—the Pacific Rim, southwestern United States, Caribbean, Mediterranean, and Southeast Asia. And **Basic Techniques IV** emphasizes more sophisticated menus and plate presentation in classic country French cuisine. Favorite dishes from this course include *Salmon en Papillote*, Ballantine of

Duck with Cherry and Port Sauce, Lobster Bisque, *Tarte Tatin*, and Chocolate Soufflé with Apricot Sauce.

In the **Asian Techniques** course you'll learn to create dishes from China, Korea, Japan, Thailand, Burma, Malaysia, and Indonesia. The French influence in Vietnamese and the Spanish flavors in Philippine cooking are also explored. This course teaches Asian methods for steaming, stir-frying, deep-frying, braising, roasting and grilling, and how to make soups, curries, and noodles. You'll learn to make Philippine Grilled Duck with Lime and Cilantro; Vietnamese Roasted Stuffed Crabs, Buddhist Seven Jade Stir-fry with Crispy Fried Noodles, Thai Sour Shrimp Soup, and Vietnamese Happy Pancakes.

The **Pastry** course teaches you how to bake with chocolate, work with meringue, properly caramelize sugar, and prepare butter creams, mousses, rolled cakes, puff pastry, pie pastry, tart shells, cream puffs, and eclairs. You'll learn to make Mocha Hazelnut Butter Cream Torte, Strawberry Almond Roulade, Puff Pastry Fruit Tart with Marzipan Cream, Meringue Mushrooms, *Dacquoise*, Brioche, Buttermilk Biscuits, and Molten Centered Chocolate Cake.

Each course includes twenty-five hours of hands-on cooking in the kitchen. Classes usually meet from 9:30 A.M. to 2:30 P.M. each day and end with the group dining together on the dishes prepared in class. Most of the courses are taught by the director of the program, Joan Brett; however, the school also hosts famous guest chefs. Alice Medrich, a two-time winner of the James Beard Cookbook of the Year award (for her cookbooks *Chocolat* and *Chocolate and the Art of Low-Fat Desserts*), and food writer and chef Joanne Weir, author of the award winning *From Tapas to Meze*, have both taught in the past.

This program is not a tour with cooking lessons. Instead, you'll be on your own in the afternoons to explore the charming cafés and shops, teahouses, art galleries, theater, and music of Boulder. You'll be at the foothills of the Rocky Mountains, and will be able to choose from many outdoor activities. Accommodations are not included, although most participants choose to stay at the Inn on Mapleton Hill, a seven-room restored nineteenth-century mansion, located on the outskirts of downtown.

THE DETAILS: The programs run five days and are offered from mid-May to mid-October. Group sizes for the Basic Techniques course are limited to twelve. Group sizes for Asian Techniques and Pastry are limited to ten. The costs include cooking lessons only. Accommodations at the Inn on Mapleton Hill include breakfast and afternoon refreshments, and access to a nearby health club.

The Cost: $475 per program
Inn on Mapleton Hill: $95–$145 per night

Contact:
Cooking School of the Rockies
637 S. Broadway, Suite H
Boulder, CO 80304
Phone: 303-494-7988
Fax: 303-494-7999
Web site: www.cookingschoolrockies.com

Inn on Mapleton Hill
1001 Spruce St.
Boulder, CO 80302
Phone: 800-276-6528; 303-449-6528
Fax: (303) 415-0470
E-mail: Maphillinn@aol.com
Web site: www.innonmapletonhill.com

• ELDERBERRY HOUSE •
COOKING SCHOOL

The Elderberry House Cooking School offers a taste of France in California. The Provençal-style *Château du Sureau* is located in California's Sierra Nevada foothills, just sixteen miles from Yosemite National Park, and offers an intimate setting for a short, intensive cooking course.

The owner of the château, Erna Kubin-Clanin, says that people thought she was crazy when she first opened the Elderberry House restaurant in this secluded location in 1984—but it's the remoteness and tranquility that attracts guests. That and the food: The Elderberry House has received numerous awards for its cuisine, including a five-diamond rating from AAA.

In 1991, Erna built *Château du Serea* as a complement to the restaurant. The château has only ten rooms and is designed to give guests the experience of staying at a private estate in France: From the lack of a front desk and other check-in procedures to the antiques in your suite to the gourmet appetizers and herbal teas brought to your room by a chamber maid, the château earned its listing in *Tattler* magazine as one of the top one hundred hotels in the world.

The cooking classes at Elderberry House, which take place in the restaurant's kitchen, are an intensive eight hours per day. A half-hour is spent discussing theory, then you move into the kitchen to start lessons. All classes are hands-on, and you'll be encouraged to work at your own pace and follow your own interests, whether it's entrees, soups, salads, or desserts.

The recipes are based on fresh, seasonal ingredients that are abundantly available in the region. Each day ends with a six-course dinner. One recent meal included Amuse Bouche of Artichoke Gratin over a Tomato Citrus Confit, Pepper-Seared Ahi Tuna in Phyllo Wafers, Polenta Leek Soup, Pan-Seared Angus Beef Tenderloin, a Bouquet of Field Lettuces and Nasturtiums, and Erna's Cham-

pagne Torte in a Raspberry Pool Laced with Mayan Chocolate. Spouses or friends can attend dinner for the cost of the evening's fare.

In addition to cooking lessons, Erna's daughter, Renee-Nicole Kubin, a cellar master who has worked with Charlie Trotter in Chicago, presents two wine courses.

Although you'll be cooking for much of your three-day stay (you are, of course, welcome to stay after the cooking course ends), other activities are also available, including hiking, biking, skeet shooting, golfing, white-water rafting, and fly-fishing—all of which can be arranged by the hotel staff. And there are also impressive sightseeing opportunities, as you'll be staying just outside of Yosemite with its breathtaking waterfalls and vistas.

Erna Kubin-Clanin was chef at the Redwood Inn restaurant, adjacent to the Wawona Hotel in Yosemite National Park, for six years before opening the Elderberry House Restaurant.

THE DETAILS: The program runs three days and is offered in March. Group size is limited to twelve. The cost includes cooking lessons, three luncheons, and a six-course dinner each night. There is a slight discount in accommodation prices for those attending the cooking course. Regular prices are listed below.

The Cost: $700
Accommodations: $315–$515 per night

Contact:
Erna Kubin-Clanin
48688 Victoria Lane
PO Box 2413
Oakhurst, CA 93644
Phone: 559-683-6800
Fax: 559-683-0800

From the kitchen of Elderberry House

∂

TRUFFLED GOAT CHEESE SOUFFLÉ
WITH SHALLOT VINAIGRETTE
SERVES 4

THE SOUFFLÉ:
$1/2$ cup heavy béchamel
$5^1/2$ ounces goat cheese
3 egg yolks
1 tablespoon truffles, julienned
$1/4$ teaspoon truffle oil
$1/2$ tablespoon onions, minced and sautéed
1 teaspoon thyme, chopped
Salt and pepper
Nutmeg

2 tablespoons unsalted butter
5 egg whites

SHALLOT VINAIGRETTE:
1 tablespoon olive oil
1 shallot, minced
$1^1/2$ tablespoons red wine vinegar
3 tablespoons orange juice
4 tablespoons chicken broth
1 tablespoon sugar
Salt and pepper to taste

To make the soufflé: In a medium mixing bowl whisk the béchamel, goat cheese, and egg yolks together until smooth. Add truffle, truffle oil, onions, and thyme. Season with the salt, pepper, and nutmeg to taste and reserve.

Coat 4 4-ounce ceramic ramekins with butter or line with plastic.

In a clean stainless steel bowl beat egg whites with a balloon whisk until they form soft peaks. Carefully fold egg whites into cheese mixture, spoon into ramekins and place in a 350° oven.

Bake for approximately 15 minutes or until risen and golden brown. When finished, remove from ramekins, drizzle with vinaigrette and serve immediately.

To make shallot vinaigrette: In a small saucepan, sauté the shallots lightly in olive oil. Add red wine vinegar, orange juice, chicken broth, sugar, and seasonings. Reduce by half and serve.

• THE GOVERNOR'S INN •

Jim and Cathy Kubec had long dreamed of owning a country inn, but it wasn't until they saw the nineteenth-century Governor's Inn that they found the one that would make their dreams come true. Located on the Ludlow, Vermont, village green, less than a mile from Okemo Mountain, the inn has received four stars from the Mobil Guide, and has been judged one of the nation's ten best inns.

For almost ten years the inn has offered Culinary Magic seminars. Chefs Cathy Kubec and Deedy Marble offer step-by-step demonstrations in the inn's kitchen that cover using fresh ingredients, planning menus, garnishing and presenting meals, and how to prepare meals ahead of time to make entertaining easier.

After you arrive on Friday, you'll be greeted with afternoon tea, welcome drinks, and a six-course gourmet dinner. Then next morning you'll be treated to breakfast created by Cathy—possibly hot apple crisp or her special "Stuffed" French Toast with Real Vermont Maple Syrup. Then class begins. You'll learn to make such dishes as Poached Chicken with Salmon, Tomato Pan-Roasted Soup, and the award winning Apricot Victorian, one of the most popular desserts at the inn. You'll also learn how to make "nightingale's nests," using a knitting needle and phyllo dough.

When not in class, you can enjoy the ambience of the nine-room inn and the outdoor activities that are available year-round in Ludlow, as well as the antique shops, the five nearby lakes, the Black River, and Okemo Mountain. There is also golf, biking, antiquing, visiting historical sites, and attending summer theater shows.

Cathy has years of experience as chef of the Governor's Inn, and is an honors graduate of the Connecticut Culinary Institute. Deedy Marble graduated from *L'Ecole de Moulin* in France.

Noncooking partners sharing a room with a cooking guest are welcome at all meals.

THE DETAILS: The program runs three days and is offered in June, August, September, and October. Group size is limited to twelve. The cost includes accommodations, luncheon, a six-course gourmet dinner, cooking lessons, and an autographed copy of *A Box of Culinary Secrets from the Inn's Kitchen*.

Double Occupancy: $385–$475
Single Occupancy: $570–$625

Contact:
Jim and Cathy Kubec, Innkeepers
The Governor's Inn
86 Main Street
Ludlow, VT 05149
Phone: 800-GOVERNOR; 802-228-8830
Web site: www.thegovernorsinn.com

· THE GREAT CHEFS ·
AT ROBERT MONDAVI WINERY

Robert Mondavi Winery has been hosting Great Chefs cooking lessons for more than twenty years—pairing the cuisine of famous guest chefs with the winery's own wines. Charlie Trotter, Roy Yamaguchi, Julia Child, Wolfgang Puck, Jacques and Claudine Pépin, and Paula Wolfert have all participated in the past, as have many other internationally known chefs.

The winery offers two cooking sessions per year: a Weekend Event and a Long Weekend Event. A typical **Weekend Event** begins on Saturday morning, with an informal question and answer period hosted by the guest chef and Robert Mondavi. Then at noon, you're treated to aperitifs and lunch in the Vineyard Room, which has a spectacular view of the winery's historic To-Kalon Vineyard. In the mid-afternoon you have a choice of a tour and tasting at Opus One (a winery co-owned by Robert and Baron Philippe Rothschild) or a History of Wine presentation. Late afternoon is reserved for a cooking demonstration by the celebrity chef, and that evening you're invited to a gala black tie dinner in the Vineyard Room.

The next day begins with another cooking class taught by the guest chef, after which there is a private tour of the Robert Mondavi Winery before your farewell lunch.

The **Long Weekend Event** begins on Friday with a tour and wine tasting at either Opus One or La Famiglia di Robert Mondavi Winery. After the tasting you'll be treated to aperitifs and lunch in the Vineyard Room, and will then return to the winery for a cooking demonstration with the guest chef, and dinner.

On Saturday morning, you're offered an optional floral design class or a wine tasting lesson. Lunch is at La Famiglia di Robert Mondavi Winery, and then your afternoon is free to explore Napa Valley. At five P.M. there is another cooking demonstration before a gala dinner in the Vineyard Room.

Sunday morning is reserved for the final cooking demonstration, followed by a private tour of the winery before your farewell lunch.

The Long Weekend Event includes accommodations at the Vintage Inn in Yountville. Partners or spouses are welcome for a reduced fee (noted below).

THE DETAILS: Programs are offered in April and November. Group sizes are limited to thirty-five for the Weekend Event and twenty-eight for the Long Weekend Event. Accommodations, most meals, and cooking classes are included in the Long Weekend Event. Only meals and cooking classes are included in the Weekend Event.

Weekend Event: $900
Weekend Event, meals only, no cooking: $500
Long Weekend Event: $1,750
Long Weekend single supplement: $200

Contact:
The Great Chefs at Robert Mondavi Winery
PO Box 106
Oakville, California 94562
Phone: 707-968-2100
Fax: 707-968-2174
E-mail: Valerie.Varachi@robertmondavi.com
Web site: www.robertmondaviwinery.com

• THE GREENBRIER—LA VARENNE •

In 1778, Amanda Anderson, crippled with rheumatism and slung on a litter between two horses, was brought to White Sulphur Springs in West Virginia, where she was immersed in the mineral water. A moment later, she leapt out of the water, completely cured. True or false, the story quickly spread, and the springs grew into a well-known healing spa. Since then, the estate that sprung up around the springs has been the summer home of Robert E. Lee, a military hospital (both during the Civil War and World War II), host to twenty-six American presidents, and, since the 1930s, the home of the Greenbrier—an elegant six-hundred-room luxury hotel and spa.

Some Greenbrier trivia: Thomas Jefferson wrote the first published mention of the Greenbrier's mineral waters in 1784; in the mid-1800s, the resort was a social center for aristocratic southern families; Sam Snead shot the best round of golf of his career (a 59) on the Greenbrier Course; a 112,000-square-foot bunker was built into the hill under the Greenbrier in the 1950s, for the purpose of housing the U.S. Congress in the event of a national crisis; and the main kitchen of the Greenbrier (which is 13,200 square feet) uses more than 26,300 pounds of chocolate a year, and 155 pounds of coffee, 100 gallons of homemade soup, and 1,400 pounds of beef, veal, and pork every day.

The Greenbrier, located on 6,500 acres in the Allegheny Mountains, is a five-star, five-diamond resort. It offers golf, horseback riding, white-water rafting, skeet shooting, croquet, tennis, swimming, fly-fishing, and much more. It's also the home of the Greenbrier Spa and Mineral Baths, where you can enjoy—in addition to soaking in the spring water—saunas, massages, mud treatments, aromatherapy, facials, and fitness consultations.

The resort has, for more than twenty-two years, offered culinary programs to nonprofessional cooks. And in 1990, it initiated the *La Varenne* Signature Series, weeklong culinary classes that focus on home entertaining. The course is offered under the direction of Anne Willan (the owner and director of *La Varenne*, see page 32), and features well-known guest chefs. Some guest chefs have been Julia Child, Mary Ann Esposito (host of PBS's *Ciao Italia* and author of several cookbooks), Abigail Kirsch, Ris Lacoste, David Rosengarten, and Martin Yan.

Classes are held daily from nine A.M. to noon, and then again in the afternoon for a short session from one to two-thirty P.M. Classes are primarily demonstration, and are based on a theme such as Entertaining at Home, How to Set up a Buffet, Wine Tasting Dinners, French Bistro Dinners, Festive Breads, Entertaining for a Crowd, and a Moveable Feast (which covers buffet dishes that can be prepared ahead of time). Other courses focus on American regional cuisine, contemporary Scottish cuisine, eclectic Northwest cuisine, classic Italian cuisine, Asian cuisine, barbecue, seafood, and wine country cuisine.

Anne Willan, who directs the course, has more than thirty years of culinary experience as a cooking teacher, food writer (she's the author of the seventeen-volume *Look and Cook*, among other books), and television host.

Children and spouses are very welcome at the resort, and there is plenty to keep them occupied. The Greenbrier also offers golf and tennis academies.

THE DETAILS: The program runs six days and is offered eight times during the spring. Group size is limited to twelve. The cost includes accommodations, meals, cooking lessons, and a one-hour treatment in the Greenbrier spa.

The Cost: $2,150

Contact:
Ricki Senn, Cooking School Coordinator
300 West Main Street
White Sulphur Springs, WV 24986
Phone: 800-228-5049; 304-536-1110
E-mail: cookingschool@greenbrier.com
Web site: www.greenbrier.com

From the kitchen of the Greenbrier

❂

ROSEMARY FLANK STEAK WITH
BALSAMIC-GLAZED RED ONIONS

SERVES 6

$^1/_2$ cup olive oil

3 large cloves garlic, minced

3 tablespoons fresh rosemary, minced, plus sprigs for garnish

$^1/_2$ teaspoon cracked black peppercorns

$^1/_2$ cup balsamic vinegar

$1^1/_2$ pounds flank steak, trimmed

2 red onions, peeled and sliced $^1/_4$-inch

Salt and pepper to taste

In a small bowl, combine $^1/_4$ cup of the olive oil with the garlic, minced rosemary, cracked peppercorns, and 2 tablespoons of balsamic vinegar.

Place flank steak in a shallow, nonreactive pan and pour marinade over. Turn steak to coat both sides, pressing spices onto steak. Marinate for 30 minutes.

Heat grill to medium high. Grill steak 2 to 3 minutes per side. Brush top of steak with $1^1/_2$ tablespoons balsamic vinegar. Turn steak over and brush other side with $1^1/_2$ tablespoons of balsamic vinegar. Cook 1 minute longer, and remove to a warm platter. Cover loosely with foil.

Brush onion slices on both sides with remaining olive oil. Season with salt and pepper. Grill onions approximately 2 minutes on each side. Sprinkle onions with remaining balsamic vinegar and cook for an additional 1 to 2 minutes.

Slice flank steak on the bias into thin slices, cutting across the grain. Arrange slices on serving platter and pour over any juices that collected on the platter that steak was placed on after cooking. Place grilled balsamic onions on platter with steak. Garnish with rosemary sprigs and serve immediately.

· GOURMET RETREATS ·
AND CASALANA

Lana Richardson, the chef and owner of Gourmet Retreats, was searching for a property to be a permanent home for her cooking program when she found more than she expected: two properties, one a professional quality kitchen and one a six-cottage bed and breakfast, within walking distance from each other.

The properties are in Calistoga, a small town in Napa Valley, known for its natural hot springs and mineral waters. The kitchen looks out over the Napa River on one side and an extensive organic herb and vegetable garden on the other.

Gourmet Retreats offers one-day cooking classes, Gourmet Weekend Retreats, and three- and five-day culinary learning vacations. The day classes have titles such as Elegant Hors d'ouvres, Celebration of Spring, Spectacular Salads and Sides, Fresh Fruit Desserts, and Biscuits, Muffins, and Scones.

The Gourmet Weekend Retreats cover ethnic cuisine, and are often taught by guest chefs. The program starts on Friday afternoon with the preparation of a four-course meal you'll enjoy for dinner. On Saturday morning you'll visit a farmer's market, specialty store, food producer, or winery, and then prepare a farewell luncheon with the rest of the group. Past retreat weekends have been A Taste of Italy, Health Cooking—Mediterranean Style, Regional Mexican Cuisine, and French Country Cooking. Guests learn to cook dishes such as *Rissotolla Milanese, Finocchio con Parma*, Creamy Curried Eggplant Soup, Bittersweet Chocolate Orange Mousse, Quesadilla de *Huitlacoche* con Salsa, *Mole Negro Oaxaqueño, Tamal de Rajas en Hojas de Platano*, Pork Loin with Tapenade and Basil, Warm Duck Confit Salad with Cabbage and Walnuts, and Red Wine Steamed Mussels with Garlic. Another class is based on the movie *Big Night*—guests learn to make the spectacular pastry "drum" filled with pasta, meatballs, cheeses, and eggs featured in the film.

The three- and five-day culinary learning vacations include daily hands-on cooking lessons, and excursions to points of culinary interest. You might visit specialty and ethnic food markets, farmer's markets, winemakers, and farmers. The three-day vacation focuses on basic cooking techniques and making stocks, broth, soups, and classic sauces. The five-day vacation goes beyond the basic techniques, and teaches how to make perfect pies and tarts, biscuits, muffins, and scones, and breads and pizzas.

When not in cooking class, you can explore Calistoga, which offers beautiful walks and bike rides, as well as health spas, shopping, and many wineries.

THE DETAILS: Programs are offered year-round. Group sizes are limited to eight. The costs include all instruction and meals prepared in class.

Gourmet Weekend Retreats: $160
Three-Day Vacations: $390
Five-Day Vacations: $650

Contact:
Lana Richardson
Gourmet Retreats at CasaLana
1316 South Oak Street
Calistoga, CA 94515
Phone: 877-968-2665; 707-942-0615
Fax: 707-942-0204
E-mail: lana@GourmetRetreats.com
Web site: www.GourmetRetreats.com

· MOVEABLE FEAST ·
IN NANTUCKET—A WALKING TRIP
WITH A CULINARY TWIST

"Nantucket may only be fourteen-and-a-half miles long and three-and-a-half miles wide," says Sarah Leah Chase, cookbook author, Nantucket resident, and your guide on this Moveable Feast. "But its vast and varied riches will make you feel you've merely dented the surface during your four intense days of cycling, touring, feasting, and learning."

The Moveable Feast in Nantucket begins with a tour of downtown Nantucket's historic center, as you are treated to a treasure trove of well-preserved Quaker, Georgian, Federal, and Greek Revival buildings. You'll stop at Sarah's specialty food shop for a short cooking demonstration followed by a buffet lunch featuring some of her favorites: cold Chinese noodles, kielbasa vinaigrette, Moroccan carrots, and Nantucket scallop puffs. Then, after a coastal bike ride on the Madaket bike path, you go to the Gallery Restaurant for dinner and live piano music.

The following day, you'll have a culinary bike tour of the island—visiting a fishmonger, brewery, winery, and farm—and will enjoy a Nantucket picnic at a farm field or on a nearby beach. You can spend the afternoon wandering around Nantucket before the next activity: a clambake on Miacomet Beach.

On your third day, you'll bike "the loop," a bike path running through one of the world's largest cranberry bogs and Nantucket's newest golf course into the charming village of Siasconset. You'll then bike past farms, fields, and woods to the village of Wauwinet on the eastern tip of the island. There you'll enjoy the four-course menu at Toppers Restaurant: drinking wine and eating Yellow Fin Tuna Tartare, Nantucket Lobster Club on Toasted Brioche, Wild Turkey Hash with Waffle Chips, and Barlett Farm Tomatoes with Buffalo Mozzarella.

On your last full day on Nantucket, you'll visit the Whaling Museum (originally built in 1847 as a candle factory), and will then have the afternoon free for more biking, shopping, and just lazing on the beach. Then, in the late afternoon, you'll meet at Straight Wharf for a harbor cocktail cruise on a restored lobster boat. Your final night's celebration takes place back at Toppers, where you'll have cocktails on the patio and a gourmet feast in the private dining room: an array of lobster, crab, scallops, and other fresh Nantucket specialties.

Note: As Nantucket is basically flat, the bicycling is not at all strenuous.

THE DETAILS: The program runs four days and is offered in June and August. Group size is limited from sixteen to twenty-four people. The cost includes accommodations, all meals, cooking lessons, all special events, guides, and entrance fees, and a customized Cannondale bicycle to use during the trip.

The Cost: $4,950
Single Supplement: $1,000

Contact:
Butterfield and Robinson
70 Bond Street
Toronto, Ontario
CANADA M5B IX3
Phone: 800-678-1147; 416-864-1354
Fax: 416-864-0541
E-mail: info@butterfield.com
Web site: www.butterfield.com

• MOVEABLE FEAST IN THE PACIFIC • NORTHWEST—A WALKING TRIP WITH A CULINARY TWIST

The Moveable Feast in the Pacific Northwest begins with a walking tour of historic downtown Victoria on Vancouver Island. "There used to be a saying that Victoria was for the newlywed and the nearly dead, but all that has changed," says Megan Vercere, the director of the tour. "It's peaceful, but it's also a funky, vibrant coastal town with fantastic gardens and museums."

After the walking tour, you'll have lunch at Camille's, one of the city's finest restaurants, and set off for the southern tip of the island. There you'll be dropped at a private walking and cycling path known as the Galloping Goose Trail, a series of old logging roads and railways which have been joined together to form a thirty-seven-mile trail. You'll follow the Goose to Sooke Harbour House, an inn built on the banks of the Strait of Juan de Fuca, where you'll attend your first cooking class—a demonstration of the use of indigenous herbs and plants in such dishes as Smoked Coho Salmon Terrine with Tea-cured Line-caught Halibut and Marinated Whiffen Spit Sea Asparagus under a Dill Crème Fraîche.

The next day begins with a hearty farm breakfast at the inn and a drive up the island for a walk to Anderlea Vineyard for a wine tasting and to Venturi-Schulze winery and fine balsamic vinegar makers for a demonstration of vinegar making. Then you'll explore the little island town of Duncan, shopping for antiques and enjoying a light lunch. Finally, you'll walk along Maple Bay (hoping to catch sight of a bald eagle) to catch a ferry to Salt Spring Island, where you'll stay for the next two days.

On Salt Spring Island, you'll stay at Hastings House hotel, a manor house overlooking Ganges Marina. While on the island, you can explore the artisan shops and art galleries of Ganges, go on a bike ride along the shores of the Trincomali Channel, hike in the

T'sa Wout Native Reserve, have a cooking lesson and lunch of Salt Spring Island specialties at an organic farmhouse, and go sea-kayaking in the harbor (where you may even see an Orca whale).

You'll then fly to the rugged west coast of Vancouver Island, where you'll stay for two days at the Wickaninnish Inn, perched on the rocks overlooking Chesterman Beach. That night, after, per-haps, a soak in your two-person tub overlooking the water, you'll have an old-fashioned beach barbecue: a clambake with fresh seafood, organic corn, baby new potatoes, local microbrews or wine, and—it should go without saying—s'mores.

The next day, you'll explore the Pacific Rim National Park—hectares of rainforest and wild coastline that begins directly next to the inn—accompanied by a naturalist and wildlife expert who'll teach you about the local flora and fauna. Then, tides permitting, you'll hike up Radar Hill, through old growth rainforest, and will emerge on the north end of Long Beach, a seven-mile strip of sandy beach and craggy shoreline. If the tides aren't so permissive, you might set out in a private boat on a cruise to Clayoquot Sound and Meares Island, home of the world's oldest cedar trees, for hiking and sea-kayaking.

You'll meet back at the inn to enjoy the award winning cuisine of Chef Rodney Butters, who will also offer a demonstration class before preparing a gourmet final dinner.

Note: This trip can be tailored to meet guests' walking needs: from avid hikers to casual walkers.

THE DETAILS: The program runs five days. Group size is limited from sixteen to twenty-four people. The cost includes accommoda-tions, all meals, cooking lessons, all private tours, guides, and entrance fees, and the use of a customized Cannondale bicycle.

The Cost: $3,950
Single Supplement: $1,250

Contact:
Butterfield and Robinson
70 Bond Street
Toronto, Ontario
CANADA M5B IX3
Phone: 800-678-1147; 416-864-1354
Fax: 416-864-0541
E-mail: info@butterfield.com
Web site: www.butterfield.com

• SANTA FE SCHOOL •
OF COOKING AND MARKET

In 1989, tired of her career in real estate, Susan Curtis decided to open a small business she could love—a cooking school/food market/gift shop specializing in the cuisine and culture of New Mexico and the American Southwest. And it wasn't long before she was also offering a culinary tour that highlights the unique tastes and history of southwestern cooking.

The first day begins with a cooking class with James Campbell, sous chef for La Casa Sena, one of Santa Fe's top restaurants. You'll learn to cook many of Campbell's favorite southwestern recipes, and will then enjoy them for lunch. You'll then spend the afternoon exploring the historic town of Santa Fe. Susan recommends visiting the Georgia O'Keeffe museum, as that evening you'll be a guest at the private estate of *Sol y Sombra* (Sun and Shadows), where O'Keeffe spent the last two years of her life. The estate is now owned by Beth and Charles Miller, who have transformed it into an organic farm with innovative water management and sustainable agriculture techniques. After watching the sun set across the desert sky, you'll enjoy cocktails and dinner prepared by *Sol y Sombra's* resident chef, Amanda O'Brien (who assisted Martha Stewart for many years).

The next day is reserved for exploring northern New Mexico. You'll visit another of Georgia O'Keeffe's residences, this one overlooking the Chama River and the foothills of the Sangre de Cristo Mountains, where admirers of O'Keeffe's work will recognize her inspiration in the surrounding landscape. Next you'll have lunch at *Hacienda Rancho de San Juan*, a small country inn, followed by a short trip to a small farm that maintains traditional New Mexican agricultural practices. Then it's back to Santa Fe for a siesta before dinner on your own at one of Santa Fe's excellent restaurants.

The next morning begins with a cooking lesson, this one taught by Flynt Payne, executive chef at the much praised Inn of the Anasazi. Chef Flynt's specialty is in contemporary Southwestern dishes made from indigenous local ingredients. After lunch, Susan suggests you visit the School for American Research which has an excellent collection of Southwestern Native American art and artifacts. The final evening is spent at the Tesuque Village home of Bill and Cheryl Jamison, where they'll treat you to an informal cooking lesson and fabulous dinner. The Jamisons are well known for their expertise in Southwestern regional cooking and are the authors of *Smoke and Spice* and *The Border Cookbook* (both of which have won the James Beard award).

It's also possible to take a day class at the school. You can study Traditional New Mexican, Contemporary Southwestern, Southwest Vegetarian, Contemporary Southwest Light, Southwest Tapas (hors d'oeuvres), or Mexican cooking.

All classes are taught by professional local chefs. Regulars include Daniel Hoyer, sous chef at the Coyote Café in Santa Fe; Kathi Long, an expert in regional Mexican cooking and author of *Mexican Light Cooking* and *Best of Mexico*; and Bill Weiland, Director of the Culinary Arts program at Santa Fe Community College and three-time winner of the annual Taste of Santa Fe competition.

Accommodations are not included, although special rates have been arranged at a country inn within walking distance of the Santa Fe Cooking School. You may, however, stay anywhere you like. And if you're interested in taking a bit of the Southwest back home with you, Susan has a well-stocked gift shop and a wonderful mail order catalog.

THE DETAILS: The course runs three days and is offered in the late summer. Group size is limited to fifteen. The cost includes two cooking classes, lunches, two evening dinners with wine, and all field trips.

Culinary and Cultural Tour: $995 per person.
Daily Cooking Lessons: $45–$85 per lesson.

Contact:
Nicole Curtis, Manager
Santa Fe School of Cooking and Market
Upper Level, Plaza Mercado
116 West San Francisco Street
Santa Fe, NM 87501
Phone: 505-983-4511
Fax: 505-983-7540
E-mail: cookin@nets.com
Web site: www.nets.com/cooking

From the kitchen of the Santa Fe School of Cooking and Market

۰

PERFECT POSOLE

MAKES 8 SIDE DISH SERVINGS

$1/2$ pound ($2^1/2$ cups) posole, picked over for any dirt or stones

3 tablespoons vegetable oil

$1^1/4$ cups onions, chopped

1 tablespoon garlic, minced

2 to 3 New Mexico dried red chile pods, washed, stemmed and seeds removed

4 cups chicken stock

1 teaspoon coriander seed, toasted and freshly ground

Salt, to taste

$1/2$ cup cilantro, coarsely chopped

Place cleaned posole in a large pot and cover with cold water by 3 inches. Cover and cook at a simmer for 2 to 3 hours, adding water as needed, until kernels are soft and beginning to burst.

Drain the posole and rinse well.

Heat the oil in large pot and sauté the onions until golden. Add the garlic and sauté for 1 minute. Add the posole, chile pods, stock, ground coriander, and $1/4$ cup of the cilantro and simmer for 30 minutes.

Add the salt and continue cooking for another 30 minutes. Stir in remaining cilantro, taste, and adjust seasonings.

• TURTLE POND •

Una Maderson, the owner of Turtle Pond Cooking School, recently bought and renovated a pre-1850 house in Quakertown, Pensylvania. "It's the most relaxing and inspiring environment I could have imagined," she says. "It has hardwood floors and beamed ceilings and a new teaching kitchen-cum-sun room with wall-to-wall windows on three sides and views of a horse farm and two ponds."

The cooking school is on twenty-four acres of land (including a two-acre pond) in Upper Bucks County, Pennsylvania, ninety miles west of New York City and thirty miles north of Philadelphia. It's home to many kinds of birds and wildlife, and offers endless hours of hiking, fishing, and lazing by the pond. The area also offers antiquing, balloon rides, and visits to historic houses, gift shops, and museums.

Una offers weekend vacations. Guests arrive Friday afternoon or evening, and dinner is provided. The first class is after breakfast on Saturday morning, and you enjoy the results, with wine, for lunch. The rest of the afternoon is free for relaxing or exploring the area, and then you have a second hands-on cooking class. The last class is after breakfast Sunday morning, and lunch brings the weekend to a close.

Una has a degree in Hotel and Restaurant Management, and is also a registered nurse, with a special interest in healthy eating. She has been the corporate chef for a major international corporate insurance brokerage since 1982, has lived and studied cooking in Hong Kong, has taught cooking privately and at NYU, and has worked as a Middle Eastern caterer.

THE DETAILS: The program runs three days. Group size is limited to six. The cost includes accommodations, breakfasts, two lunches, and two dinners.

The Cost: $350

Una Maderson
Turtle Pond Cooking School
210 Axehandle Road
Quakertown, PA 18951–4904
Phone: 215-538-2564
E-mail: turtlepond@erols.com

·5·

MEXICO

 MEXICAN FOOD in the United States is to authentic Mexican cuisine what string cheese is to fresh mozzarella. If you want to discover the true flavors of Mexico—based on pre-Hispanic cuisine and incorporating Spanish and French influences—you have to travel to the source. Each of Mexico's regions has its own singular culinary traditions: you might make plantain *empañadas* with black beans and a chili chipotle sauce in Cuernavaca, *cheviches* with fresh-caught river shrimp in Jalisco, tortilla soup in Tlaxcala, *mole poblano* in Puebla, and tamales with pumpkin seeds and *chaya* (a chardlike green) in Yucatan.

You can also study local medicinal plants, enjoy long siestas in a riverside hammock, and feel the heat of the salsa (both the dish and the dance). Or you can relax with a massage, shop for tropical fruits and fresh flowers at local markets, explore archeological sites, see how tequila and *pulque* (a pre-Hispanic alchoholic beverage) are made, visit a Oaxacan cheese farm, and have overnight trips to indigenous villages.

• CHOCOLATE, CHILIES, AND COCONUTS: •
A CULINARY JOURNEY TO THE
HEART OF MEXICO'S CULTURES,
MEDICINES, AND HISTORIES

The Center for World Indigenous Studies

Travel to the west coast of Mexico, into the subtropical zone, to explore the flora and fauna, traditional medicines, and culinary delights of the local region and peoples. The Center for World Indigenous Studies is a nonprofit organization dedicated to fostering a wider understanding of indigenous peoples, and their cooking vacation study trip focuses on the food and cooking traditions of Mexico's indigenous and colonizing cultures.

You'll gather herbs and plants and use them both in gourmet buffets and in medicine making. You will learn to prepare a variety of traditional dishes and will explore the value of many foods that have been marginalized since European contact. And, in addition to cooking classes, you'll attend lectures examining politics, economics, agriculture, and the environment. Over sumptuous meals, you'll discuss ethnobotany, culture, and the state of the indigenous community and cuisine in the early twenty-first century.

Your travels begin in Puerto Vallarta, where you'll catch a *ponga* (boat taxi) to Yelapa, a small coastal town in Jalsico. As you travel down the coast you'll see dolphins, seabirds, and manta rays who may escort the boat as you pass Mismaloya, where John Huston filmed the movie *Night of the Iguana*.

Upon your arrival in Yelapa, you'll settle into *Casa Xipe Totec*, your home during the trip. Your days will begin with fruit and tea, followed by an optional exercise or yoga class and then breakfast. Then you'll have lectures and discussions, which break for lunch and an extended siesta. You can nap in a hammock, go swimming on the beach, practice your Spanish, work in the garden, or go on boat trips, hikes, or herb walks to neighboring villages.

After siesta, you meet again for cooking, food gathering, and field activities. Or you can try a polarity treatment or massage, take a private lesson in scuba diving or windsurfing, or ride a gentle horse up-river with *Doña* Alisia, who is well versed in the medicinal use of local flora.

CWIS also offers other culinary trips to Mexico, such as one that explores Western Mexico's ancient celebration of the winter solstice. "The ancient peoples of Western Mexico organize their yearly calendar around three weeklong feasts," says Dr. Ryser of CWIS. "In keeping with that tradition, this trip is a celebration of native food and feasting. The focus is on the peoples, past and present, and the foods and rituals, that bring harmony and propitiate the gods and goddesses."

The program has many instructors. Dr. Rudolph Ryser is a chef and professor who specializes in the cooking traditions of indigenous peoples. Dr. Leslie Korn is an authority in the use of traditional methods of healing using foods and herbs as medicines. Ken Rubin is a professional cook and a degree candidate in anthropology. And *Doña* Alisia Rodriguez is native to Yelapa and a cook who learned from her great-grandmother.

The accommodations at *Casa Xipe Totec* are rustic, but include hot running water, full toilets, and double beds. There is limited electricity—everything runs on propane and solar power, as *Casa Xipe Totec* is an ecological, low-tech facility.

Noncooking partners are welcome on the trip, as are children older than twelve.

THE DETAILS: The program runs one week and is offered in winter, spring, summer, and fall. Group size is limited to twenty. The cost includes accommodations, breakfasts and lunches, cooking lessons, and excursions.

The Cost: $1,900

Contact:
Chocolate, Chiles, and Coconuts
Center for World Indigenous Studies
Dr. Leslie Korn
1001 Cooper Pt. Rd. SW, Ste. 214
Olympia, WA 98502
Phone: 360-754-1990
Fax: 360-786-5034
E-mail: lekorn@cwis.org
Web site: www.cwis.org

From the kitchen of
Chocolate, Chiles, and Coconuts

●

TOMATILLO SALSA (GREEN SALSA)

1 1/2 pounds of tomatillos
6 serrano chilies
2 cloves of garlic
4 tablespoons of onion
Cilantro
A tablespoon of honey (or to taste—just enough
    to reduce the tartness)
Salt to taste

Boil the tomatillos for 15 minutes. Roast the garlic and chilies over a comal or fire (or fry with a little oil on your stovetop). Mix the tomatillos with the chilies, the garlic, the onion, cilantro, and honey in a blender until smooth. Salt to taste. Serve warm or cold, with guacamole, beans, and rice, or chips.

· CULINARY ADVENTURES ·
OF MEXICO

This culinary adventure in Mexico begins with a drive through the rugged countryside typical of Mexico's central highlands to San Miguel de Allende. Once in San Miguel—one of four Mexican towns designated as an official National Historic Treasure—you'll be greeted by pastel-colored colonial houses, centuries-old churches, and cobblestone streets. You'll settle into your room in a private villa, restored colonial mansion, or luxury bed-and-breakfast, and then meet the other guests for a sunset cocktail reception and elegant dinner at one of San Miguel's oldest restaurants.

Over the next week, you'll discover the unique cuisine and charm of San Miguel. One day you may go on a guided walking tour of the city, visit colonial churches and archeological museums, have a traditional Mexican lunch, and then spend the evening exploring, shopping, and enjoying San Miguel's nightlife. Another day may begin with a trip to the local market to shop for tropical fruits and vegetables, fresh and dried chilies, herbs, and flowers, followed by a cooking lesson and lunch featuring homemade *moles* and *pipians*. In the afternoon you may decide to tour studios where artisans make tinware, papier mâché, brass, and pewter goods, or you may decide to search for treasures at a local crafts fair.

On another day you'll be taught regional specialties by a guest chef before traveling to Pozos, an abandoned silver mining town near San Miguel. After lunch with the owners of a nearby hacienda, you'll work off your meal by exploring their estate and touring an abandoned mine. That evening, you can have drinks in a restored wine cellar or a night of salsa dancing.

You'll also enjoy a class that features Southwest cooking with a Mexican twist, a spa treatment by one of the program's staff of masseuses, dinner at *Casa de Sierra Nevada* with a talk with the chef, a day in Guanajuato (including lunch at the famous Count of

Valencia Restaurant), a class on salsas and chiles, and relaxing, shopping, and sipping margaritas.

The itinerary is flexible, though, and much depends on the season: Some highlights of past trips include attending a fashion show, a traditional Indian *concera* dance, a talk by a Pulitzer Prize–winning poet, the Day of the Dead festivities, and a Mexican rodeo. Other activities include tennis, golf, horseback riding, aerobics, yoga, dancing, and concerts. Culinary Adventures of Mexico can also arrange classes and workshops in painting, drawing, jewelry making, Spanish language lessons, and many other subjects.

Kristen Rudolph, the director of Culinary Adventures of Mexico, taught cooking at the University of Massachusetts and owns a café in San Miguel that specializes in Mexican and southwestern cuisine.

Noncooking guests are welcome.

THE DETAILS: The program runs eight days and is offered in April and October. Group size is limited from six to sixteen. The cost includes accommodations, most meals, cooking lessons, field trips, studio visits, spa treatments, optional Spanish or salsa dance classes, and transfers to and from the airport. The noncooking guests cost includes everything except the cooking lessons and the meals that accompany them.

The Cost: $1,800
Single Supplement: $400
Noncooking guests: $1,500

Contact:
Culinary Adventures of Mexico
Kristen Rudolph
432 Mainsail Ct.
Lake Mary, FL 32746
Phone (in Mexico): 52-4117-8228
Fax/Messages (in Mexico): 52-4117-8228
E-mail: culadv@unisono.ciateq.mx

• THE FLAVORS OF MEXICO •
Culinary Adventures, Inc.

Every year, Flavors of Mexico leads culinary tours through different regions of Mexico—Oaxaca, Veracruz, Pueblo, Michoacan, Tlaxacala, Yucatan, Compeche, and Tabasco. Each trip focuses on the cuisine, architecture, and history specific to that region.

For example, the Oaxacan Valley has been home to the Zapotec and Mixtec Indians for thousands of years, and their influence is strongly felt in the crafts and cuisine of Oaxaca—and in your cooking classes. You'll be taught both by local cooks and by Diana Kennedy (author of *Cuisines of Mexico* and *The Art of Mexican Cook-*

ing) while traveling through Oaxaca. One night you might dine in a village *barbacoa*, the next in an intimate *cena* in a private garden, and the third in a Zapotec home, where you'll sample traditional foods created by using the *metate* and *mano* to grind the corn, chiles, and cacao beans.

You'll also visit the ancient cities of Mitla, Monte, and Alban, discovering the pottery, weaving, wood-carving, and jewelry of the local artisans. And you'll learn from local culinary artists as well— the secrets of *mezcal*, the most traditional of Mexican intoxicating beverages and the techniques of creating the distinctive Oaxacan cheeses on a small farm in the Etla Valley.

Or you may choose to visit the port city of Veracruz, which Marilyn Tausend (Flavors of Mexico coordinator, co-author of *Mexico the Beautiful Cookbook* and author of *Cocina de la Familia*) calls "the New Orleans of Mexico." You'll learn to create the favorite dishes of this distinctive cuisine, as demonstrated by regional cooks and chefs. Later in the week, you'll visit Xalapa, high on the slopes of the Sierra Madres and surrounded by coffee and banana plantations, and Tlacotalpan, a small seventeenth-century port town on the banks of the "River of Butterflies," where you'll enjoy local dishes as a guest in the butterfly-hued homes that line the streets. And finally, you'll take a day trip to Papantla to visit farms growing fragrant beans of the vanilla orchid, and another trip to El Tajin, the ruins of the sacred city of the Totanac Indians.

Or you could have your cooking holiday in Puebla, which is noted for its baroque buildings and locally produced Talavera tile, and its profusion of ex-convents and monasteries, chapels, and churches. Puebla is also known for its *moles* and *pipians*—complex sauces of many spices, herbs, seeds, and nuts that are considered the epitome of classical Mexican cooking.

Or you might view the Orozco murals and visit the Mercado San Juan de Dios, one of Latin America's largest enclosed markets, on a trip to Guadalajara, Mexico's second largest city. But you won't spend much time in the city itself—you'll be too busy touring the countryside and nearby towns, and visiting the distilleries that produce 100 percent blue agave tequila.

The dishes you'll learn to make depend entirely on which region you visit. In Jalisco you'll make *tortas ahogadas* (overstuffed sandwiches on thick, chewy rolls, slathered in fiery chile sauce); in Yucatan you'll make tamales with pumpkin seeds and *chaya* (a chardlike green); and in Puebla you'll make the famous *mole poblano*, with its many ingredients ground together to form a rich sauce to cover the turkey or chicken, and *tinga poblana*, shredded pork with a tomato and chipotle sauce.

As you travel through a region, you stay in a variety of local hotels, and cook in private homes, outdoor sites, and occasionally in restaurant kitchens.

The nature of the trip precludes bringing young children. Spouses and partners can usually participate in all but the major classes for a somewhat reduced rate, although sometimes this is impossible due to the structure of the trip.

THE DETAILS: The programs vary from year to year, but the average trip runs eight to ten days. Group size is limited to twelve. The cost includes accommodations, meals, cooking lessons, and excursions.

The Cost: $2,500

Contact:
Culinary Adventures
Marilyn Tausend
6023 Reid Drive NW
Gig Harbor, WA 98335
Phone: 253-851-7676
Fax: 253-851-9532
E-mail: cul_adv_inc@ibm.net

From the kitchen of Flavors of Mexico

❧

SOPA DE CILANTRO (CILANTRO SOUP)

SERVES 6

4 small zucchini, cooked in
salted water until crisp-
tender
6 cups chicken broth
1 cup cilantro leaves, tightly
packed
4 tablespoons butter or vegetable oil
$1/2$ medium size onion,
minced

2 tablespoons cornstarch
2 serrano or jalapeño chiles
4 day-old corn tortillas, cut
into $1/2$-inch squares
$1/2$ pound fresh mozzarella (or
queso fresco), cubed
Jalapeño chiles, diced, to taste
$1/4$ cup crème fraîche
(optional)
Salt to taste

Purée the zucchini in a blender with the chicken broth. Add the cilantro, and blend completely or partially, as you prefer.

Melt the butter in a pot and sauté the onion until transparent. Add the broth and cilantro mixture, the starch (diluted in a bit of cold water), and the whole chiles. Add salt, if necessary.

Simmer for 10 minutes. Add crème fraîche if you want a creamier soup, and heat a few minutes more, but do not allow to boil.

Fry the tortilla squares in the butter or oil, then add the squares, mozzarella, and diced chile to the serving bowls. Pour the soup in, and serve.

• LAS CAMPANAS •
COCINA Y CULTURA

Las Campanas teaches an authentic Mexican cuisine that goes far beyond what's available in most Mexican restaurants. Instead of burritos, it's *Chiles Poblanos* Stuffed with Squash Flowers and Oaxaca Cheese, wrapped in puff pastry and served with cilantro sauce and pomegranate seeds. Instead of tacos, it's plantain *empañadas* filled with refried black beans and a chili chipotle sauce. And instead of tamales and enchiladas, it's Smoked Duck Breast and Mesclun Salad with *Xoconostle* Vinaigrette, Filet Mignon Stuffed with Goat Cheese and *Pulque* Sauce, Cold *Chile Poblano* Soup with Green Grapes, or a Pyramid of Three Chocolates with Coffee Crème *Anglaise* and Balsamic Caramel Sauce.

The classes cover traditional and contemporary Mexican cuisine, from pre-Hispanic recipes to Spanish and French influences to the most current reinterpretation of traditional dishes. Guests learn techniques such as cooking on a *comal*, preparing fresh chilies, and using the *molcajete*; spicing with avocado leaves, *epazote*, cilantro, and vanilla; and using jicama, nopales, *masa*, tomatillos, corn, and *huitlacoce*.

On one day, the class may focus on appetizers, salsas, and drinks. The next, you may visit the central market in Cuernavaca for identification and selection of ingredients, followed by a class in soups and salads. Then, after a visit to a local dairy ranch to see special cheeses being made, you may move on to main courses. And there's also a day set aside for pastries and desserts—using tropical fruit, nuts, vanilla, and chocolate.

Cooking classes take place at *Rancho Cuernavaca*, a private estate and bed-and-breakfast which has a large working kitchen, spacious reception halls, stables and a riding ring, a lap pool, and a bar. You'll cook both at the *Rancho Cuernavaca* and in kitchens in private homes in the area—and, as the city is known as "the City of Eternal Spring," you'll often enjoy your meals in beautiful garden surroundings.

Las Campanas can also organize side trips to Indian villages, mountain towns, archeological sites, and cigar and coffee plantations. Or you can just wander around Cuernavaca: Before Hernan

Cortes established Cuernavaca as his base, it was a Tlahuica city known as a center of learning and religious ceremonies, and a vacation destination for Aztecs who wanted a break from the winter chill. The city has plazas, colonial architecture, lush gardens, museums, churches, galleries, and many delightful restaurants.

Classes are taught by Chef Vanessa Musi Batty. Chef Vanessa has worked in kitchens in France, England, Israel, and Austria (where she was chef for the Mexican Embassy in Vienna). In Mexico, she has worked with some of Mexico's best chefs, including Monia Patino of La Galvia and La Taberna and Alicia D'Angeli of El Tajin.

THE DETAILS: The program runs four days and is offered in June, July, August, and October. If you have a group of five or more people, *Las Companas* will organize a program at your convenience. The cost includes cooking lessons, some meals, and excursions. Accommodations are not included, but you may stay at *Rancho Cuernavaca* for an additional price, or other arrangements can be made for you.

The Cost: $300
Rancho Cuernavaca: $75–$300 per night, ranging from a single
    room to a self-contained bungalow.

Contact:
Las Campanas
Apt. 292-3
Cuernavaca, Morelos
C.P. 62250
MEXICO
Phone/Fax: 52 (73) 172 678
E-mail: lascampanas@infosel.net.mx
Web site: www.campanas.com

• MEXICAN HOME COOKING •

Tlaxcala

"What I teach," says Estela Salas Silva, "goes beyond what is generally understood in the United States to be Mexican food. It's really a sophisticated cuisine originating in pre-Hispanic times. It was added to and enhanced by the Spanish and French following their invasions, resulting in a kitchen as rich, subtle, and complex as any in the world."

The kitchen in question is in Tlaxcala, the capital of the smallest state in Mexico. It's located in a valley surrounded by three volcanos—Popocatepetl, Ixtaccihuatl, and La Malinche—and is a short drive from the brilliantly colored murals at the ruins at Cacaxtla and La Malinche State Park. The town itself offers Baroque churches, pre-Hispanic ruins, and a quiet central square surrounded by sixteenth- and seventeenth-century buildings and sidewalk cafés shaded by a graceful arcade.

Guests stay in Estela's hacienda-style home. "Although we have spacious double rooms with private baths and fireplaces, it's not a hotel or resort," her husband, Jon, says. "It's a comfortable family home where guests can experience the routines of a Mexican family in their kitchen." (Or, if you prefer, there's also a hotel with a swimming pool twenty minutes away.)

The kitchen is decorated in Talavera tile and has a view of La Malinche (a dormant volcano) directly out the window, and an outdoor kitchen with a traditional wood-burning oven and barbecue is being constructed as of this writing. A typical meal might start with *Sopa de Veradura*, *Sopa de Abas*, or *Sopa de Tortilla*. Then you'd have *Ensalada de Nopales* (a cactus salad), *Chiles Rellenos*, or *Gorditas con Requeson*. Follow that with Guacamole and Salsa *de Pulla*, or *Tortas de Papas con Espinaca* (potato tortas with spinach), or *Chuletas de Puerco en Chipotle Qeumada* (pork chops with charred chipotle

chiles). And then finish it all off with Flan, *Capirotada* (bread pudding), *Tejocotes* (a local fruit).

Mexican Home Cooking offers a Basic Course, which focuses on main dishes, soups, salads, and salsas; a Dessert Course; and a Seafood Course. Classes run three to four hours a day, during which guests prepare four or five dishes. A Mexican Mushroom Culinary Tour is also available. Seven days of mushroom hunting and cuisine, during which you'll taste most of the more than thirty species of mushrooms in Tlaxcala (call or email for more information). The classes are hands-on and structured to meet the interests of the guests. Mexican Home Cooking focuses on providing a relaxed, informal, and fun atmosphere—all the better for imparting a genuine knowledge of the cuisine.

The program also offers many noncooking activities, including Spanish language classes and excursions to archeological sites (such as Cacaxtla and Teotihuacan). You can go on a day trip to see the local production of *pulque* (a pre-Hispanic alcoholic drink), or spend the night in indigenous villages (including hotel, meals, visits to homes, lectures on food and herbal medicine, and, of course, cooking classes). You can also go hiking and mountain climbing or attend carnival celebrations in Huejotzingo (during which thousands of local residents re-enact the Battle of Cinco de Mayo in traditional costumes) or the running of the bulls in Huamantla. You'll also have a chance to see other festivals, depending on the time of your visit, such as the Feast of the Assumption of the Virgin (in which carpets of flowers cover the streets) and Holy Week.

Estela has had more than twenty years experience as a chef in Mexico City and the United States. She recently returned to Mexico after many years as the head chef in her family's restaurant in San Francisco. She is assisted by her brother, Rogelio Salas Silva, who has also had many years experience, including owning and managing a restaurant in Mexico City.

Noncooking spouses and family members are welcome.

THE DETAILS: The Basic Course runs one week and is offered year-round. The Dessert Course and Seafood Course also run one week and each is offered twice per year. Group size is limited to six. The cost includes accommodations, meals, cooking lessons, and some excursions.

The Cost: $1,000 per course

Contact:
Mexican Home Cooking
Apdo. 64
Tlaxcala, Tlaxcala 90000
MEXICO
Phone: 52-246-8-09-78

Fax: 52-246-2-48-98 (If you fax, please write "Estela Salas Silva
Tel. 8-09-78" on the top of each page.)
E-mail: mexicanhomecooking@yahoo.com or
jon_jarvis@servired.com.mx

From the kitchen of Mexican Home Cooking

●

MANCHA MANTEL CON CONEJO (RABBIT)

You can substitute pork, lamb, chicken, or shrimp for the rabbit.

4 or 5 dried ancho chiles, stems and seeds removed	1 pound meat, thinly sliced, or whole shrimp
1/4 onion	2 apples, cut into 1-inch pieces
2 cloves of garlic, uncooked	1/2 cup pineapple, cut into 1-inch pieces
4 or 5 small tomatoes, charred (on grill or, if you have, a *comal*)	2 tablespoons olive oil
	2 tablespoons butter
4 or 5 cloves of garlic, charred as above	1/2 cup sugar
Dried oregano	1 to 2 tablespoons vinegar (to taste)
Cumin seed	1 cup chicken or meat stock

Cook the chiles with the onion and the two fresh garlic cloves in a
small amount of water, until soft (5 to 10 minutes). Blend the chile
mixture with the charred tomatoes and garlic, then add a little
water or stock and the oregano and cumin seed. Fry the meat (or
shrimp), apples, and pineapple in the oil with a little salt.

In a large pot, heat a little olive oil with the butter. Add the
sugar and let caramelize slightly. Keep stirring until the sugar melts.

Add *adobo* sauce (the mixture of chile, tomato, garlic, and spices). If the sugar crystallizes, stir it until it melts again. Add stock or water for consistency and stir occasionally for about 10 minutes as it simmers on a low heat.

Add the vinegar, stock, and meat, making sure to get as much of the juices from the meat possible. Simmer for about 15 minutes.

Garnish with onion and avocado slices on top, and radish and lettuce leaves on the side, or with fried pineapple and apple pieces, and serve.

• SEASONS OF MY HEART •

While selling her husband's produce door to door (native crops of corn, beans, squash, tomatoes, and flowers), Susana Trilling was invited into the kitchens of her Oaxacan neighbors . . . and there discovered the traditional cuisine of the region. Inspired, she revived **Seasons of My Heart**, the catering business she'd started in New York in 1980, and began teaching international cooking to local women, and Oaxacan cuisne to foreigners.

"The cooking techniques here are ancient," Susana says. "Customs in some villages have been preserved for over a thousand years, and that's what gives the food its unique flavor. Every dish has its own magic, and its own traditional sauce to make it even more special. Oaxacans are proud of their food, and rightly so, for its flavor can be subtle or very intense, but always pure."

The classes range from one day to one week, and cover everything from making tamales to the lost art of grinding chocolate for mole on the metate. Classes include Seven Regions of Oaxaca, Food of the Gods, *Dia de Muertos* Festival, To Grandmother's House We Go, *Navidad y Tres Reyes*, and Regional Oaxacan Cuisine.

You'll visit local markets, molinos, and cheese makers, and harvest herbs and vegetables from Susana's fields. Archeological and cultural tours are included, as well as classes and visits which cover everything from pineapple plantations to folk dances to rug-weaving.

The weeklong *Dia de Muertos* (Day of the Dead) Festival class is typical. Lessons are hands-on, and cover traditional chocolate and bread making, altar building, and black mole making. You'll be invited into local homes to participate in the fiesta, and will visit markets, a mezcal factory, cheese and bread makers, and archaeological ruins.

The culinary focus is on pre-Hispanic food and its modern adaptations. A sample menu is: *Sopa de Esquites*, Tostadas de Pipián, Ensalada de Nopales Asados, *Mole Coloradito* or *Amarillo*, *Arroz Blanco con Platanos Fritos*, and *Patel de Mi Abuela Relleno con Guayaba*. Other dishes you may learn to make include *Sopa de Ajo con Flor de Calabaza*, *Ensalada de Piña, Jícama y Aguacate, Estofado de Pollo*, and *Flan de Coco*.

Rancho Aurora, Susana's home, is a hillside farm located between San Lorenzo Cacaotepec and San Felipe Tejalapan (a Zapotec village where handmade tortillas are the major cottage industry) and overlooking the pueblo of San Lorenzo Cacaotepec, Etla. You can stay in a private bungalow at the ranch or in Oaxaca City at Casa Colonial or Posada de Chencho, which are comfortable bed and breakfasts with lovely gardens.

Susana recently published her cookbook, *Seasons of My Heart, A Culinary Journal through Oaxaca, Mexico*, and produced the accompanying PBS television series.

THE DETAILS: Classes run from one day to one week and are offered year-round. Group size is limited to twelve. Costs will include accommodations, all meals (except the one-day classes), hotel accommodations, and airport transfers. Credit cards are not accepted.

One day group: $65 per person (minimum of four people)
One day private: $250 (for one to three people)
Weekend: $850
One week: $1,595

Contact:
Susana Trilling
Seasons of My Heart Cooking School
Rancho Aurora
AP #42 Admon. 3
Oaxaca, 68101 MEXICO
Phone/Fax: 52-951-87726
E-mail: seasons@spersaoaxaca.com.mx
Web site: www.seasonsofmyheart.com

· 6 ·

AUSTRIA, BRAZIL, ENGLAND, GREECE, IRELAND, MOROCCO, SPAIN, AND TURKEY

WHAT DO A CASTLE in Ireland, a yacht off the coast of Greece, a pasha's palace in Morocco, a sixteenth-century estate in the Suffolk countryside, and fine hotels in Vienna and Spain and Greece have in common? They all offer cooking vacations—with enlightening lessons, delicious feasts, cheerful company, and extraordinary excursions.

You can stay in San Sebastián, and learn the secrets of traditional and contemporary Basque cuisine. You can cruise down the Aegean coast, exploring ancient ruins when you're not cooking regional specialties. You can see the snake charmers of Marrakesh or the produce markets of Crete, or visit the palaces of Vienna or the artisan food producers of Ireland (where you'll visit traditional pubs as well). You can stay in Rio de Janeiro or Ouro Preto, a seventeenth-century colonial town in the Brazilian mountains. Or you can stay at a fifteenth-century manor house five miles from Oxford, enjoying the luxurious rooms, Michelin two-star restaurant, delightful gardens, and delicious lessons.

Perhaps you want to explore the Gothic Quarter in Barcelona. Or the English food market in Cork. How about the ruins of an ancient Dorian port (famed for its cult of Aphrodite) or the antique shops of Woodbridge or the souks of Fez? They're all here, in this section of less common, but outstanding, destinations.

• THE ART OF LIVING TOURS •

France, Ireland, Italy, Morocco,
Spain, and the United States

"It's something of a moveable feast," says Sara Monick of her Art of Living tours. "Every year I do different programs: I've been in France, Italy, Spain, Morocco, Ireland, and California. The one thing they have in common is I never plan a trip I wouldn't love to go on!

"The trips reflect my interests: cuisine, wine, regional style and culture, markets (I'm a true market maven), decorative arts and artisans. My guests and I have done everything from truffle hunting to visiting an escargot farm. We've visited modest houses inhabited by delightful people and very elegant homes inhabited by aristocrats. We've eaten at simple regional restaurants to those that carry Michelin stars. I run the gamut, because I think it all contributes to understanding the culture of a region."

For example, her trip, **The Treasures of the Mediterranean Spain—Barcelona, Catalonia, Mallorca**, offers an insider's look at the art, architecture, artisans, markets, and cuisine of this lovely corner of Spain. You will visit the Gothic Quarter in Barcelona and tour many museums (including a lecture at the Picasso Museum and a visit to the Miro Foundation). You'll also stroll past the bird and flower markets on the Ramblas, enjoy lunches, dinners, and cocktails in many private homes, and be taught regional specialties by local chefs—learning, for example, how to make Mallorca's most beloved pastry, *ensaimada*.

Sara also offers vacations in France and Italy. Her trip, **Cooking** in *Provence at Hostellerie de Crillon le Brave*, includes five days of classes in the *Hostellerie*'s kitchen. Guests explore the fundamental elements of Provençal cuisine while covering the basic techniques of fish and meat cookery, stocks and sauces, and desserts. There are also excursions to markets and wine cellars, visits to Avignon and Carpentras, and even a hunt for the elusive black truffle. "For a hands on experience," Sara says, "this program is absolutely top notch. Chef Phillipe Monti imparts as much information as students can absorb . . . in a wonderfully relaxed atmosphere."

There's also her **Treasures of Venice and the Veneto** trip: Live in a twelfth-century antique-filled palazzo, go on guided tours of the Sacred Gardens of Venice and many private gardens, cruise the Grand Canal, visit artisans' workshops, and enjoy local specialties and wines in private homes and restaurants.

And Sara also offers **At Home in the Loire—From Market to Kitchen:** Stay in a private château, *La Mahaudiere*, and visit gardens and markets, join an art historian for trips to museums and historic châteaux, attend a lesson on flower arranging, and learn to prepare (and be prepared to enjoy!) the cuisine of this region that was once the playground of French royalty.

"I seek out the opportunities that are so hard to find on your own," Sara says. "Cuisine is a marvelous entrée into a country: It isn't just food, it's agriculture, history, culture, and pleasure."

THE DETAILS: The details of Sara's trips vary. The programs usually run from a week to a week and a half. Group size is limited from six to fourteen. The costs generally include accommodations, all breakfasts, most lunches and dinners, all travel within the trip, cooking lessons, and, sometimes, additional guides and lecturers. Noncooking partners may attend at a reduced (sometimes significantly reduced) price.

The Costs: $2,300–$4,700
Single Supplement: $300–$800

Contact:
The Art of Living Tours
Sara Monick
4215 Poplar Drive
Minneapolis, MN 55422
Phone: 612-374-2444
Fax: 612-374-3290
E-mail: Monick4215@aol.com

The Art of Living Tours
Hilliard and Olander Ltd.
608 Second Avenue South
Minneapolis, MN 55402
Phone: 800-229-8407; 612-333-1440
Fax: 612-333-3554
E-mail: Diane@Hilliardolander.com

• A TASTE OF VIENNA •

Austria

The American awareness of Viennese food tends not to extend beyond wiener schnitzel. But the cuisine of Vienna is a complex and tasty melange of regional adaptations from countries that were once all united under the Hapsburg crown: Germany, the Netherlands, Czechoslovakia, Hungary, Yugoslavia, Romania, Italy, part of Russia and France, and even Spain. The Taste of Vienna tours offers the chance to discover this misunderstood (and sometimes unpronounceable) cuisine—featuring dishes such as *palatschinken, tafelspitz, sacher torte,* and *mehlspeisen.*

Guests live in a four-star hotel while attending hands-on cooking classes at Vienna's leading professional cooking school, AM

Judenplatz (which was featured on Robin Leach's *Gourmet Getaways* TV show—he made the apple strudel). In three or four half-day classes, guests learn to prepare traditional and contemporary dishes. The traditional recipes, some of which are more than a thousand years old, include Viennese potato soup and wiener schnitzel. Contemporary recipes include Steamed White Asparagus with Bread-Crumb Butter Sauce, Pike or Perch in Horseradish Sauce with Saffron Rice, French Beans with Dill Sauce, and Poppyseed Cake.

Classes are taught by professional chefs, who work under the director of the school, Franz Zodl, well known in Austria for his cooking television appearances. The trip is led by native Austrian Susanne Marie Servin, so you're sure to get an authentic experience.

You'll also have a chance to tour the city and surroundings. You'll see the Inner City, the famous Ring Strasse, St. Stephen's Gothic Cathedral, the Imperial Winter Palace, the Schönbrunn Palace, the (former Imperial) Augarten Porcelain Factory, and Palais Esterhazy. Susanne also offers walking tours throughout the city, and will arrange for you to attend one of the many classical music concerts that take place more or less constantly in the concert halls and palaces of the city.

Susanne is happy to accommodate spouses and children. The lodging is the same and the programs for children include activities that are interesting to kids.

THE DETAILS: The program runs one week and is offered March through May and October through December. Group size is limited to eighteen. The cost includes round trip airfare, accommodations, two meals per day, cooking lessons, and excursions, entrance fees, and guides.

The Cost: $2,475
Single Supplement: $255

Contact:
Susanne Marie Servin
Herzerl Tours
127 West 26th Street
New York, NY 10001
Phone: 800-684-8488; 212-366-4245
Fax: 212-366-4195
E-mail: sm@herzerltours.com
Web site: www.herzerltours.com

From the kitchen of A Taste of Vienna

❧

VIENNESE *RINDSGULASCH*
(VIENNESE GOULASH)

Susanne Marie Servin writes: In Vienna, when ordering goulash in a restaurant, the waiter will assure diners that it is freshly made. "How many days ago?" asks the prudent diner, knowing full well that goulash tastes best when warmed up. As for vitamins that supposedly get destroyed by reheating the goulash—anyone in Vienna will assure you that a good goulash gives you strength, no matter what.

1½ pounds beef	Fat for frying
1½ pounds onions	Salt
1 tablespoon paprika	A pinch of marjoram
1 tablespoon tomato purée	A pinch of caraway seeds
(optional)	A dash of vinegar

Slice the onions finely and cut the beef into cubes. In a saucepan, fry the onions in fat until golden brown. Add paprika and stir once, then add 2 tablespoons water. Add the beef, stirring until water has evaporated. Add the tomato purée, salt, a dash of vinegar, the mar-joram, and the caraway seeds.

Cover and simmer very gently until meat is tender, adding water only in very small quantities as it becomes necessary. When the meat is soft, add a little more water, increase the heat under the saucepan, stir well, and cook for a few more minutes.

If you want more gravy, add a scant tablespoon of flour (mixed with a little water) before adding of water. Stir and then proceed as described above, adding more water as necessary.

There are 101 tricks to create the perfect goulash. Some people add a crushed clove of garlic with the caraway seeds, or a green or red pepper cut into strips instead of the garlic. Some people add a dash of strong black coffee while others insist that an extra table-spoon of vinegar or a teaspoon of grated lemon rind is the secret. Explore and enjoy—and serve with bread dumplings or plain boiled potatoes (having added a pinch of caraway seeds to the potato water while cooking).

• ACADEMY OF COOKING •
AND OTHER PLEASURES

Ouro Preto, Brazil

Ouro Preto is a seventeenth-century colonial town in the mountains of Minas Gerais. It's one of the world's best preserved exam-
ples of colonial baroque architecture, and was declared a "Cultural
Patrimony of Humankind" by UNESCO. It's also the home of Yara
Castro Robert's Academy of Cooking and Other Pleasures.

"Cooking is an art form, an anthropological window, and a historical bridge," Yara says. "I want to bring people together who are
interested in the culinary arts from many points of view."

Her emphasis on the many pleasures of Brazilian cuisine and life
are apparent from the first night. After you arrive in Ouro Preto—
you'll be staying at the Hotel *Solar do Rosario*, a five-star hotel—
you'll have drinks, appetizers, an introductory lecture about the
people and cultures of Brazil, and will then enjoy live Brazilian
music at the hotel or in the neighborhood.

Starting on the second day, there are four or five hours of activities—cooking classes, walking tours, field trips—in the morning,
followed by individually tailored activities in the evening, specifically organized for any of the guests' special or newly discovered
interests.

For example, you might start the day with a field trip to
Cachacaria, to watch the manufacture of sugar cane alcohol, and a
visit to various artists' studios. Then you'd have a cooking class
focusing on Brazilian cookies, cakes, and pastries, followed by a traditional Brazilian "high coffee" and a visit to a religious or popular
festival or carnival. Finally, you'd enjoy a gourmet dinner at Restaurant *Casa do Ouvidor*, with dishes prepared and presented by Chef
Goncalves.

The next morning you might visit a colonial farm or a three-
hundred-year-old coffee plantation for a walking tour followed by a

short lecture and a coffee tasting. A cooking class focusing on the cuisine of Bahia or the Amazon would then precede a music performance by classic musicians performing an outdoor Serenata. Dinner and dancing might be at the hotel or at *Le Coq d'Or*, where Chef Milton Schneider will demonstrate his creations.

You can also look forward to a demonstration of Brazilian candy making, a classical music performance in a nearby church, a tour of a traditional miller's business, horseback riding or hiking, a day of driving the old colonial gold route through nearby mountain villages, or a visit to a colorful and lively farmer's market.

Yara was born in Belo Horizonte, the capital of Minas Gerais, where she began her culinary education under the directon of her mother, Belita de Castro, a well-known chef, caterer, and cooking school owner. Yara is also the subject of the video, *Brazilian Cuisine with Yara Roberts*, and was the host of an Emmy-nominated PBS-WGBH cooking show that focused on cuisine and cultural tradition. She has taught at a number of universities and cooking schools and organizations.

Arrangements can be made for people who want to accompany a participant without attending cooking sessions.

THE DETAILS: The program runs one week. Group size is limited to ten. The cost includes accommodations, all breakfasts and gourmet meals, cooking lessons, events, field trips, and transportation to and from the airport. The cost also includes an optional night in Rio de Janeiro.

The Cost: $2,650

Contact:
Yara Castro Roberts
256 Marlborough Street
Boston, MA 02116
Phone: 617-262-8455

Fax: 617-267-0786
E-mail: rbr2@earthlink.net

Judy Ebrey
Cuisine International
PO Box 25228
Dallas, TX 75225
Phone: 214-373-1161
Fax: 214-373-1162
E-mail: CuisineInt@aol.com
Web site: www.cuisineinternational.com

*From the kitchen of the Academy of Cooking
and Other Pleasures*

●

QUINDIM DE YAYÁ (COCONUT CUSTARD)

SERVES 8

9 egg yolks
3 whole eggs
1 pound sugar
3 tablespoons butter
1 medium coconut, grated (about 2 1/2 cups) or
    1 bag of grated unsweetened coconut
1/2 cup raisins

Heat 1/2 gallon of water, and preheat oven to 350°. Using a whisk, beat the whole eggs lightly. Add the yolks, beating until the mixture is homogeneous. Melt 2 tablespoons of the butter. Add the sugar and coconut, mix well, and add the melted butter.

Coat a mold with the remaining 1 tablespoon of butter, and sprinkle with sugar. Shake to remove excess. Place the raisins around the bottom of the mold and gently pour in the mixture.

Place the mold in the center of a roasting pan, and carefully fill the pan with water. Bake the mold in this double-bath for 1 hour. Check with a toothpick for doneness (the toothpick should come out dry). Allow to cool and unmold on a serving dish.

Decorate with tropical flowers and sprigs of mint. Serve at room temperature.

• SANDY'S BRAZILIAN CUISINE •
Brazil

This Brazilian culinary tour begins in Rio de Janeiro, where you'll be greeted with a welcome cocktail party and a light dinner at your four- or five-star hotel. The next morning, you go on a city tour, visiting Copacabana and Ipanema, and then drive to Barra da Tijuca, where you'll visit the Tijuca rainforest and Corcovado Mountain (site of a 125-foot Christ the Redeemer statue) before enjoying dinner and a samba show at a local restaurant.

Over the next several days, you'll go on a full day excursion to Angra dos Reis island, attend hands-on cooking classes with Margarida Nogueira of *Aventuras na Cozinha* (Adventures in the Kitchen) cooking school, and have dinner at local restaurants, such as *Mistura Fina* in Lagoa Freitas (where you'll be served the famous drink *caipirinha de lima*).

You also visit Buzios, home of some of the most beautiful beaches in the world, for sunbathing, swimming, scuba diving, snorkeling, and boat riding. You stop at Niteroi for lunch and a visit to the art museum, followed by dinner. You make a morning visit to an open market in Ipanema, where you'll inspect the tropical fruits and vegetables before returning to Margarida's for another cooking class.

And you spend a day at Petropolis, with lunch at the Gourmet Valley in Itaipava, and see the famous *Dedo de Deus* Mountain in Terezopolis Park.

Sandy Allen, your tour direction, has taught in Santa Barbara, Paris, New York, and New Jersey. And Margarida Nogueira, who teaches most of the classes, is a food writer, restaurant critic, and chef.

DETAILS: The program runs ten days. Group size is twenty to thirty. The cost includes accommodations, all breakfasts, most lunches and dinners, cooking classes, excursions, and round-trip airfare from New York (although individual arrangements can be made for guests coming from other gateways).

The Cost: $3,895
Single Supplement: $1,500

Contact:
Sandy Allen
827 Oronoke Road, #8-3
Waterbury, CT 06708
Phone: 203-596-9685
E-mail: Sandyna@juno.com

Lily Levy-Harhay
Celestial Voyagers, Inc.
Phone: 800-676-7843; 718-237-2312
Fax: 718-237-2031
E-mail: lilytti@aol.com

From the kitchen of Sandy's Brazilian Cuisine

●

CHEETAH'S MILK (*LEITE DE ONCA*)

A very popular drink in Brazil, often served as an after dinner liqueur.

> 1 quart white rum
> 1 quart coconut milk
> 1 cup cold water
> 2 14-ounce cans of sweetened condensed milk
> Mint leaves or cinnamon sticks for garnish

Blend all the liquid together for about 1 minute (you may have to blend this quantity in 2 batches). Serve well chilled in small aperitif glasses with mint leaf or cinnamon stick.

To preserve: Pour into quart-sized sterilized glass bottles and refrigerate, or give as gifts. Cheetah's Milk will keep in the refrigerator for about 6 months.

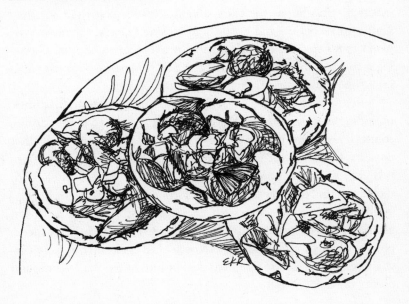

· The Ashburton Centre— · Vegetarian Cookery Course

South Devon, England

When the Ashburton Centre first opened in 1994, as a resort and learning center, it didn't offer a cookery course. But the guests, delighted with the meals they were being served, started requesting classes—now cookery is the most popular course. The Ashburton Centre is located in the South Devon countryside, directly next to a moor leading into Dartmoor National Park, and close to downtown Ashburton, known for its colorful secondhand bookstores, antiques and local crafts, quiet lanes and small alleyways, and Georgian houses.

The cookery course is vegetarian and focuses on learning to cook "from the heart." Chef Stella West-Harling says that many guests, even those with a strong background in cooking, lack the self-confidence to throw away the cookbook and follow their own instincts. She hopes to teach students to develop their intrinsic ability to recognize and create fine cuisine. That's not to say you won't follow recipes in this course—you'll receive a cookery booklet at the beginning of class—but the goal is to move beyond recipes into a more direct experience of food and cooking.

You'll spend three days learning to make vegetarian dishes, including sauces, nut loaves, Indian curries, bean and savory dishes, soups, breads and croissants, cheesecakes, party cakes, and other desserts. Classes, which combine demonstration and participation, take place in a farmhouse kitchen designed by the chef, with reclaimed timber and old granite flagstones on the floor.

"Students' experiences with cooking vary," says Stella. "I am always delighted to hear little cooking 'secrets' which I can incorporate into my work. And the inexperienced cooks do not feel overwhelmed either. There is a great deal of fun during our lessons, and plenty of work."

The cooking class allows plenty of free time to explore the surrounding area and the center itself: You might want to take a dip in the spring-fed heated outdoor swimming pool, wander around the center (which is a Georgian property built in 1819), enjoy a book by one of the marble fireplaces or in the courtyard, or relax in the sauna.

Stella has been an organic and vegetarian cook for the past twenty-five years, and has been a restaurant owner and caterer.

THE DETAILS: The program runs three days and is offered throughout the year. The cost includes accommodations, all meals, and cooking lessons.

The Cost: £195 (approx. $320)
Single Supplement: £10 per night (approx. $17)

Contact:
The Ashburton Centre
79 East Street
Ashburton
South Devon TQ13 7AL
ENGLAND
Phone: 44-1364 652 784
Fax/Message: 44-1364 653 825

From the kitchen of the Ashburton Centre

◦

CAN'T GO WRONG PASTRY WITH TOMATO, OLIVE, AND FETA FILLING

This pastry can be used for quiche or pie. Included below is a tomato, olive, feta filling. Makes one 9-inch quiche base or five small pie bases.

1/2 cup flour
1/2 teaspoon of salt
1/4 cup Crisco or other solid vegetable fat
2 tablespoons of ice water
1 tablespoon of vegetable oil, mixed with the ice water

Mix flour and salt together in a bowl.

Cut the vegetable fat into small pieces and rub into the flour. (The trick is to use the tips of your fingers—the less you touch it the better the pastry.) It should look like bread crumbs.

Slowly fold the mixed ice water and vegetable oil into the flour with a metal spoon. As soon as it starts to bind together, stop.

Press firmly into a ball and roll out onto a floured surface. Lay the rolled dough into a pie dish or five ramekins, let set in the refrigerator for 10 minutes, then fill with your choice of filling.

TOMATO, OLIVE, AND FETA FILLING
FOR FIVE RAMEKINS

PER RAMEKIN:
3 cherry tomatoes, halved (6 halves per pie)
3 or more pitted black olives
A healthy sprinkling of feta cheese

Salt and pepper to taste
Fresh basil

Fill each ramekin with the tomatoes, olives, feta, and salt and pepper.
Bake at 350° for 15 minutes, or until pastry is light golden brown.
Sprinkle fresh chopped basil leaves over the top before serving.

• THE EARNLEY CONCOURSE •

West Sussex, England

The Earnley Concourse is a retreat center that offers courses in a
variety of subjects, including history, literature, music appreciation,
dance, health and fitness, painting and sketching, and, of course,
food and wine.

The cooking courses include Better Baking: Tea Time Favorites,
in which you'll learn the basics of making cakes, scones, muffins,
cookies, meringues, biscuits and teabreads; Cooking and Eating the
Japanese Way, in which you learn to cook sushi and tempura; and
Chinese, Italian, and French cooking. There are also courses in
cooking with wine, cooking for Christmas, and a "Chocoholics"
weekend which promises to "expand your mind, not to mention
your waistline." Finally, Earnley offers courses in wine tasting and
beer brewing (which takes you through the whole process of brewing from raw ingredients to the actual drinking).

Located on ten acres of countryside, close to the sea, Earnley
offers a relaxed and comfortable atmosphere: All rooms have en
suite bathrooms, refreshment trays, color televisions and full or twin
size beds. Meals are served in the self-service dining room—a full
English breakfast and homemade lunches and dinners. When not in
cooking class you can take advantage of the indoor swimming pool,

games and recreation room, the ten acres of garden and parkland, and the newly created indoor garden.

All of the cooking classes are taught by professionals in a kitchen workshop with a demonstration area, dining facilities, and work areas for students. Some of the courses include a self-prepared dinner as part of the class.

THE DETAILS: All programs run three days and are offered year-round. Group size is limited to twelve. The costs include accommodations and one cooking course. Some of the programs have additional fees requested to cover the cost of ingredients, usually no more than £30.

Cooking courses: £155 (approx. $255)
Wine and beer courses: £175 (approx. $290)

Contact:
The Earnley Concourse
Earnley, Chichester
West Sussex, PO20 7JL
ENGLAND
Phone: 44-1243 670392
Fax: 44-1243 670832
E-mail: info@earnley.co.uk

• HINTLESHAM HALL •

Suffolk, England

Built in the 1570s by the grandson of the Duke of Norfolk and set on more than 175 acres of Suffolk countryside, Hintlesham Hall is a lovely estate house that incorporates more than four hundred years of elegant architectural influence.

The hall offers a weekend retreat of relaxation and sightseeing combined with a one-day cooking course. It is within easy traveling distance of a traditional sixteenth-century wool merchant's village, Gainsborough's (the portrait artist) house, the Newmarket race courses, the coastal town of Aldeburgh (famous for its music festival), Melford and Woodbridge (both full of antique shops), Cambridge, and the cathedral city of Norwich.

Not that you ever have to leave Hintlesham Hall: there's an eighteen-hole (par seventy-two) golf course, an elegant restaurant, a fitness gym, and a pool, and trout fishing, clay pigeon shooting, horseback riding, snooker, and croquet.

The cookery course begins in an elegantly appointed drawing room with fresh coffee and homemade shortbread. You then move into the kitchen for a cooking demonstration from Alan Ford, the head chef. Seasonal produce is always used and Chef Alan organizes the demonstration around the best quality of food available—often incorporating fresh herbs from the hall's garden. You'll learn recipes for two appetizers, two main courses and two desserts, and will then partake in a leisurely three course lunch in the dining room hosted by the chef.

Chef Alan Ford has been at Hintlesham Hall since 1988, and has cooked for restaurants in London and Australia for over twenty years.

Travel partners and children are welcome, and will have no trouble finding something wonderful to occupy their time. There is a zoo and wild animal park close by for children's amusement; however, children younger than ten are not allowed in the dining room or lounge at dinner.

THE DETAILS: The program runs one day and is offered in the winter, spring, summer, and fall. A special Christmas program is offered as well. Group size is limited to twelve. Accommodations at the hall range from a small double room to a suite with a separate sitting room and include a generous continental breakfast, complimentary newspaper, and service. A slight discount is applied the eve of the cookery program. It's also possible to stay in a local bed-and-breakfast instead of at the hall.

Cooking Class: £47 (approx. $80)
Hintlesham Hall: £105–£300 (approx. $175–$495)

Contact:
Hintlesham Hall
Hintlesham, Ipswich
Suffolk, IP8 3NS ENGLAND
Phone: 01473-652334
Fax: 04173-652463
E-mail: reservations@hintlesham-hall.co.uk

COCKTAILS FROM HINTLESHAM HALL

ALL AROUND THE WORLD
1 part banana liqueur
1 part whiskey
$1/2$ part cointreau
$1/2$ part orange juice

Put all ingredients into a cocktail shaker over ice. Shake and pour into a cocktail glass. Garnish with orange and banana.

BLUE LAGOON
2 parts vodka
1 part blue curacao
1 part fresh cream
1 part lemonade

Mix vodka and blue curacao together in a shaker. Pour over ice into a tall glass. Add lemonade and float the cream on top. Garnish with coconut and fruit kebab.

· LE PETIT BLANC, · L'ECOLE DE CUISINE

Great Milton, England

"Fun is the word most often used by our cookery students to describe their days in *L'Ecole de Cuisine*," says director Alan Murchison. "Many students arrive a little worried about the level of their cooking skills, but they realize very quickly that the only qualifications required are a love of food and the desire to learn more about preparing and cooking it."

The school is located at Chef Raymond Blanc's *Le Manoir aux Quat' Saisons* restaurant housed in a fifteenth-century manor house in the Cotswold village of Great Milton, eight miles from Oxford. Everything is luxury: from the superb guest quarters (Raymond says, "A room tells you how to behave. I wanted rooms that would give the message that you're here to enjoy and celebrate life.") to the flower and vegetable gardens to blazing log fires and afternoon tea to dining in the Michelin two-star restaurant and enjoying brandy and sweets in the parlor after dinner.

You check in on Sunday, settle in to your room, explore the

Manor, and then enjoy a three-course dinner at the restaurant. Classes begin the next morning after your continental breakfast. You begin with an introduction to the kitchen, and then learn how to make hot and cold starters, including soufflés and homemade ravioli.

"The first recipe," Alan says, "is a ravioli of wild mushrooms. Students already look nervous, because pasta is so tricky and time consuming. Then I get out the food processor, throw all the ingredients in, and whiz. The pasta is made and the myths dispelled in just two minutes."

After lunch, the class reconvenes until afternoon tea. You're then free until dinner is served in the restaurant. On Tuesday, you focus on the selection of fresh fish, accompanied by vegetables, such as nage de poissons and papillote de saumon et turbot. Wednesday's course focuses on meats and sauces, and on Thursday the class covers patisseries, including a chocolate demonstration, and ends with a seven-course menu *gourmand* and presentation of certificates.

L'Ecole de Cuisine welcomes budding cooks, from the complete novice to the experienced enthusiast—and also partners of participants, who can stay throughout the course, and are charged only for meal and drinks.

THE DETAILS: The program runs for four days and is offered year-round, excluding June and July. Group size is limited to ten. The cost includes accommodations, all meals with wine, and cooking lessons.

The Cost: £1,375 (approx. $2,700)
Single Supplement: £225 (approx. $370)

Contact:
Le Manoir aux Quat' Saisons
Church Road, Great Milton
Oxford, OX44 7PD ENGLAND

Toll free, North America only: 800-845-4274
Phone: 44-1844 278-881
Fax: 44-1844 278-847
E-mail: lemanoir@blanc.co.uk
Web site: www.manoir.com

In the United States:
Judy Ebrey
Cuisine International
PO Box 25228
Dallas, TX 75225
Phone: 214-373-1161
Fax: 214-373-1162
E-mail: CuisineInt@aol.com
Web site: www.cuisineinternational.com

• WORLD CULINARY ARTS— •
CULINARY JOURNEY TO GREECE

Athens and Crete, Greece

"In the global society, the identity or 'flavor' of each country can get lost in translation," says Nikki Rose, the director of World Culinary Arts. "The history behind a unique dish is forgotten—its origins unknown. But our **Culinary Journey to Greece** immerses guests in the distinctive culinary history of Greece. We discover the array of flavors of traditional and modern Greek cuisine, we meet farmers who maintain a passion for producing the highest quality (often organic) culinary items such as cheese, honey, olive oil, and wine, and we learn from noted chefs who specialize in traditional, eclectic, and international Greek cuisine."

The program is an intensive educational tour that begins in Athens and continues in Crete. It includes classes with experts in the fields of agriculture and organic farming methods, anthropology, gastronomy, nutrition, and viticulture, as well as cooking demonstrations and kitchen sessions with guest chefs.

The tour was originally designed for professional chefs, but is now open to nonprofessional culinary enthusiasts—and, in fact, includes a few classes in the fundamentals of cooking techniques to ensure that all participants know the basics. Still, it's an intensive course, not just a casual romp between restaurants (although there is time set aside for exploring the countryside, fishing, and general relaxing).

After your arrival in Greece, you'll spend several days in Athens—eating traditional and modern Greek meals, attending a lecture series, visiting the Acropolis, enjoying lunch near the ancient Plaka, touring Central Market in Athens for produce identification and tasting, and enjoying a banquet of regional specialties.

Then you'll travel to Hania, Crete—the center of Minoan civilization, where age-old agricultural and cooking techniques still live in today's farms and kitchens. Your first night will feature a traditional Cretan dinner and a lecture of the culinary history of Crete. Over the following days, you will meet local producers of specialty items, attend lectures covering indigenous produce, organic farming, and the health benefits of the Cretan diet, and enjoy meals prepared by host chefs.

Then you'll journey from Hania to Eolounda, stopping on the way at the ancient palace of Knossos where you'll tour the ruins and surrounding farmland. In Eolounda, you'll go on a fishing trip with local fishermen, and attend a fish cooking session before enjoying a seafood dinner at a local restaurant. You'll cook with chefs from small taverns and large resorts, experimenting with products indigenous to the region, some of which you will have collected yourself from the land or sea.

During the next few days in Eolounda, you will have a field trip to the eastern edge of Crete (Sitia and surrounding area), will attend a number of cooking sessions, and will eat lunch in village restaurants, dinner at the renowned Ferryman Taverna, and a farewell feast.

Nikki is currently developing culinary cruises in Greece.

THE DETAILS: The program runs ten days and is offered in May and September. The group size is limited to twenty. The cost includes hotel accommodations (single occupancy), breakfast daily, designated lunches and dinners, all lectures and demonstrations, and travel within Greece.

The Cost: $3,250–$4,500 (depending on itinerary and season)

Contact:
Nikki Rose
1627 R Street NW #401
Washington, DC, 20009
Phone: 202-462-6225
Fax: 202-518-6958
E-mail: NRoseWCA@aol.com

• THE BALLYMALOE •
COOKERY SCHOOL

County Cork, Ireland

Ballymaloe House, once a Geraldine castle, has been remodeled for modern convenience and aesthetics throughout the centuries. It now features contemporary comforts, while still retaining its fourteenth-century keep, Norman tower, and elegant, old-world feeling. The estate is also a working farm, and sits on almost four hundred acres of beautiful Irish countryside near the sea.

In the early 1980s Tim and Darina Allen, the current owners, opened a professional cooking school at Ballymaloe which as been an integral part of the estate ever since. The culinary emphasis is on Irish country cuisine, combining the traditional cooking of Myrtle Allen, the matriarch of the Allen family, with modern recipes and tastes. Darina, head chef at the school, is the author of many cookbooks based on the recipes of Ballymaloe and has her own television series on Irish television.

On the day you arrive at Ballymaloe, you'll tour the ornamental herb, vegetable, and fruit gardens and attend a talk about the current renaissance in Irish cuisine before sitting down to a welcome dinner.

Your second day begins with a visit to the local "strand" (shoreline) to collect periwinkles. Then you'll visit the workshop and showroom of Ireland's foremost potter, Stephen Pearce, have afternoon tea with Lana Pringle in her delightful cottage on the edge of the village, and then either return to Ballymaloe to relax, or travel on to St. Coleman's Cathedral in Cloyne.

On the following day, you'll visit a dairy farm in Schull to see how Gubbeen Cheese is made, take a short trip to Hare Island for

lunch at the acclaimed Island Cottage (only accessible by boat), and then wind your way home in the afternoon through the charming villages of West Cork, stopping at local craft and antiques stores.

The fourth morning you'll find yourself back in the kitchen at Ballymaloe, learning how to make such dishes as Fish Mousse with Mussel Sauce, Roast Goose, Spicy Lamb with Eggplant, and Calf's Liver Flamed in Irish Whiskey, as well as Ballymaloe's famed dessert, Irish Mist Soufflé. You'll spend the afternoon exploring the farm, swimming in the pool, playing tennis, croquet, or golf, or taking a leisurely walk on the beach.

The final day includes another cooking lesson, lunch in the garden, and a visit to a fish smokery to taste smoked salmon, mussels, and eel. You'll also visit the English food market in Cork for its overflowing stalls of local produce, olives, cheeses, patés, and Cork delicacies such as tripe and drisheen.

You'll spend every evening at dinner with the Allens—in the estate dining room or garden café, or at a private home in Shanagarry—and at least one night at a traditional Irish pub.

Children and spouses are welcome, and there is plenty to keep them entertained on the farm. For children, there is a sandpit, pool, and tea room, and the Allen grandchildren to play with.

Ballymaloe also offers a twelve-week professional training program as well as shorter one- to three-day courses in a wide variety of subjects—not limited to cooking. Some of the cooking courses include Valentine's Day Cooking, Irresistible Breakfasts, Pub Grub, Bread Making, A Taste of Mexico, and A Taste of India (both favorite international cuisines of Darina's). Noncooking courses include Organic Gardening, Grow Your Own Herbs, Seed Saving—a Forgotten Skill, The Power of Relationships, Paint Finishes, The Wisdom of Vulnerability, and Wonderful Weddings.

THE DETAILS: The program runs one week and is offered in September. The cost includes accommodations, all meals, and excursions.

The Cost: £ 1,950 (approx. $3,210)
Other Courses Cost: £75–£265 ($125–$440)

Contact:
The Ballymaloe Cookery School
Kinoith, Shanagarry
Co. Cork, IRELAND
Phone: 353 21 646785; 353 21 646727
Fax: 353 21 646909
E-mail: enquiries@ballymaloe-cookery-school.ie
Web site: www.ballymaloe-cookery-school.ie

From the kitchen of Ballymaloe

◦

BALLYMALOE CAULIFLOWER SOUP

SERVES 6

3 cups water	Pinch of nutmeg, freshly
2 1/2 pounds cauliflower,	grated
leaves reserved	Salt and freshly ground
2 tablespoons (1/4 stick)	pepper
unsalted butter	Parmesan cheese, freshly
2 tablespoons all-purpose flour	grated
2 cups milk	1 cup croutons, sautéed in
5 tablespoons Parmesan	butter until golden brown
cheese, freshly grated	

Bring 3 cups water to boil in a large heavy saucepan. Coarsely chop cauliflower leaves. Set aside 1/2 cup; add remainder to water. Cover and simmer 25 minutes.

Strain, pressing on leaves to extract as much liquid as possible. Discard the pressed leaves. Return cooking liquid to saucepan. Cut the cauliflower into florets and add to liquid with reserved $^1/_2$ cup leaves. Cover and simmer until cauliflower and leaves are very tender, about 30 minutes.

Meanwhile, melt butter in a small heavy saucepan over low heat. Add flour and cook 2 minutes, stirring frequently. Whisk in the milk. Increase heat and bring to boil, stirring constantly. Reduce heat and simmer 5 minutes, stirring frequently. Mix in 5 tablespoons of Parmesan cheese and nutmeg.

Purée cauliflower with cooking liquid in batches in blender. Return to saucepan. Mix in cheese sauce. Bring to simmer, stirring constantly. Season with salt and pepper. Ladle soup into bowls. Garnish with Parmesan and sautéed croutons and serve.

• COME WITH ME TO THE KASBAH •

Morocco (Casablanca, Fez, Marrakesh, and more)

Kitty Morse, the author of seven cookbooks (including three about North African cuisine) was born and raised in Casablanca. She has offered this culinary tour since 1983, and draws on an extensive network of personal friends and culinary experts to offer guests an authentic Moroccan experience.

Kitty will meet you at the airport and escort you to her family home—a restored pasha's residence within the old city of Azemmour, overlooking the Oum er Rbia river and just ten minutes from the ocean. You'll then spend two days relaxing and enjoying Kitty's cooking classes: you'll learn to make *b'stila* (sweetened chicken and almond phyllo "pie"), traditional couscous, *tangines* (exotic stews), and will prepare dough and bring it to the neighborhood public oven to be baked.

Then you'll travel along the Atlantic coast, from the quaint fishing port and artist colony of Essaouira to Marrakesh, where

you'll spend two nights at a deluxe hotel. While in Marrakesh you'll explore the medina and museums of the fabled Pink City and see the snake charmers and fire-eaters at Djemaa el Fnaa Square.

You'll also cross the High Atlas mountains, past dozens of fortified Berber *Kasbahs*, and descend to the lush, pre-Saharan oases of Ait ben Haddou, Ouarzazate, and Tinerhir. You'll follow the Kasbah trail north to the cedar forest of the Middle Atlas mountains and the Alpine resort *Ifrane*. You'll then spend two nights in Fez, Morocco's cultural capital, visiting the city's labyrinthine, twelve-hundred-year-old *medina*, bustling *souks*, and historic *medersas*. Enjoy elegant meals at private homes, tour the Roman ruins, and visit Volubilis, the holy city of Moulay Idriss, and the eighteenth-century Imperial City of Meknes.

After Fez, you'll travel to Rabat for more sightseeing and a special feast at the Touarga Cooking School on the royal palace grounds. Finally, you'll return to Casablanca to meet local artists, do some last-minute shopping, and enjoy a special farewell *diffa* (Moroccan feast). There's also time for swimming, tennis, and golf (you'll have access to world-class golf courses).

THE DETAILS: The program runs two weeks and is offered in the spring. Group size is limited to eighteen. The cost includes accommodations, most meals, cooking lessons, services of a trilingual guide, all transportation, museum admissions, and round-trip airfare from New York to Casablanca.

The Cost: $4,150

Contact:
Kitty Morse
Adventures in Food and Travel
PO Box 433
Vista, CA 92085-0433
Phone/Fax: 760-758-8631
E-mail: kmorse@adnc.com
Web site: www.kittymorse.com

Natalie Toumi
Carlsbad Travel
2727 Roosevelt Street
Carlsbad, CA 92008
Phone: 800-533-2779; 760-729-9282
Fax: 760-729-9053

From the kitchen of Kitty Morse—
Come with Me to the Kasbah

●

COUSCOUS TIMBALES WITH SHRIMP AND ROASTED RED PEPPER COULIS

SERVES 6

RED PEPPER COULIS:

2 red bell peppers, roasted,
  peeled, and seeded
$1/2$ cup chicken broth
1 garlic clove, minced
2 teaspoons lemon juice

TIMBALES:

3 tablespoons olive oil
1 teaspoon paprika
$1/2$ teaspoon ground cumin
2 cloves garlic, minced
8 ounces medium shrimp,
  shelled and deveined

1 to $1^1/2$ cups chicken broth
$1^1/2$ cup instant couscous
1 red bell pepper
$1/4$ cup fresh cilantro
  (or Chinese parsley),
  minced
3 inner celery stalks, diced
2 teaspoons lemon rind,
  diced
3 tablespoons fresh lemon
  juice
Pepper to taste
6 fresh cilantro leaves for
  garnish

For the coulis: Purée the roasted peppers, chicken broth, and garlic in a blender or food processor. Season with the lemon juice. Set aside.

For the timbales: Heat half the olive oil in a medium skillet over a medium-high heat. Add the paprika, cumin, and garlic. Cook, stirring, until fragrant (1 to 2 minutes). Add the shrimp and cook until they turn pink, about 3 or 4 minutes. Then, with a slotted spoon, transfer the shrimp to a cutting board, cut them crosswise into 4 pieces, and set them aside.

Pour the juice from the skillet into a measuring cup. Add enough chicken broth to make $1^1/2$ cups, then add the remaining olive oil and bring this liquid to a boil in a medium saucepan. Gradually stir in the couscous and remove from heat. Cover and let stand for 5 minutes. Transfer the couscous to a bowl and fluff with a fork. Let cool. Add half the diced pepper, the cilantro, celery, lemon rind, lemon juice, ground pepper, and shrimp. Set aside.

Pack the couscous mixture into a small ramekin and cover with a salad plate. Turn it upside down to unmold the timbale. Repeat the process to make more timbales. Spoon some of the coulis around the base of each timbale, and garnish with the remaining diced red pepper and a cilantro leaf.

• A CULINARY TOUR OF MOROCCO •

Morocco

From the first night's dinner at *Dinarjat*, one of the finest restaurants in Casablanca, to the final Berber lunch at the *Tiout* Oasis, this culinary tour offers a unique taste of Morocco.

You'll visit a seventeenth-century city built by a sultan, with a stable that housed twelve thousand horses and a palace once guarded by twelve hundred eunuchs. You'll spend an afternoon at an ancient Roman outpost, with villas and brothels and mosaic floors. You'll travel to Marrakech (stopping for lunch of mountain trout on the way) to enjoy the Majorelle Gardens (now owned by Yves Saint-Laurent), a museum of Islamic art, and the bazaar. You'll stop at an apricot farm owned by your guide, travel the Road of one thousand Kasbahs, and have dinner in your hotel—which used to be a pasha's palace.

Demonstration cooking courses are offered at *Maison Bleue* (a fourteenth-century palatial home recently converted into a deluxe bed-and-breakfast) and *Yacout* (one of the most famous Moroccan restaurants). And two participation courses at private homes—one in the old city in Marrakech, one in Ouarzazate—will give you hands-on experience.

You'll be eating and cooking Moroccan specialties such as *bastila* (layers of phyllo pastry stuffed with pigeon meat, egg yolks, and almonds, infused with honey and rose water, and covered with cinnamon and sugar icing) and *tajine* (stews made with chicken, pickled lemon, and olives, or mutton and prunes or green peas). You'll also have couscous, *harira* (lentils and chickpea soup), *brochettes* (grilled meat), and honey cakes.

THE DETAILS: The program runs two weeks and is offered in October. Group size is limited to twenty. The cost includes round-trip airfare from New York, accommodations, breakfasts, entrance fees, cooking lessons, and about half the meals.

The Cost: $3,981
Single Supplement: $678

Contact:
Specialty World Travel
186 Alewife Brook Parkway
Cambridge, MA 02138–1102
Phone: 617-476-1142
Fax: 617-661-3354
E-mail: dma@fpt.com
Web site: www.specialtyworldtravel.com

• ANDALUSIAN PANTRY •

Andalusia, Spain

You'll spend your first three days in Spain relaxing at the *Alqueria de Morayma*, a beautiful restored farm-turned-hotel located in the Alpujarras, a mountainous region in the Sierra Nevada Nature

Park. You'll have daily cooking classes on the covered terrace over-looking the valley, and can spend your free time in the swimming pool, hiking to town, on the nature trails, or taking an optional horse trail ride into the mountains.

You'll then travel to Granada, stopping on the way to visit the cave dwellings in Guadix and the ceramics of Purellana. In Granada, you'll visit the Alhambra Palace and Generalife Gardens before having lunch and a cooking presentation at the sixteenth-century Parador de San Francisco. You'll also have a morning walk-ing tour of Granada, lunch at *Galatino* restaurant, a visit to a goat cheese farm, a baking class given by the cloistered nuns of Santa Clara, and lunch at a typical *taberna*. On your last day in Granada you'll visit the outdoor markets, have an Arabic bath and massage, and enjoy a farewell-to-Granada dinner.

The next day you'll travel to Seville by way of Cordoba. In Cor-doba, you'll tour the city and then enjoy a Mozarabe meal at the *Caballo Rojo* restaurant and a cooking class and historical presenta-tion on Andalusian cuisine.

Your stay in Seville also begins with a walking tour, followed by a visit to the cathedral and the eighth-century Alcazar. After a typ-ical paella for lunch, you'll visit Maria Luisa Park and the Santa Cruz Quarter and will dine at the Parador Nacional in Carmona.

Your last two days you'll spend in Costa del Sol. You'll explore Jerez, have lunch in Algeciras, and visit Gibraltar. Finally, before your farewell dinner, you'll have a day of leisure to enjoy the Mediterranean Sea and have a Talaso therapy session.

Your tour leader is Tom Lacalamita, who spends part of each year in Spain (he's married to an Andalusian woman) after having fallen in love with Spain and Spanish cuisine while attending college in Seville. Tom is the author of *The Ultimate Bread Machine* and sev-eral other cookbooks, and is assisted by Madeline Rasmussen who, while American born, has lived in Granada well over thirty years, where she teaches Spanish cooking and language classes.

THE DETAILS: The program runs for ten days. Group size is limited to twenty to thirty guests. The cost includes accommodations, most meals, cooking lessons, excursions, and airfare from New York (although arrangements can be make for guests coming from other gateways).

The Cost: $3,650
Single Supplement: $1,200

Contact:
Lily Levy-Harhay
Celestial Voyagers, Inc.
Phone: 800-676-7843; 718-237-2312
Fax: 718-237 2031
E-mail: lilytti@aol.com

Main office:
Celestial Voyagers, Inc.
79 Watermill Lane
Great Neck, NY 11021
Phone: 800-651-6262; 516-829-1525
Fax: 516-829-0703
E-mail: celestial@isecom.com

• EL CENADOR DE SALVADOR •

Moralzarzal, Spain

El Cendador de Salvador is a four-star hotel in the elegant mountain town of Moralzarzal, twenty-five miles from Spain's capital. The hotel is warm, relaxing, and small—only seven rooms—and boasts such luxuries as private jacuzzis in each air-conditioned room. And,

in addition to the rooms and the excellent restaurant, it offers a cooking course.

Class meets for five hours each morning, and emphasizes "fresh, homemade-quality food infused with a love for the art of cooking." Past favorite recipes have been Salmon and Tuna Tartaré with *Acedera* Sauce, *Pil Pil Hake Coins*, Andalusian Gazpacho with Lobster, Presalted Lamb with Lyonnaise Potatoes, and Chocolate Soufflé with Honey Ice Cream. Classes take place in the hotel's kitchen— a combination of professional stainless steel counters, high-tech cooking equipment and homey touches such as shiny copper pots, bowls of hen fresh eggs, and ceramic spice jars.

Moralzarzal is a lovely small town that offers many cultural opportunities, including trips to museums, art galleries, the theater, and flamenco shows. If you're interested in more active options, horseback riding and golf are also available. And if you're there purely for gastronomic pleasures, wine lessons and dinner reservations at fine restaurants can be arranged.

The classes are taught by Chef Salvador Gallego Jimeniz. Chef Salvador's restaurant in Madrid won a Michelin star, and he has been awarded "Best Chef of the Year," by the Real Gastronomy

Academy of Spain. *El Cenador*, of which he is the owner, was rated the third best restaurant in the Madrid community, the eighth in all of Spain, and the *Gourmet Tour Guide* ranked it as having the best reception and service available in Spain. He has been a guest lecturer at the James Beard Foundation in New York and at the Culinary Institute of America.

THE DETAILS: The program runs five days and is offered January through May. Group size is limited to fourteen. The cost includes accommodations, breakfast, lunch, and cooking lessons. Accommodations range from simple double rooms to suites.

The Cost: 137,000–185,000 pesatas (approx. $875–$1,175)
Single Supplement: 72,000–120,000 pesatas (approx. $450–$750)

Contact:
El Cenador de Salvador
Avda. España 30
28411 Moralzarzal–Madrid
SPAIN
Phone: 91 8577722/10
Fax: 91 8577780

• Luis Irízar Escuela de Cocina •

Basque Country, Spain

Since the 1970s, there has been a renaissance in Basque cooking. Influenced by French nouvelle cuisine, innovative Basque chefs created a new Basque cuisine, offering a modern approach to traditional dishes. Luis Irízar, one of the best-known Spanish chefs, was at the forefront of this movement and now offers a cooking vacation at his cooking school in San Sebastián on the Basque coast.

The *Escuela de Cocina* is primarily a professional cooking school, but it also offers summer programs for nonprofessionals. These vacation programs last two weeks, giving guests a chance to immerse themselves in Basque cuisine and culture—cooking with seafood fresh caught off the coast or in traditional fishing grounds, using fresh ingredients purchased daily in the market, and visiting small coastal fishing towns, nature reserves, ancient Roman ruins, museums, and local festivals.

Each two week cooking session focuses on one theme. Past themes have included: Traditional Basque Cuisine; Salads, Cold Appetizers, and Basic Rices; Assorted Desserts in Today's Cuisine; Great Cuisine in Miniature: *Pintxos* (Tapas); and The Exciting World of Vegetables.

Classes are held in the mornings, and you'll have your afternoons free to explore the beaches, aquarium, cathedrals, and fish and vegetable markets of San Sebastián. Or you can go on excursions to the Guggenheim Museum in Bilbao, surf at the Zurriola beach, play golf, and enjoy the lively San Sebastián nightlife. Peaceful mountain views, removed from the hustle and bustle of the city, are only a short walk from the town center—which also offers several summer festivals: International Jazz in July, Classical Music/Ballet/Opera in August, and International Film in September.

The old part of town is full of bars famous for their tapas (locally known as *pintxos*), with counters overflowing with an array of delicious dishes, from simple potato omelets to *gilda* (chili pepper, salted anchovies, and olives). The bars offer the most sophisticated of fare reduced to its minimum expression—known to Basque chefs as "miniature cooking"—which offer an excellent way to sample typical Basque cuisine.

Classes are taught in Spanish, with English translation available.

THE DETAILS: Classes run Monday through Friday for two weeks, and are offered July through September. Group size is limited to fifteen. The cost includes cooking lessons and some excursions. Guests have to make their own arrangements for lodging; however, the school is happy to make recommendations, and a large variety of options, from one to four stars, is available in San Sebastián.

The Cost: $265

Contact:
Luis Irízar *Escuela de Cocina*
C. Mari
5 Bajo 20003 San Sebastián
SPAIN
Phone: 34-943 431 540
Fax: 34-943 423 553
E-mail: cocina@escuelairizar.com

From the kitchen of Luis Irízar Escuela de Cocina

●

FRESH TUNA WITH ONIONS
AND GREEN PEPPERS

SERVES 4

2 tuna fish steaks (approx. 1 pound each)
$^1/_2$ pint of tomato sauce
$^1/_2$ cup onions, sliced
2 green peppers
1 clove of garlic, thinly sliced
1 cup olive oil
Salt

Heat the olive oil in a saucepan and add the onion and green peppers. When cooked, discard the excess oil, add the tomato sauce and garlic, and simmer for 10 minutes.

Meanwhile, salt and oil the tuna steaks and cook them in the broiler. Once cooked, remove the skins and bones, cut the steaks in 2, and place them in a serving dish. Pour the sauce over the fish and serve.

From the kitchen of Luis Irízar Escuela de Cocina

●

FRIED MILK

3 $^1/_3$ cups of milk
Lemon peel
$^1/_2$ stick of cinnamon
1 cup sugar
$^1/_2$ cup cornstarch

2 tablespoons butter
Flour
1 beaten egg
Olive oil, for frying
Cinnamon to taste

Boil the milk with the lemon peel and $^{1}/_{2}$ stick of cinnamon. Mix the sugar and the cornstarch. Discard the lemon peel and cinnamon stick and add half the milk to the sugar mixture. Dissolve the sugar in the milk and then add the rest of the milk. Boil the mixture slightly, taking care not to let it stick to the bottom of the pan.

Spread the mixture over a tray greased with butter and sprinkle with sugar. Butter the top of the mixture, then leave it to cool.

Once cool, cut it up into rectangles, dip into flour and the beaten egg, and fry them in hot oil.

Strain them well, sprinkle them with sugar and cinnamon, and enjoy.

• EXPEDITIONS IN TURKEY •

Turkey (Istanbul, Gaziantep, the Aegean and Mediterranean Coasts, and more)

Cruise the Aegean and Mediterranean seas on an eighty-foot gulet, a traditional wooden yacht designed for coastal waters, while learning to prepare Turkish specialties such as stuffed eggplant, vegetable salad with yogurt and garlic sauce, and red lentil *koftes*. Study food history, spice use, and regional cuisines, visit small coastal settlements and historical sites and ruins, explore peaceful anchorages, and swim and snorkel in beautiful blue bays.

Kathleen O'Neill of Culinary Expeditions in Turkey offers two culinary cruises and one land-based culinary adventure. Her **first cruise** begins at Bodrum, a resort town (where Kathleen has lived for years) on the Aegean coast. Guests spend the first day on shore, exploring the weekly food market, buying local vegetables, fruits, herbs, spices, and other produce. Then, after a walking tour of the city, a visit to a nearby Crusader castle, and a welcome dinner on the *gulet*, the voyage begins.

You travel along the ancient coastline, cross into the Mediterranean sea, and explore Knidos (the ruins of a Dorian port city famed in antiquity for its cult of Aphrodite), the rock tombs of Caunos, and the remains of the Hellenistic fortress at Loryma on your way toward Gocek harbor in Fethiye Bay, your final destination.

Kathleen's **second cruise** travels through Lycia in the Mediterranean, along the Turquoise Coast. You'll see the underwater ruins at Aperlae, the sunken city at Kekova, the famous Lycian city of Xanthos, and the harbor towns of Kas and Kalkan.

Both cruises offer much time to explore the shore and seas, visit ancient sites, and cook and eat—menus are designed to showcase national and regional (such as Aegean, southeast Turkish, and Ottoman) specialties. Several mornings and afternoons are set aside for demonstration and hands-on cooking classes on board.

The **land-based tour** begins with three days in Istanbul. You'll explore the alleys and streets on both sides of the Golden Horn, visit and shop in food stalls and markets (including the famous Egyptian Spice Market and the Flower Passage), and see the magnificent Topkapi Palace, Aya Sophi, and Blue Mosque. You'll enjoy meals at an Ottoman restaurant, a traditional *meyhane* in the old Beyoglu district (offering an impressive array of *meze*, or appetizers), and will sample the varied offerings of street shops.

Then you travel to Gaziantep. Situated on the western edge of the Euphrates River plain in southeast Turkey, Ganziantep and the surrounding area offers a unique cuisine, influenced by the ancient spice trade routes and drawing heavily on Arabic culinary history. Accompanied by Kathleen and food writer, researcher, and local resident Filiz Hosukoglu, you'll attend cooking sessions with the region's best home cooks. You'll dine with local families in their homes, have dinner at fine restaurants, and savor the distinctive Ganziantep street cuisine.

In the home kitchens, you'll discover regional ingredients such as aromatic red pepper pastes, pistachios, bulgur wheat, chickpeas, and yogurt. You'll eat lentil and bulgur wheat pilaf, and stews of lamb, chickpea, and *koftes* (red lentil patties seasoned with fresh herbs and spices, and tomato and pepper pastes). At street stalls, you'll taste the art of the grill: from wood-fired ovens come mouthwatering kebabs, *koftes*, and vegetables and fruits, grilled to perfection and served with flat bread and *ayran*, a refreshing yogurt drink. And in restaurants, you'll sample baklava, kebabs, and other southeastern Turkish delights.

Other activities include market trips, visits to artisans' workshops, a Ganziatep potluck with a gathering of local residents, and several journeys east, through a landscape of pistachio groves and grapevines. For example, on one day trip, you'll join a local family for lunch in a small village overlooking the banks of the Euphrates and then travel to Sanli Urfa for a walking tour of the covered bazaar and Islamic pilgrimage sites. Or you might visit Antakya (the ancient city of Antioch), near the Syrian border, where you'll see Roman ruins, visit the mosaic museum, and tour the old quarter.

Kathleen also offers private tours, private *gulet* charters, market tours in the Aegean and Istanbul, and more. Noncooking partners and children are welcome on her trips.

THE DETAILS: The cruises run twelve days and are offered May, June, October, and November. Group size is limited according to the yacht; some can accommodate eight to ten, others six to seven. The land-based tour runs ten days and is offered in September. The cost for the cruises includes accommodations, all meals, cooking lessons, and excursions. The cost for the land-based tour includes accommodations, all meals, excursions, and transfers to and from airport.

Cruises: $ 2,100 (eight to ten guests); $2,400 (six to seven guests)
Land-based tour: $2,200

Contact:
Culinary Expeditions in Turkey
Kathleen O'Neill
PO Box 1913
Sausalito, CA 94966
Phone: 415-437-5700
Fax: 925-210-1337
E-mail: koneill@evocative.net
Web site: www.evocative.net/~turkey

From the kitchen of
Culinary Expeditions in Turkey

◉

KISIR (BULGUR SALAD)

SERVES 6 TO 8

This dish comes from the Gaziantep region in southeastern Turkey, where red pepper paste features in many of their notable dishes. (*Note:* Bulgur wheat, red pepper paste, and pomegranate syrup can be found at many gourmet or Middle Eastern grocery shops.)

2 cups fine-grain bulgur
1¼ cups hot water
1½ tablespoons tomato
    paste
1½ tablespoons red pepper
    paste
⅓ cup olive oil
2 tablespoons pomegranate
    syrup

2 tomatoes, peeled and diced
1 cup sweet red onion, finely
    chopped
1 cup fresh mint, finely
    chopped
1 cup flat-leaf parsley, finely
    chopped
Salt to taste
Crushed red chile (optional)

In a large pot, pour the hot water over the bulgur and stir briefly. Cover and set aside for 30 minutes until the bulgur softens and swells.

Add the tomato paste, red pepper paste, and the olive oil to the bulgur and knead the mixture until the pastes are well distributed. Add the pomegranate syrup and knead again.

Stir in the chopped tomatoes, onion, mint, and parsley. Add salt to taste and crushed red pepper if desired. Place on a serving platter and refrigerate. Bring to room temperature and serve.